# DIVINE INSPIRATION

# DIVINE
# INSPIRATION

*The Life of Jesus in World Poetry*

ASSEMBLED AND EDITED BY

Robert Atwan, George Dardess,
and Peggy Rosenthal

NEW YORK   OXFORD

OXFORD UNIVERSITY PRESS

1998

Oxford University Press

Oxford  New York

Athens  Auckland  Bangkok  Bogotá  Bombay
Buenos Aires  Calcutta  Cape Town  Dar es Salaam
Delhi  Florence  Hong Kong  Istanbul  Karachi
Kuala Lumpur  Madras  Madrid  Melbourne
Mexico City  Nairobi  Paris  Singapore
Taipei  Tokyo  Toronto  Warsaw

and associated companies in
Berlin  Ibadan

Published by Oxford University Press, Inc.
198 Madison Avenue, New York, New York 10016

Oxford is a registered trademark of Oxford University Press

Library of Congress Cataloging-in-Publication Data
Divine inspiration : the life of Jesus in world poetry / assembled and
edited by Robert Atwan, George Dardess, and Peggy Rosenthal.
p.  cm.
Includes bibliographical references and index.
ISBN 0-19-509351-8
1. Jesus Christ—Poetry.  I. Atwan, Robert.
II. Dardess, George.  III. Rosenthal, Peggy.
PN6110.J4D58      1997
808.81'9351—dc20      96-41983

1 2 3 4 5 6 7 8 9

Printed in the United States of America
on acid-free paper

To our dear friend

John W. Wright

# Contents

## PART EIGHT: THE PASSION

# Preface and Acknowledgments

*Divine Inspiration: The Life of Jesus in World Poetry* is an anthology of world poetry inspired by the language of the Gospels. As such, it is not primarily a book of religious or devotional poetry—of poetry, that is, written by believers for believers, and restricted in tone, quality, or dogma. It is instead an effort to bring together examples of the fresh, varied, and unpredictable ways in which the words of the Gospels have inspired poets in the past and continue to inspire poets today.

Some of those poets translate the words of the Gospels into their own poetic idiom (for instance, Sor Juana Inés de la Cruz); some imaginatively expand and meditate upon episodes, sayings, and parables (Rainer Maria Rilke); some find correlations between events in the Gospels and the circumstances of their own day (Léopold Senghor, Anna Akhmatova); some use the Gospels to express their personal faith (Charles Péguy, Vassar Miller), their religious skepticism and even their hostility (René Depestre), some their irony and humor (D. H. Lawrence), or their social or political views (Federico García Lorca, Wole Soyinka); and some view the Gospels from other faiths (Primo Levi, Badr Shākir al-Sayyāb).

This variety of response isn't merely personal. Much of it derives from the time period and the culture in which the poets wrote. We have in fact favored poems in which the local culture makes the Gospel its own. In this way *Divine Inspiration* differs in its outlook from an earlier twentieth-century bias of "World Religious Poetry" anthologies toward "universalism": such collections chose poems in which anything culturally distinctive was absent, in order to posit an untroubled unity of belief. We sought instead to show how poems reflecting vastly different cultures and time periods follow from the same Gospel passage. The resulting unity is suggested, not asserted; it is stimulating, not soothing.

The variety of work inspired by the Gospels through the ages is represented here in almost 300 poems. The collection also represents nearly every culture or nation exposed to Christianity, even those (as in the Middle East, China, and India) where it is not the major religion. Naturally we included a greater proportion of poems from cultures with the longest traditions of Christian belief, such as those of Europe (including Russia) and the Americas. But since our intention was to introduce readers to world poetry on this subject, we deliberately downplayed the major British and American poets, assuming readers would already be familiar with their work. A previous two-volume Oxford anthology, *Chapters Into Verse*, represents this work comprehensively.

The fact that about half of the poems in *Divine Inspiration* are from the twentieth century indicates our preference for poetry that appeals to current tastes and concerns. Among poems included from previous centuries, we've favored those that appeal to our contemporary poetic sensibility. Our collection isn't meant to have only antiquarian interest; something in the poem must seem alive for us today. The few exceptions to this rule include poems representing a major usage of the Gospels for the poetry of an era (the typology of Adam of St. Victor) or poems of extraordinary persistence in their popular appeal over the centuries ("Gloria, Laus, et Honor," "Veni Creator Spiritus," "Stabat Mater"); for these we've retained the Latin titles by which they're best known. In choosing twentieth-century poems, we've avoided heavily anthologized poems in favor of ones not easily found in other books.

For freshness, we've included some less known contemporary writers whose poems have a striking angle on a Gospel text. Freshness and a sense of discovery can come from older poems as well. Our seventeenth-century Chinese poems, suppressed in their time, have been rediscovered by scholars only in the past few years and just published in English for the first time in scholarly books of the 1990s. Our book is the first to anthologize them for a wider English-speaking audience.

In making all choices, our preference was for self-contained poems, not excerpts. But since certain longer poems are too important to be excluded—e.g., those by Dante, Péguy, and Milton—we've excerpted a self-contained part linked to a particular Gospel text.

Translations have been chosen not only for their accuracy but also for their energy and appeal to contemporary taste. With only a very few exceptions, all translations are recent ones, done for the most part within the last fifty years. As such, they reflect "modernist" poetic standards: use of conversational diction as well as restraint and variety in the use of rhyme and rhythm. Where we felt published translations to be obsolete (e.g., nineteenth-century translations of Latin hymns and sequences), new ones were done especially for this volume. A certain number of poems, all those written originally in Hungarian and several in German, were translated into English for the first time for use in this volume. Also translated for the first time were poems previously kept in obscurity by a bias we call "secular screening"; religious poetry tends to be excluded from twentieth-century anthologies of the poetry of a country and of collections of a major poet. For example, though Sor Juana Inés de la Cruz, Mexico's major poet, is included in every anthology of Latin American poetry, her delightful *villancico* on Peter had never been translated into English.

In organizing the volume we wanted, as much as possible, to emphasize the Gospels' strong narrative element: we wanted the poems to tell the story of Jesus's life from his birth to his resurrection. Yet our desire to order the poems narratively had to be tempered by our understanding of what the Gospels *are*—i.e., not "biographies" of Jesus but efforts to strengthen the faith of the Evangelists' own communities. The Gospel writers arranged their material—which consisted of not only narratives of Jesus's actions but also recordings of his sayings, parables, and other teachings—to suit their homiletic purpose, not to tell a story. As a result, the Gospel writers were extremely attentive to narrative detail in some places (especially when describing the Passion), and very loose in others (especially in the accounts of Jesus's ministry). Since they seemed to feel no need to "harmonize" their own narrative elements with each other's, their accounts at times differ greatly, making very problematic any attempt to impose a narrative order in those places where none was apparently intended. Taking these difficulties into account, we tried to group the poems in ways people have come to expect: as moments in the drama of Jesus's life (especially at its beginning and at its end) and as aspects of his wisdom or healing power during the three years of his ministry. Our structure follows Jesus's career in Parts I–II (Birth and Infancy, and Preparation for Public Ministry) and again in Parts VII–IX (Final Jerusalem Ministry, The Passion, The Resurrection). Parts III–VI (Healings and Miracles, Encounters, Parables, Sayings and Discourses) make use of the various categories of Jesus's ministry most commonly used today in Biblical discussion and most familiar to churchgoers, though where possible even within these categories we tried to arrange material narratively (e.g., in Healings and Miracles, we group the healings and exorcizings before the raising of Lazarus).

Only those Gospel passages were used, however, that had a clear and explicit verbal connection to the poetry. Or, to put our criterion for selection the other way, each poem had to contain a direct reference to the language or events described in a particular Gospel passage. Yet such references could not be made in passing; the poem had to reflect on that passage, or to be "inspired" by it (hence our title, *Divine Inspiration*). Omitted therefore were poems that loosely reflect on Christ's life; poems with a religious slant or reference but without a link to a Gospel text; and most of the grand body of mystical poetry, which usually generates metaphors for the poet's direct experience of God without the mediation of a Scriptural text.

Within each group of poems related to a particular Gospel passage, we usually placed first the poem whose connection to the Gospel passage was closest (most direct or literal), establishing in this way an "anchor" for the entire unit. We placed subsequent poems in each group according to their degree of departure from the original Gospel text into more private reflections or more public, political ones. But we also ordered poems to bring out interesting contrasts and juxtapositions in tone, language use, cultural expression, and era. Often poems were clearly connected to a particular version of a Gospel episode; in those cases, we printed that version. Otherwise our choice of evangelist was determined by which Gospel passage was shortest.

We used the New Revised Standard Version of the Bible for all Gospel citations because it is an up-to-date, non-sexist, readable translation. And for a book devoted to world poetry, with poets relying on all sorts of Gospel translations, the NRSV seemed preferable to other more distinctively "English" ones, such as the King James. Furthermore, the NRSV is the current standard ecumenical translation, held in high regard by mainstream Christian churches, and increasingly familiar to their congregations.

In an international anthology of this nature, we had to make certain decisions about spelling and alphabetizing. For words with different American and British spelling (judgment/judgement for instance), the American spelling prevails except where the poet or translator uses the British or alternative spelling. Likewise with Biblical names (Magdalene, Zacchaeus, and others) we used the NRSV spelling in the Biblical passages and headnotes, while in the poems themselves we retained the spelling of the poet or translator. In the headnotes and index, the form and alphabetizing of foreign names follows the custom of the poet's own country. We should note, too, that some foreign poets (for example, in Nigeria and the Philippines) write in English; where no translator is named in the headnote, the poem was written in English.

A project of this scope naturally draws on the expertise of many people. For invaluable help in locating poems from other countries, we thank Daniel H. Bays, Dalma Hunyadi Brunauer, John Dardess, Rev. Lawrence E. Frizzell, Aimée Lim, RSCJ, D. E. Mungello, D.N. Premnath, Jon Roberts, the Trappist Monks of the Abbey of the Genesee, Jonathan Spence, and Laurance Weider. Others who generously suggested material include Anne Coon, Marvin Krier Mich, Charles O'Neill and William Vesterman. We appreciate very much the fine research assistance we received from Joy Briggs, Matthew Howard, Peter Krass, Ann Moirier, and Shelley Salamensky, as well as the original translations provided by Dalma Hunyadi Brunauer, David Curzon, Y. R. Pérez, Jack Roberts, and Shelley Salemensky. Finally, our deepest thanks to the editorial and production staff at Oxford University Press, who attended to this multi-faceted project with an inspired professionalism.

RA, GD, PR

# Introduction

"Who do you say that I am?" The question Jesus posed to his disciples in Caesarea Philippi has continued for two thousand years to challenge people in every place on the globe that has been touched by the Christian Gospels. As we turn the corner of the second millennium, we're naturally drawn to take stock of how various eras and cultures have responded to this unique figure in human history. The poetry inspired by the canonical Gospels over this time period is a rich resource for discovering what people in different parts of the world have made of the person of Jesus, since poetry focuses a culture's imagination as no other verbal medium can. In the shape and substance a poem gives to the figure of Jesus of Nazareth, in a poem's reinvention of Scriptural moments, we can see how a local culture conceives the meaning of Jesus's life and makes the Gospels its own.

How a culture conceives of poetry—what poetic forms and occasions the culture offers, what roles it defines for the poet—will naturally come to bear on its poetry's treatment of the Gospel texts. So will the place of Christian faith in the society at large and in the poet's own life. With such an immense span of time and geography to cover, and with so many permutations of religious and poetic practice to consider, I can only attempt here a quick historical survey of the material. Actually, when we get to the twentieth century, with poetry on Jesus coming from every continent out of an unprecedented array of cultures and of attitudes toward Christianity, categories other than the historical will be best for grasping the trends. But chronology will work at the start.

The earliest poetry about Jesus was composed by theologians. The Greco-Roman Christian subculture had no separate role of "poet." Rather, the men spreading the Gospel message, teaching the new faith to converts, and defending the faith from heresies would move into a hymn of praise at the high point of a prose treatise. The best of the hymns entered the community's worship.

These celebratory poems see Jesus's whole life in a flash: in the dazzling light of Easter. For Christians of the first few centuries after Jesus's death, the central reality of his life is the Resurrection. All other moments of the Gospel story, and of the Hebrew Scriptures as well, are transformed in their eyes into that glorious Easter instant. Our anthology's earliest poem, the hymn with which the important second-century theologian Clement of Alexandria ends his catechetical treatise, *Paedagogus*, is a chain of names for Jesus inspired by images from all over the Bible but fused by the triumphant figure of "Christ the King": "you the Shepherd, Cultivator, . . . Fisher of men, . . . you the Wing that lifts to heaven all the company of saints, . . . Jesus Christ, celestial Milk out-pressed from a young bride's fragrant breasts (your Wisdom's graces) . . . " Similarly, a third-century treatise on Easter by Hippolytus includes verses transforming Matthew's cautionary Parable of the Laborers of the Vineyard into a joyous hymn with "Christ is risen" as its theme.

This first poetry on the Gospels, like all early Christian literature including the Gospels themselves, was written in Greek, which was the language of the Hellenized Roman Empire into the third century. After that, distinct Eastern and Western churches started developing, with different languages and different cultural influences on their poetry.

In the East, the fourth-century Syriac poet Ephrem wrote verses that are still staples of Eastern Christian liturgy. (He was one of those artists who so engage their culture's imagination that the subsequent centuries' cultural expressions are inconceivable without their original creativity.) Writing within a Semitic-Asian literary tradition, Ephrem thinks his theology through metaphor. He argues against heresy and teaches doctrine as much as the Greek and Roman Christians did, but he does it all in hymns. Taking the complex Syriac stanzaic forms of his time and pondering the meaning of Jesus's life, Ephrem shapes paradox after paradox. The mind-bending wonder of the Incarnation, in particular—the Creator of the universe tucking himself into the womb of his creature—refracts in Ephrem's vision into hundreds of paradoxical gems. "As indeed He sucked Mary's milk/He has given suck—life to the universe"; "As again He dwelt in His mother's womb/in His womb dwells all creation." (Clearly Ephrem and Clement had no problem with female images for Jesus; only later did the official Church develop a blind spot about them.) Ephrem's prosody influenced the greatest Byzantine poet, the sixth-century Romanos, famous for his intricately structured poetic sermons dramatizing—in delightful invented dialogue—the Biblical text for each occasion of the Eastern Church calendar. And Ephrem's paradoxical mode was still shaping Byzantine poetry centuries later. The ninth-century poet Kassia, the single woman poet whose work survives from Byzantine Greek, has Mary Magdalene lament at Jesus's tomb in these turns of phrase: "Accept this spring of tears,/you who empty seawater from the clouds./Bend to the pain in my heart, you/who made the sky bend to your secret incarnation . . ."

The Western Church had meanwhile, by the end of the fourth century, exchanged Greek for Latin as its language. Christians who wanted to play any part in Roman society had to be educated in the powerful Roman school system, so inevitably the Latin classical poets became their literary model. A fourth-century versification of the Gospels as Virgilian epic, by the Spanish priest Juvencus, was one result that is now a mere curiosity. But from more creative fourth-century writers, such as Ambrose (Bishop of Milan) and Prudentius (civil servant to the emperor Theodosius), came Christian verse that enriched the Latin language and Church life alike. Ambrose wrote hymns to hearten his flock under persecution. Their lyric expression of Christian belief made them immensely popular; Augustine confesses that their beauty moved him to tears. Ambrose's hymns, blending Eastern hymn styles with Western classical moods such as the evocation of nature's cycles, are considered the most original product of fourth-century Latin literature, as well as the model for subsequent hymnody in the Western Church. Prudentius, judged the first great Christian poet of the West, also composed hymns for church celebration, some of which are still used today. With Prudentius, the Gospels become Virgilian pastoral. Christ the Shepherd seeks the parable's One Lost Sheep through "sylvan mazes"; finding it, he carries it back to "open woodland,/ Where the lush grass bends its green leaves, and laurels/ Shade the glassy streamlet of living water/ Ceaselessly flowing." This early instance of a local poetic idiom making the Gospels its own could hardly be more charming.

The world of Ambrose and Prudentius had no national or even linguistic boundaries. Ambrose became Bishop of Milan though he was born in the Alsace region; Prudentius lived in what is now Spain. But, along with all Western writers from the fourth century to around the fourteenth, they were citizens of a Europe that had Latin as its common language and Roman Christianity as its common culture. The immense output of medieval Latin Christian poetry was written primarily for specific feasts on the Church calendar, or for specific parts of the Mass or of the monastic daily Liturgy of the Hours. It was created to be chanted or sung, to put in a pleasing form the dogmas of faith for a congregation largely unable to read. As liturgical poetry, it was inherently public poetry, meant to express communally held beliefs. Individual authorship was unimportant. Hence the many anonymous medieval poems, or poems ascribed (probably wrongly) to a famous person.

Since the Church calendar was full of feasts for extra-Biblical saints, the poetry inspired by that calendar doesn't tend to include Gospel figures. Where it does, saints like John the Baptist and Peter and especially the Virgin Mary get as much attention as Jesus does. And the poetry on Jesus focuses on those Gospel events or Church doctrines for which the Church celebrated feasts: chiefly the Nativity, Transfiguration, Palm Sunday, Exaltation of the Cross, and Easter.

No matter what Gospel subject medieval poetry is focusing on, the main lens through which it is seen is that of Biblical typology. This mode of seeing the meaning of Jesus's life—as the fulfillment of events and characters whose "types" are pre-figured in the Hebrew Scriptures—begins with the New Testament authors themselves. Elaborated in minute detail by the early Church Fathers, typology informs more than a millennium of Christian writing and visual art.

One predominant typological figure is the Cross as Tree. To Jesus's first disciples, his Cross was a scandalous disgrace, because crucifixion was the means of execution for common criminals. But Paul, in his Epistles, helped transform the Cross into the sign of Christ's victory. Typology, too, helped in the transformation. Already in the late second century, the Church Father Irenaeus could write: "The Lord . . . by his obedience in the tree renewed and reversed what was done by disobedience in connection with a tree." The typological vision sees Christ's Cross, because it is wood, as the reversed renewal of the Tree in the Garden of Eden. The Cross becomes the Tree of Triumph. So in Fortunatus' sixth-century poem "Vexilla Regis Prodeunt," which the Middle Ages made its favorite processional hymn and Dante quoted in the *Inferno's* final canto, everything about the Cross as Tree is victorious: it's the "Tree of beauty and of light" from which God rules the nations; it's dyed "with royal purple"; it's "blessed" that on its branches "hung the ransom of the world." (The Cross as Tree has persisted to the present as a poetic image, though its royal purple has had to mix with shades more subdued and even dark; to the eye of contemporary Welsh poet R. S. Thomas, for instance, it's painfully stark, a grim shadow falling on the fields in one poem, in another "a bare tree" toward which starved people reach waiting "for a vanished April/To return to its crossed/Boughs.")

Another favorite typological figure is the Eve-Mary coupling: Eve is the Old Testament type of the Virgin Mary, who reversed the harm Eve did in the Garden. Medieval poetry and visual art play with the linkage in endlessly imaginative ways. A representative variety can be found in the twelfth-century poems of Hildegard of Bingen, who—besides writing major theological and scientific works—composed the words and music for the liturgical verses chanted by her nuns in the Benedictine monastery of which she was abbess. An antiphon (verses introducing a psalm or other liturgical song) for the Feast of the Annunciation, for instance, has Mary, on receiving the Holy Spirit into her body, being "purged of the poison Eve took." Whereas Eve "soiled all freshness when she caught that infection from the devil's suggestion," Mary allowed God's Son to "blossom" in her body. Mary is pictured as herself a garden, "swelling with the breath of God," nurturing the "seedbed of holiness," and hence reversing Eve's reception of the devil's word in the original garden.

Typology isn't the only way that the medieval imagination treated the Gospels. Other complex allegorical systems abounded, finding Christ hidden in every detail of the universe. In the intricacies of these cosmological allegories, however, Christ can be so hidden that the Gospel story disappears; figures representing, say, the Virtues and their corresponding Vices take over the Christian drama. Or, put another way, the Christian vision came to include the whole natural, historical, and moral world. In the grand allegorical system of *The Divine Comedy*, Gospel texts are indeed privileged reference points, but within a dramatic arrangement of a vast array of other cultural materials. The *Paradiso*'s celestial vision of Christ on the Cross—a Tree no longer made of wood or any earthly matter, but of rays of the divine light (Canto 14)—is a meditation less on the Gospel moment than on a millennium of Exaltations of the Cross.

Standing at the peak of a medieval vision of Christ (note that we have to say "of Christ," not "of Jesus of Nazareth," so far is this salvific figure from his human being), Dante also already has a foot in the poetic era to come. He has left Latin for the Italian language, and he isn't writing for liturgical use. Not that there aren't any earlier vernacular or non-liturgical poems on Christ; and liturgical verse, even some in Latin, continued into the Renaissance. But trends toward the vernacular as poetry's language and away from liturgy as its occasion are manifestations of a major change in the relation between religious and literary culture by around the sixteenth century.

The Renaissance-Reformation period is one of those historical moments of substantial redefinition for both poetry and religion. Though poetry on the Gospels certainly remains Christian poetry—that is, poetry assuming Christian faith—it is no longer necessarily the voice of an institutional Church whose dominance in the intellectual and sociopolitical culture is taken for granted. The Renaissance invention of the self put the poet's individuality at the center of the creative process, while the Reformation made religion a matter between the individual and God, mediated only by the Scriptures. Originality became a value in poetry at the same time as one's personal relation with God was becoming Christianity's core.

That personal relation could be strained. Indeed, when explored in a poetic medium shaped soon by the Baroque sensibility of sixteenth-

and seventeenth-century Europe, it almost had to be. "Baroque" is one of those hopelessly loose literary terms, but critics agree that it was a psycho-aesthetic response to political, economic, scientific, and religious crises that ripped apart the harmoniously ordered medieval cosmos, yanking into anxious tension the things of this world and the source of their meaning beyond. "This psychic and moral discord," as Octavio Paz puts it, "was resolved in a violent, dynamic art permeated with the dual awareness of the world's fragmentation and its unity, a chiaroscuro of contrasts, paradoxes, twisted inversions, and scintillating affirmations."

Of course, paradox was nothing new for poetry on Christ. We've seen that mind-bending inversions were always the Byzantine mode, and in the West as well, Christian theology was fond of twists like "God became man so that man could become God" and "Jesus became a slave to set us free." Indeed, the Christian story can't be told without paradox at its heart. So what Helen Gardner once noted about the religious poetry of the English metaphysicals is true also of the continental Baroque: that much of its famed "wit" is not particularly original, but draws on traditional Christian turns of thought and phrase. Yet the dynamically tense Baroque sensibility did transform religious verse. To spell out how, we might ask what happens to the figure of Jesus in Baroque poetry that hadn't happened before.

He becomes, for religious poets adapting Petrarch, the Beloved addressed in passionate sonnets. Though invented for the theme of secular love, the sonnet—with its play of emotion and wit, its acrobatic mental twists—was perfect for elaborating the Christian paradox of a God loving us so much that he became human to make us divine. In sacred sonnets like those of Miguel de Guevera, prizes of seventeenth-century Spanish literature, that paradox in all of its variants is run through the love sonnet's tropes, as the poet plays with what it means to exchange love with such a Lord. I wouldn't say that Guevara and his brilliant contemporaries—Lope de Vega, John Donne, George Herbert, Jean de La Ceppède—are any more inventive than Ephrem was in spinning turns of mind and phrase within an intricately tight stanzaic form. But what's new is the central theme being spun: the poet's intense personal relation with a Savior of whom the poet feels too sinful to be worthy. This dynamic isn't limited to sonnets. Even when Jesus isn't addressed in Baroque verse as the Beloved, he can be called into the poet's soul, which becomes the site of a Gospel episode transformed into the poet's own spiritual drama. Henry Vaughan's "The Dwelling-Place" follows the characteristic plot. From the disciple's question in John 1:38—"Lord, where are you staying?"—the poem moves through various proffered answers, all external locales (mountain, tent, star), to conclude: "But I am sure, thou dost now come/Oft to a narrow, homely room, . . . My God, I mean my sinful heart."

The single Gospel moment stayed with and played with: while not new to the Baroque, it does get now a new treatment. Romanos in his sixth-century verse homilies would take one scene and expand it, would pull back the camera (to use an anachronistic metaphor) and pan the crowd, letting the participants speak invented dialogue at length. The Baroque camera is more likely to zoom in and freeze the frame, to hold still the instant while heightening its visual effects. Master of this mode is Jean de La Ceppède, who composed an astounding sequence of 520 sonnets visualizing, instant by instant, the four Gospels' final chapters. (Since the sonnets were written as Catholic apologetics during the religious wars in post-Reformation France, the poet's fortunes were tied to which religious group was in power; his work was buried after his death and has been only recently rediscovered.) La Ceppède used the Baroque's own favorite metaphor for its aesthetic when he called his poetry *peinture parlante*: "talking picture." The Baroque poet's brush swept its subjects with sensuous imagery, intensifying the physical world's delights. When treated in this manner, Jesus moves amidst lush color: a "crimson blossom" falls on his manger in Gongora's "Nativity"; he treads a "green tapestry" in Marino's "Palm Sunday" procession. Other Gospel figures besides Jesus also get this treatment. The Polish poet Andrzej Morsztyn's "To St. John the Baptist" is a case study of the chiaroscuro that Paz points to: John is "grey brightness which the sun breaks through"; his blood "gushes on the world" like the dawn sun's "blood-red stream." As often happens in Baroque art, the poem's real subject seems to be less the story alluded to in its title than the dramatic play of color and light.

Though Western poetry was redefined in the Renaissance-Baroque period as primarily a private art, a vehicle for personal expression, public poetry continued to be composed. Courts commissioned verse for special occasions, and the Church—especially in Catholic Spain and New Spain—continued commissioning poetry for religious festivals. Spanish liturgical verse of the era draws on popular song and dance forms, with their abbreviated assonant lines, to teach the faith in a way engaging to the populace. The mystic Teresa of Avila used this method in the convent she founded; for occasions such as a nun's veiling or a church feast, she composed instructional verse that had the carefree fun of folk songs. Also developed from folk culture, and popular throughout the Spanish world, was the *villancico*, a dance-song interlude for feast-day liturgies. New Spain's most celebrated colonial poet, Sor Juana Inés de la Cruz, had *villancicos* commissioned by the cathedrals of Mexico City, Puebla, and Oaxaca. Baroque to her bones, Sor Juana delighted in the genre's literary constraints, within which she could let her imaginative wit and spoofing humor run wild. A *villancico* for St. Peter is typical in inventing a scene of schoolchildren learning from Peter, whose lesson becomes a showcase of Baroque conceits and puns.

With Sor Juana in the seventeenth century, poetry of the highest quality on the Gospels moved beyond Europe, though it was still in the Western tradition. But poetry on the Gospels made a real cultural leap during the same century when the Jesuits brought Christianity to China. Their converts tended to be from the *literati* class, for whom writing poetry was an expected activity. Official persecution soon forced Christianity underground, and most of its artistic expressions were lost, but two major bodies of this first Chinese Christian poetry have just recently been rediscovered and made available to the scholarly world, both by way of English translations by American historians. These poems do something utterly new: they reconceive "the Lord of Heaven Teaching," as Christianity was called, in Confucian terms and in Chinese literary conventions. So in the poetry of Zhang Xingyao, designed to show Christianity as a harmonious continuation of Confucianism, Peter the Rock, for instance, becomes "a sage who was a great cornerstone for the Teaching/ . . . A massive mountain of shining light." Model of Confucian virtues, Peter "swore an oath to totally commit his time,/and sincerely believed in complete self-cultivation." And in a brilliant cultural blending by the accomplished painter and poet Wu Li, the traditional Chinese figure of the fisherman finds himself in the Gospel episode where "some friends of his have changed their job/they now are fishers of men." Both Wu Li and Zhang Xingyao knew what they were about; they were deliberately transforming the Christian story into their own cultural idiom. Possibly a comparable project went on as well in southern Japan, where a Jesuit community flourished during the seventeenth century. But there, the repression that followed was so fierce that no poetry, if any was composed, seems to have survived.

Back in Europe, the next major redefinition of poetry that bears on our subject is Romanticism. In European Romanticism, poetry was reconceived as an act of the poet's imagination, in tune with nature's forces but often at odds with society. Coming at the same time, out of German intellectual developments, was Christian theology's major nineteenth-century movement: historical criticism and its "quest for the historical Jesus," a search for what could be known of Jesus of Nazareth's human life. From poets engaged in the quest with Romanticism's eye, a strikingly new sort of poem emerged: a Gospel scene imagined from Jesus's human point of view, with Jesus given a personal psychology and with the poem dramatizing his personal response or a change in his mind. This was a bold step. But it's important to note that, at this stage, the psychologizings of Jesus are respectful. Though he is no longer the medieval salvific figure so distant from humanity that he can only be called the "Christ," his divinity isn't in doubt; it's just not where the interesting action is for Romantic poets. What engages them is imagining how it might have felt to be this central character of the Gospel story.

Not surprisingly, the Jesus they imagine is a Romantic hero: the Solitary, suffering his aloneness from other people but deeply in touch with nature. A poem by the nineteenth-century Italian Giovanni Pascoli re-imagines the Gospel incident of Jesus blessing the little children as his lonely response to foreseeing his fate; in an inventive touch, the poem has Jesus, "with sadness in his voice," bless particularly the son of Barabbas. In the "Gethsemane" of the German poet Annette von Droste-Hülshoff, Jesus moves from mood to mood as he imagines in advance the experience of his Crucifixion, with each of his psychological states presented through correlates in nature: as he lay down, "the breezes seemed nothing but sighs"; as he pictured his Cross, "the air went dark. In the grey ocean/A dead sun swam." In the final stanza, nature becomes not merely a correlative but an active force in his ability to accept the Father's will: "The moon swam out in quiet blue,/ Before him, on the dewy green,/A stem of lily stretched up its length./ Then out of the calyx-cup/An angel stepped/And gave him strength." Nature also acts on Jesus in Hans Benzmann's "Jesus Walks on the Water," but here the mood is lighthearted, as the poet imagines the miracle from inside Jesus's being. Resting alone on the shore, Jesus is peacefully listening to the evening crickets when "Some force moves the Holy One" to rise and think: "O dance of souls all around me,/Beloved Nature, a longing seizes me . . . to join the play with all the rest! . . . His feet hover and take flight–/And Jesus walks–walks on the water!–And under his feet the waves in silver flutter . . . " This Romantic Jesus is literally in touch with and moved by Nature in a marvelous sense.

The Romantic re-envisioning of Gospel texts had ramifications that reached throughout the twentieth century. It was the start of the secularization of Christianity, because it made God vulnerable. Imagining Jesus with a personal psychology had the effect of saying: Well then, if you're human, here's what follows. And what followed was modernism. Of course, modernism followed from other forces as well. One was the iconoclastic spirit that, beginning with Europe's political revolutions at the end of the eighteenth century, developed in Romanticism into a stance of revolt against all forms of authority and tradition. In poetry, the Romantic Revolt's most influential expression was Baudelaire's *Fleurs du Mal*, with its deliberately, provocatively satanic vision. Spitting out disgust at the very idea of sacrificial death, one *Fleurs du Mal* poem directly challenging Jesus ends with the cry: "Peter denied his Master?–He did right!" From such defiance, something like modernism had to come.

"Modernism" is a term even harder to pin down than "Baroque," since it refers to a literary aesthetic and also to a *Weltanschauung*. (It also refers, in Church history, to a progressive turn-of-the-century movement that has surprisingly little in common with the literary and cultural modernism that is our subject.) As both aesthetic and *Weltanschauung*, modernism had particular moments of historical origin but has also remained hovering in the air over the whole twentieth century, materializing in one part of the globe or another at different times. For twentieth-century literature does become unprecedentedly global. In the first half of the century, European colonialism spread Western intellectual movements around the world (though local appropriation was often delayed until after World War II). Usually coming in the independence movements characteristic of the century's second half, these local appropriations freely turn Western materials into native products. So a paradox of the century's poetic theories and practices is that they're at once more universal and more culturally specific than ever before. And the concept of literary culture itself splits into a general and a specific sense as well. Radiating from the historically Christian West is the culture called secular, effectively the opposite of Western culture a millennium before: where medieval poets had assumed a communal religious belief, modern poets presume communal doubt. At the same time, throughout the non-Western world, the poetry of particular ethnic and religious cultures takes over Christian stories and symbols, making them its own. Because this range of twentieth-century poetic responses to Christian material has happened all over the globe nearly at once, I think the clearest way to present it is—after a brief grounding in modernism's origins—to leave chronology behind in favor of categories of treatment of Jesus and the Gospel texts.

As a literary aesthetic, modernism began with the French Symbolist poets of the 1880s. Seeing traditional structures—whether religious, political, or literary—crumbled and discredited, the Symbolists proclaimed poetry freed from external reality. Only the poet's inner being was a reliable subject, to be evoked through images of color and music since the senses were the only perceptions the poet could trust. To liberate poetry's fluidity of sound, the Symbolists invented *vers libre* (free verse). Symbolism's program was immediately grabbed up by Latin Americans longing for a revitalization of poetic language; led by the Nicaraguan Rubén Darío, they developed a vibrant, iconoclastic modernism that was their culture's first original poetic voice. In Britain after the turn of the century, Ezra Pound and T. S. Eliot refocused the Symbolist vision onto the fragment. The isolated image, pulled from the wreckage of civilization's lost coherence, became modernism's characteristic literary unit. Then World War I brought modernism out of the literary journals into the general culture. The war's devastation made horribly relevant, even requisite, all the Symbolist stances: the disgust with authoritative tradition, the *fin de siècle* world-weariness, the disillusionment about ultimate meanings. "Cultural modernism" became a popular mode.

Because modernism is in part a spiritual response—to the perceived loss of transcendent meaning—its poetry on the Gospels comes right out of its core vision. Romanticism had explored Jesus's human dimension without denying the divine, but for modernism there is only the human. Jesus of Nazareth is not the Christ. At the Nietzchean proclamation that God is dead, however, modernism doesn't celebrate; nor does it gloat cynically over the corpse as postmodernism will do. Modernism goes wistfully to the wake. "Weep for Jesus," writes Danish poet Ole Wivel in a poem mourning the loss of all divinity, not only the Christian, from our world. Wivel deliberately removes from the Gospel story any belief in the Resurrection, so that when Jesus, "powerless like mortal men," appears after his death, "his disciples would/ Not believe that it was he who spoke—Would but see his bleeding hands and wounds." This is all that the Russian poet Vladimir Lvov can see either: "That yellowed body of the Lord/Hanging on the cross, The face tormented with loss." And the poet's response to this unglorious sight? "We do not adore him . . . We can only pity Christ today,/So, of course, he's no longer great." To see only Jesus's wasted mortal body, not to see also the Risen Christ, is to look at the Gospels without Christian faith. Modernism marks the end of the assumption that poetry on the Gospels is Christian poetry.

But, surprisingly, it doesn't at all mark the end of poetry on the Gospels. One might expect that this particular body of poetry would yellow and dry up along with the body of Jesus that modernism sees. Yet the opposite has been the case for our century. Freed from the requirement of belief, poets in historically Christian societies have felt liberated to explore any personal attitude toward religion whatever:

they can doubt it, scorn it, ignore it, test it out, even believe in it if they will. This freedom has given an astonishing vitality to poetry on the Gospels. Poets, who are children of the century like the rest of us, are energized by a sense of choice, so that when they do choose to treat a Gospel text or the person of Jesus, there's often a remarkable freshness in their product. At the same time, the Asian, Caribbean, and African postcolonial poets who are freeing themselves from Western control bring to the Gospels the fresh approaches of their native heritage, while the worldwide interfaith dialogues that are the twentieth century's major religious development have also inspired some Muslim and Hindu poets to appropriate Jesus and the Gospels in unprecedented ways. So when we ask what happens to the figure of Jesus in twentieth-century poetry, instead of finding—as in previous eras—two or three characteristic images, we discover a plethora of new figures popping up practically at once.

We've looked already at modernism's shrunken, pathetically human Jesus. There are other twentieth-century poets for whom a remnant of the Romantic Jesus remains, but after modernism's diminution of his grandeur, he's less hero than anti-hero, moved to the margin of his own story, his essence—like all reality to the modernist mind—impossible to grasp. This figure of an unknowable Jesus fascinates Rainer Maria Rilke, who has poem after poem re-imagining some Gospel scene from the point of view of characters who are baffled by Jesus and yet transformed by him, touched by a contact with the divine that they don't understand. For Australian poet James McAuley, it's precisely this contact that is now impossible; his poem "Jesus" deliberately places a grand Romantic Jesus in a post-Romantic world that is utterly unresponsive to him, turning to him only "muted faces." Polish poet Tadeusz Rózewicz invents a striking image for our absolute inability ever to know who Jesus was: in "Unknown Letter," expanding on the Gospel incident where Jesus writes with his finger on the earth (in the scene of the woman taken in adultery), the poet imagines a Jesus so disgusted at being continually misunderstood that "when Matthew Mark Luke and John approached him he covered the letters and erased them forever." What poets like these are doing with the figure of Jesus is projecting onto him a twentieth-century puzzlement about religious faith. Whether Jesus was God or not, they ponder, why are we so uncomfortable with the possibility of divine presence in our world? It's a question about the cultural psychology of belief and disbelief characteristic of the secularized West.

Elsewhere in world poetry, very different kinds of concerns can get projected onto the figure of Jesus. For black poets in Africa and the

Americas, political concerns have been preeminent in this century, and a useful figure for their race's experience of slavery and colonialism has been Christ on the Cross. An influential early case is Haitian poet Jacques Roumain's 1939 "New Negro Sermon," in which Christ is a "poor nigger" and, conversely, the black race victimized by injustice is the suffering Christ. When the poem appeared in Leopold Senghor's revolutionary 1948 anthology of black poetry, its final eight lines—calling for a militant black liberation—became a motto of the movement known as negritude, an effort by black intellectuals to throw off the European culture imposed on them and reassert their African heritage. It's intriguing that the figure of Christ Crucified, drawn from the very Western culture they're rejecting, has continued to be for postcolonial African poets a privileged image for the suffering of their particular country or tribe. No other archetype of sacrificial suffering, apparently, has the universally recognized power of the Cross. So a poet like Nigeria's Wole Soyinka, who otherwise rarely draws on the Gospels, chooses Crucifixion images to construct his lone figure of the contemporary political martyr in "The Dreamer" and other poems. South Africa's Oswald Mbuyoseni Mtshali, too, in his poem "Ride Upon the Death Chariot," identifies the suffocation of three black victims of apartheid as "their Golgotha." And even for a writer whose life work has been devoted to recovering native religion and culture lost under colonialism, Nigeria's Chinua Achebe, the Passion can still be the chosen image for his people's suffering in the Nigerian civil war: "We are the men of soul/men of song we measure out/our joys and agonies/too, our long, long passion week/in paces of the dance. We have/come to know from surfeit of suffering/that even the Cross need not be/a dead end nor total loss/if we should go to it striding/the dirge of the soulful *abia* drums . . . "

The poem goes on to warn against following another Gospel moment, the Ascension, away from the call of native ancestral gods. This tension between tribal gods and a Christ set down in their midst is a motif especially among African poets who have been practicing Christians. Kofi Awoonor's "Easter Dawn" has the two religious practices contending with nearly equal strength in the poet's own being. Abioseh Nicol's "African Easter," reflecting on the poet's identity as a Christian intellectual in the midst of native religions, ends by affirming Christ (the "sun") as his continent's hope for restorative love: "The great muddy river Niger,/Picks up the rising equatorial sun,/Changing itself by slow degrees/Into thick flowing molten gold." It's a rare postcolonial image of Africa taking in Christ and being thereby richly transformed.

Sometimes the figure of Christ (and as archetype, it is indeed "Christ," not Jesus) is made not to contend against other gods but to conflate with them. While in general archetypal modes of seeing are, since Jung, as predominant for the twentieth century as the typological were for the Middle Ages, the sourcebook for this kind of conflation is Frazer's section, in *The Golden Bough*, on Tammuz and Adonis as murdered-reborn fertility gods. "Killing a god dates from the most remote times according to Frazer," writes Nicaragua's Ernesto Cardenal, whose book-length *Cosmic Canticle* embraces seemingly every relevant god in the archetype of Christ. More focused is the conflation of Christ and Tammuz in post-World War II Arab poets, who actually came to Tammuz through "The Waste Land." Palestinian poet Jabrā I. Jabrā explains in his essay "Modern Arabic Literature and the West" what excited his generation about the poem: seeing in T. S. Eliot their own "experience of universal tragedy, not only in World War II, but also, and more essentially, in the Palestine debacle," they adopted the wasteland motif of a thirsting land with fertility restored through the murdered god's blood. Yet, interestingly, the poems written by these Arab poets, Muslim as well as Christian, make explicit an identification between Tammuz and Christ that is not present in "The Waste Land," where Christ stays buried. For the Arabs, what brings fertility to the land is "love and sacrifice," writes Jabrā, so they reached for the Cross "as a symbol of great immediacy, and Christ and Tammuz were made one, and the poet was identified with them." Political exigencies could also make an archetypal Christ figure useful to Muslims: Iraqi poet Badr Shākir al-Sāyyab said that in his poem "City of Sinbad," he couched his message—a call to his people to make sacrifices to bring about a political rebirth—in terms of the Christ/Adonis story in order to veil his revolutionary intentions from the Iraqi regime.

In "City of Sinbad," al-Sayyāb gives a shockingly modernist twist to one Gospel episode. When Christ awakens Lazarus from the dead, the poet cries out "Let him sleep"—because a city of death is all he can be reborn into. A wasteland vision of near despair haunts even the Christian poet Yūsuf al-Khāl (Lebanon); his poem "The Eternal Dialogue" agonizes over whether human sinfulness is so great that even "God's cross . . . raised on the hill of time" can't blot it out. This nightmare view of a world perhaps too evil to be redeemed isn't at all limited to Arabs, however. It's a dominant twentieth-century vision, transcending cultural boundaries—a response to the brutal wars, genocides, nuclear terror, and attendant collective moral collapse of the second millennium's close. Filipino poet Ricaredo Demetillo, in "The Scare-Crow Christ," presents modern humanity's grim choice as follows: in our "endless dreariness of days/ Where no oasis greens the sand-choked waste," each of us is either "man diminished . . . crucified" or else this scraggly figure's betrayer, "Judas to this scare-crow Christ." When poets set the figure of Jesus into this moral wasteland, chilling things can happen. Hungary's György Rónay, in his poem "Stones and Bread," invents a terrifying scene blending the Gospel healings with the Temptation. Crafting in a pounding rush of words the way we sinners clamor for healing yet shrink from sacrifice, the poet reinterprets Satan's challenge to Jesus to turn stones into bread: the stones are the hard hearts of the throngs whom Jesus has healed but who, when he asks that they share in "just one of the thorns which tear my forehead ragged," all slink away. Satan taunts Jesus: "Behold . . . the blessed/people your people! . . . hearts stone only stone no hearts . . . so change the stones to bread!" But Jesus, though grieved at humanity's utter desertion of him, resists the temptation to force us to goodness. "No/said Jesus wearily/What for/said Jesus discouraged/Depart from me Satan/said Jesus sadly/ I WILL NOT CHANGE THE STONES TO BREAD."

In a world so abandoned to heartlessness that even Jesus is tempted to despair, poets can be hard put to find grounds for hope. Yet the very act of composing a poem—any creative act—is inherently a hopeful gesture; a new creative work is a birth. Belgian-American poet May Sarton finds in the death-resurrection story of Lazarus a way to figure the struggle personally experienced by many twentieth-century poets in their movement from modernist disillusionment to a discovery of poetry's resurrecting power. Her poem "Lazarus" begins with the poet facing a statue of Lazarus and wondering what it means to come alive in "this heavy world." Like al-Sayyāb, she suggests that Lazarus might better have remained dead, for on awakening "Lazarus relearns despair./His look is grave; his gaze is deep/Upon us, men carved out of sleep/Who wish to pray but have no prayer." The lines capture a characteristic twentieth-century instant: the human spirit hanging by a thread of hope that life isn't as bereft of meaning as it appears. For to "wish to pray" isn't quite to despair. And modernist poems that choose a Gospel text to figure their pain are reaching to touch the hem of a divine cloak in hope of healing. In the poem's second part, the poet experiences her resurrection; her "heavy thickness" gives way to "weightless feet" as her poem takes shape. Yet, significantly, it's not Jesus but Lazarus who calls forth her poetic power. Jesus is utterly absent from the poem.

It's striking how many twentieth-century poems take a Gospel story and remove Jesus from it. The point of his absence can be, as in Sarton's "Lazarus," that divine power is indeed operative in our world, though it now resides in our own human potential for the miraculous.

Or the point can be that we still search for the missing person of God in a modern world that seems to exclude him. "Where is He today?" asks Swedish poet Anders Österling in "Unemployed." Why, asks Russia's Nikolai Gumilyov in "The Progeny of Cain," "do we stoop in impotence,/Feeling, perhaps, that Some One has forgotten us, / . . . Whenever any hand unites/Two sticks . . . in a casual, momentary cross?" Amid these expectant absences, Jesus's sudden entry into a contemporary scene can be transfiguring, whether he steps into an Indian street in Nirendranath Chakrabarti's "Christ of Calcutta"; into a Moscow bread line in Mikhail Pozdnyayev's "Remembrance of Five Loaves"; or into a frozen French morning in Leopold Senghor's "Snow in Paris."

Of course, there are poets for whom Jesus never left the scene, major twentieth-century Christian poets who write out of a more or less traditional faith. Yet they can't help but set their faith in the context of the century's varieties of unbelief. So France's Charles Péguy booms out a seemingly timeless narrative voice presented as that of God himself presiding with infinite patience and wry wit over a world that only half hears him. Wales's R. S. Thomas shares his century's pained sense of God's absence, but meditates on "the hidden God" without losing hope. Greek poet Tákis Papatsónis defies modern disbelief with a classic mysticism that testifies to his own personal encounters with Christ. New Zealand's James K. Baxter plays the prophet, crying out against the injustices of our modern moral wilderness. Vassar Miller, of the United States, asserts her religious and poetic orthodoxy by taking on rigorous Renaissance-Baroque verse forms, through which she tangles with the tangible, even sensual, presence of Jesus in her own flesh. England's W. H. Auden, conscious of how odd a believing voice can sound in his time, plays with levels of diction as he recasts Gospel stories in contemporary dress. Korea's Ku Sang sets his faith in its Eastern environment by writing Christian poems with a Zen feel.

These twentieth-century poets for whom Jesus is without doubt a salvific figure are in a sense like the original evangelists, proclaiming "He is risen" to a questioning world. Yet the features of him who has risen have considerably altered. Reviewing how the figure of Jesus has looked to twenty centuries of poets is like watching the Gospels' central character change costume and reinterpret his part on the changing stage of successive cultures' construction of life's meaning. First we see a glorious Christ the King who is all at once every good figure, from Cultivator to protective Wing to celestial Milk out-pressed from a young bride's fragrant breasts. Then the fourth-century East produces the mind-bending figure of the Creator tucking himself into his creature's womb, while the West shows us the Virgilian Shepherd moving through sylvan mazes to recover his lost sheep. The Middle Ages develop the typological figure who redeems every detail of past history, culminating in a Christ as Celestial Center from whom all meaning radiates through an allegorical system of correspondences, over a stage swelled to cosmic size. With the Renaissance and Reformation, the figure of Jesus comes down to earth, indeed into each human being's individual core, where meaning is now seen to reside. On the stage of the individual heart, the Baroque drama of anguished love between God and the unworthy human lover is played out. Jesus's own human feelings then take center stage for Romantic poets; without losing his divinity, Jesus becomes a Romantic hero, sadly alienated from society but moved by a sympathetic nature. With modernism, Jesus is no longer God but merely human, a shrunken yellowed body hanging purposelessly on a dim stage, where the light of trust in any transcendent meaning has gone out.

But along with this diminished figure, the twentieth century produces many other figures of Jesus as well, so that the century's stage shows us simultaneously a variety of different characters, some playing off each other, some acting in worlds of their own—indeed as in a postmodern drama. So we see one Jesus at the very edge of the stage, moved to the margin of his own story, pondered by poets suspicious that he or anything else can be known. Elsewhere Jesus is actually pushed offstage altogether, though his place can be taken by a humanity now itself possessing divine creative potential. Or, absent, Jesus can be searched for, sensed, or in an unexpected spot suddenly seen. In other places, Jesus is not only present but is an imposing archetypal figure: as political symbol of a nation's sacrificial suffering or of its resurrecting power, he can appear dressed as the divinity of another religion or made to join the native dance in one spot and to contend against native gods in another. The vast center of the twentieth-century stage is, however, a wasteland—a world shattered by evil and nearly empty of hope. Set down in this grim world, Jesus himself can almost despair.

The drama goes on. Poets, whose vocation it is to give voice to their culture's deepest perceptions, show no signs of losing interest in the challenge posed by the Gospels' central figure. And those who will help shape who Jesus is for the poetry of the third millennium are already writing.

*Peggy Rosenthal*
Rochester, New York
July, 1997

# PART ONE

# BIRTH AND INFANCY

# The Incarnation

## *John 1:1–4*

In the beginning was the Word, and the Word was with God, and the Word was God. He was in the beginning with God. All things came into being through him, and without him not one thing came into being. What has come into being in him was life, and the life was the light of all people.

# Words

NIKOLAI GUMILYOV

Russia, 1886–1921. A well-traveled student of philogy and leader of an anti-symbolist poetry movement, Gumilyov fought in World War I and afterwards returned to Russia where he participated in a variety of literary and publishing activities. The first husband of ANNA AKHMATOVA (they divorced in 1918), Gumilyov was executed in Petrograd by a Bolshevik firing squad on charges of conspiracy. "Words" is translated from the Russian by Simon Franklin.

In ancient days, when God cast down his gaze
Upon the newly created world,
Words could stop the sun,
Words could shatter cities.

Eagles didn't spread their wings,
And stars huddled, horror-stricken, round the moon,
Whenever words, like pink flame,
Drifted through the heights.

But lower down in life came numbers,
Like domestic, subjugated cattle;
Clever number can convey
All shades of meaning.

The gray, old sage, who had transcended good and evil
And subdued them to his will,
Had not the nerve to risk a sound,
So, with his staff, he traced a number in the sand.

But we've forgotten that only words
Stay radiant among earthly troubles,
And in the Gospel of St. John
It does say that the word is God.

We have set their limits
At the meager boundaries of matter,
And, like bees in a vacated hive,
Dead words smell foul.

# The True Appearance of the Word

KU SANG

Korea, 1919 –. Journalist, essayist, playwright, Ku Sang has also published many volumes of poems. Seeing the person of Jesus of Nazareth as key to the mystery of daily realities, he often sees those realities with an Eastern, particularly Buddhist, eye: the unexpected minute detail, the paradoxical fullness in "emptiness." "The True Appearance of the Word" is translated from the Korean by Brother Anthony of Taizé.

As the cataract of ignorance falls
from off the eyesight of my soul,
I realize that all this huge Creation
round about me is the Word.

The hitherto quite unattended fact
that these familiar fingers number ten,
like an encounter with some miracle,
suddenly astonishes me

and the newly-opened forsythia flowers
in one corner of the hedge beyond my window
entrance me utterly,
like seeing a model of Resurrection.

Smaller than a grain of sand
in the oceanic vastness of the cosmos,
I realize that this my muttering,
by a mysterious grace of the Word,

is no imagined thing, no mere sign,
but Reality itself.

# The Incarnation

## JOHN OF THE CROSS

Spain, 1542–1591. Influenced by TERESA OF AVILA, John labored to spread the reform of the Carmelite order. For this he was imprisoned by the Carmelite prior general. In prison, suffering brutal treatment, he began writing the mystical poetry for which he is famous. In Spain's extraordinary tradition of mystical writing, John stands out as the master poet. "The Incarnation" is translated from the Spanish by Kieran Kavanaugh and Otilio Rodriguez.

Now that the time had come
when it would be good
to ransom the bride
serving under the hard yoke
of that law
which Moses had given her,
the Father, with tender love,
spoke in this way:
"Now you see, Son, that your bride
was made in your image,
and so far as she is like you
she will suit you well;
yet she is different, in her flesh,
which your simple being does not have.
In perfect love
this law holds:
that the lover become
like the one he loves;
for the greater their likeness
the greater their delight.
Surely your bride's delight
would greatly increase
were she to see you like her,
in her own flesh."
"My will is yours,"
the Son replied,
"and my glory is
that your will be mine.
This is fitting, Father,

what you, the Most High, say;
for in this way
your goodness will be more evident,
your great power will be seen
and your justice and wisdom.
I will go and tell the world,
spreading the word
of your beauty and sweetness
and of your sovereignty.
I will go seek my bride
and take upon myself
her weariness and labors
in which she suffers so;
and that she may have life,
I will die for her,
and lifting her out of that deep,
I will restore her to you."

# The Coming

R. S. THOMAS

Wales, 1913 –. An Anglican priest considered the leading twentieth century Welsh poet in English, Thomas has devoted a lifetime of poetry to meditating on "the hidden God." In tune with the stark Welsh landscape and harsh living conditions of his rural parish, Thomas writes a primarily dark poetry, pained by God's apparent absence. Against this background, a poem like "The Bright Field" (p. 229) is startlingly light.

> And God held in his hand
> A small globe. Look, he said.
> The son looked. Far off,
> As through water, he saw
> A scorched land of fierce
> Colour. The light burned
> There; crusted buildings
> Cast their shadows; a bright
> Serpent, a river
> Uncoiled itself, radiant
> With slime.
>                     On a bare
> Hill a bare tree saddened
> The sky. Many people
> Held out their thin arms
> To it, as though waiting
> For a vanished April
> To return to its crossed
> Boughs. The son watched
> Them. Let me go there, he said.

# The Annunciation

## Luke 1:26—38

In the sixth month the angel Gabriel was sent by God to a town in Galilee called Nazareth, to a virgin engaged to a man whose name was Joseph, of the houses of David. The virgin's name was Mary. And he came to her and said, "Greetings, favored one! The Lord is with you." But she was much perplexed by his words and pondered what sort of greeting this might be. The angel said to her, "Do not be afraid, Mary, for you have found favor with God. And now, you will conceive in your womb and bear a son, and you will name him Jesus. He will be great, and will be called the Son of the Most High, and the Lord God will give to him the throne of his ancestor David. He will reign over the house of Jacob forever, and of his kingdom there will be no end." Mary said to the angel, "How can this be, since I am a virgin?" The angel said to her, "The Holy Spirit will come upon you, and the power of the Most High will overshadow you; therefore the child to be born will be holy; he will be called Son of God. And now, your relative Elizabeth in her old age has also conceived a son; and this is the sixth month for her who was said to be barren. For nothing will be impossible with God." Then Mary said, "Here am I, the servant of the Lord; let it be with me according to your word." Then the angel departed from her.

# Antiphon for the Virgin

### HILDEGARD OF BINGEN

Germany, 1098–1179. Famous throughout Europe during her lifetime, Hilde-
gard was a composer and poet, a writer on scientific and theological subjects,
abbess of a monastery in her native Germany, and a prophet whose visions
were approved by the reigning Pope. She wrote her poems to be chanted by the
nuns of her monastery; she also composed the music to which the poems were
set. "Antiphon for the Virgin" is translated from the Latin by Barbara Newman.

Pierced by the light of God
Mary Virgin,
drenched in the speech of God,
your body bloomed,
swelling with the breath of God.

For the Spirit purged you
of the poison Eve took.
She soiled all freshness when she caught
that infection
from the devil's suggestion.

But in wonder within you
you hid an untainted
child of God's mind
and God's Son blossomed in your body.

The Holy One was his midwife:
his birth broke the laws
of flesh that Eve made. He was coupled
to wholeness
in the seedbed of holiness.

# Annunciation

PRIMO LEVI

Italy, 1919–1987. A chemist from Turin, Levi was arrested as an antifascist and deported to Auschwitz in 1944. His memoirs of the Holocaust and his several collections of lyrical essays are internationally famous. His "Annunciation" grimly places the gospel of Luke in the context of the Book of Revelation. "Annunciation" is translated from the Italian by Ruth Feldman and Brian Swan.

Don't be dismayed, woman, by my fierce form.
I come from far away, in headlong flight;
Whirlwinds may have ruffled my feathers.
I am an angel, yes, and not a bird of prey;
An angel, but not the one in your paintings
That descended in another age to promise another
      Lord.
I come to bring you news, but wait until my heaving
      chest,
The loathing of the void and dark, subside.
Sleeping in you is one who will destroy much sleep.
He's still unformed but soon you'll caress his limbs.
He will have the gift of words, the fascinator's eyes,
Will preach abomination and be believed by all.
Jubilant and wild, singing and bleeding,
They'll follow him in bands, kissing his footprints.
He will carry the lie to the farthest borders.
Evangelize with blasphemy and the gallows.
He'll rule in terror, suspect poisons
In spring-water, in the air of high plateaus.
He'll see deceit in the clear eyes of the newborn,
And die unsated by slaughter, leaving behind sown
      hate.
This is your growing seed. Woman, rejoice.

# Mary's Poem

KATHLEEN WAKEFIELD

U.S., 1954–. Poet and teacher, Wakefield lives in Rochester, New York. Her
poetry has appeared in *The Georgia Review*, *Poetry*, and other journals; her
chapbook, *There and Back*, was published by State Street Press (1993). Wake-
field frequently turns to Gospel scenes to explore the relation between the
Word and lived experience. "Mary's Poem" was originally commissioned to
be set to music.

> When she heard infinity
> whispered in her ear, did the flashing
> scissors in her fingers fall
> to the wooden floor and the spool unravel,
> the spider's sly cradle
> tremble with love? Imagine
>
> How the dry fields leaned
> toward the news and she heard, for a moment,
> the households of crickets—
> When she answered, all things shifted, the moon
> in its river of milk.
>
> And when she wanted to pluck
> her heart from her breast, did she remember
> a commotion of wings, or the stirring
> of dust?

# The Visitation

## Luke 1:39−55

In those days Mary set out and went with haste to a Judean town in the hill country, where she entered the house of Zechariah and greeted Elizabeth. When Elizabeth heard Mary's greeting, the child leaped in her womb. And Elizabeth was filled with the Holy Spirit and exclaimed with a loud cry, "Blessed are you among women, and blessed is the fruit of your womb. And why has this happened to me, that the mother of my Lord comes to me? For as soon as I heard the sound of your greeting, the child in my womb leaped for joy. And blessed is she who believed that there would be fulfillment of what was spoken to her by the Lord."

And Mary said,
"My soul magnifies the Lord,

and my spirit rejoices in God my Savior,

for he has looked with favor on the lowliness of his servant.
Surely, from now on all generations will call me blessed;

for the Mighty One has done great things for me,
and holy is his name.

His mercy is for those who fear him
from generation to generation.

He has shown strength with his arm;
he has scattered the proud in the thoughts of their hearts.

He has brought down the powerful from their thrones,
and lifted up the lowly;

he has filled the hungry with good things,
and sent the rich away empty.

He has helped his servant Israel,
in remembrance of his mercy,

according to the promise he made to our ancestors,
to Abraham and to his descendants forever."

# The Visitation

ROBERT SOUTHWELL

England, c.1561–1595. A Jesuit educated at Douai and Paris, Southwell resided for several years at the English College in Rome, where he became acquainted with Italian secular poetry. Requesting he be sent to England, he returned at a time perilous for Catholics. Arrested in 1592, he was continually interrogated, occasionally tortured, and finally executed by hanging. Unlike many Roman Catholic poets, Southwell often drew direct inspiration from scriptural passages; "The Visitation" is part of a sequence of poems reflecting on the first chapter of Luke.

> Proclaimed Queen and mother of a god,
> The light of earth, the sovereign of Saints,
> With Pilgrim foot, up tiring hills she trod,
> And heavenly stile with handmaid's toil acquaints;
> Her youth to age, her health to sick she lends,
> Her heart to God, to neighbor hand she bends.
>
> A prince she is, and mightier prince doth bear.
> Yet pomp of princely train she would not have.
> But doubtless heavenly Quires attendant were,
> Her child from harm, herself from fall to save;
> Word to the voice, song to the tune she brings,
> The voice her word, the tune her ditty sings.
>
> Eternal lights enclosed in her breast
> Shot out such piercing beams of burning love
> That when her voice her cousin's ears possessed,
> The force thereof did force her babe to move.
> With secret signs the children greet each other,
> But open praise each leaveth to his mother.

# The Birth of John the Baptist

## Luke 1:57–66

Now the time came for Elizabeth to give birth, and she bore a son. Her neighbors and relatives heard that the Lord had shown his great mercy to her, and they rejoiced with her.

On the eighth day they came to circumcise the child, and they were going to name him Zechariah after his father. But his mother said, "No; he is to be called John." They said to her, "None of your relatives has this name." Then they began motioning to his father to find out what name he wanted to give him. He asked for a writing tablet and wrote, "His name is John." And all of them were amazed. Immediately his mouth was opened and his tongue freed, and he began to speak, praising God. Fear came over all their neighbors, and all these things were talked about throughout the entire hill country of Judea. All who heard them pondered them and said, "What then will this child become?" For, indeed, the hand of the Lord was with him.

# To St. John the Baptist

ANDREZJ MORSZTYN

Poland, 1613?–1693. A statesman and courtier whose work circulated largely in manuscripts, Morsztyn fled to France in 1683 under charges of treason and died a French citizen. He was a prolific translator, particularly of the work of MARINO. "To St. John the Baptist" is translated from the Polish by Jerzy Peterkiewicz and Burns Singer with Jon Stallworthy.

Of course you are the messenger, you who
   Shed the grey brightness which the sun breaks
      through.
As when pale dawn provokes the birds to play
   Their music glorifies the shape of day,
So your birth violates your father's tongue
   Till, from his lips, a shriek of praise is wrung.
And as the sun burns red when the last gleam
   Of styptic dawn admits a blood-red stream,
Your blood, too, gushes on the world whose fate
   The sun you herald will illuminate.

# Joseph

## *Matthew 1:18–24*

Now the birth of Jesus the Messiah took place in this way. When his mother Mary had been engaged to Joseph, but before they lived together, she was found to be with child from the Holy Spirit. Her husband Joseph, being a righteous man and unwilling to expose her to public disgrace, planned to dismiss her quietly. But just when he had resolved to do this, an angel of the Lord appeared to him in a dream and said, "Joseph, son of David, do not be afraid to take Mary as your wife, for the child conceived in her is from the Holy Spirit. She will bear a son, and you are to name him Jesus, for he will save his people from their sins." All this took place to fulfill what had been spoken by the Lord through the prophet:

> "Look, the virgin shall conceive and bear a son,
>   and they shall name him Emmanuel,"

which means, "God is with us." When Joseph awoke from sleep, he did as the angel of the Lord commanded him; he took her as his wife.

# The Temptation of St. Joseph
## from *For the Time Being*

W. H. AUDEN

England, 1907–1973. Born in York, Auden graduated from Oxford in 1928 and
that year published his first volume of poetry. A few years later it was revised
and reissued at the urging of T.S. Eliot, who helped launch his literary career.
Auden married Thomas Mann's daughter Erika in 1935 to help her escape Nazi
Germany. After witnessing the Spanish Civil War, Auden grew increasingly re-
ligious. In 1946 he became a U.S. citizen and published *For the Time Being: A
Christmas Oratorio*, which he dedicated to his Anglo-Catholic mother.

I

JOSEPH
My shoes were shined, my pants were cleaned and pressed,
And I was hurrying to meet
   My own true Love:
But a great crowd grew and grew
Till I could not push my way through,
   Because
A star had fallen down the street;
   When they saw who I was,
The police tried to do their best.

> CHORUS [*off*]
> *Joseph, you have heard*
> *What Mary says occurred;*
> *Yes, it may be so.*
> *Is it likely? No.*

JOSEPH
The bar was gay, the lighting well-designed,
And I was sitting down to wait
   My own true Love:
A voice I'd heard before, I think,
Cried: "This is on the House. I drink
   To him
Who does not know it is too late;"

When I asked for the time,
Everyone was very kind.

> CHORUS [*off*]
> *Mary may be pure,*
> *But, Joseph, are you sure?*
> *How is one to tell?*
> *Suppose, for instance . . . Well . . .*

JOSEPH

Through cracks, up ladders, into waters deep,
I squeezed, I climbed, I swam to save
   My own true Love:
Under a dead apple tree
I saw an ass; when it saw me
   It brayed;
A hermit sat in the mouth of a cave:
   When I asked him the way,
He pretended to be asleep.

> CHORUS [*off*]
> *Maybe, maybe not.*
> *But, Joseph, you know what*
> *Your world, of course, will say*
> *About you anyway.*

JOSEPH

Where are you, Father, where?
Caught in the jealous trap
Of an empty house I hear
As I sit alone in the dark
Everything, everything,
The drip of the bathroom tap,
The creak of the sofa spring,
The wind in the air-shaft, all
Making the same remark
Stupidly, stupidly,
Over and over again.
Father, what have I done?
Answer me, Father, how
Can I answer the tactless wall

Or the pompous furniture now?
Answer them . . .

GABRIEL
No, you must.

JOSEPH
How then am I to know,
Father, that you are just?
Give me one reason.

GABRIEL
            No.

JOSEPH
All I ask is one
Important and elegant proof
That what my Love had done
Was really at your will
And that your will is Love.

GABRIEL
No, you must believe;
Be silent, and sit still.

# The Nativity

*Luke 2:1—7*

In those days a decree went out from Emperor Augustus that all the world should be registered. This was the first registration and was taken while Quirinius was governor of Syria. All went to their own towns to be registered. Joseph also went from the town of Nazareth in Galilee to Judea, to the city of David called Bethlehem, because he was descended from the house and family of David. He went to be registered with Mary, to whom he was engaged and who was expecting a child. While they were there, the time came for her to deliver her child. And she gave birth to her firstborn son and wrapped him in bands of cloth, and laid him in a manger, because there was no place for them in the inn.

# *from* Hymn on the Nativity #4

EPHREM

Syria, d.373. A deacon of the Christian church in Asia Minor, Ephrem was also
an influential theologian whose medium was poetry. His hymns, written in
Syriac (a dialect of Aramaic, the language Jesus himself spoke), burst with
paradox and symbol. They were popular in his day and are still used in the
liturgy of the Syrian Christian Church. "Hymn on the Nativity #4" is translated
from the Syriac by Kathleen McVey.


Mary bore a mute Babe
though in Him were hidden all our tongues.
Joseph carried Him, yet hidden in Him was
a silent nature older than everything.
The Lofty One became like a little child, yet hidden in Him was
a treasure of Wisdom that suffices for all.
He was lofty but he sucked Mary's milk,
and from His blessings all creation sucks,
He is the Living Breast of living breath;
by His life the dead were suckled, and they revived.
Without the breath of air no one can live;
without the power of the Son no one can rise.
Upon the living breath of the One Who vivifies all
depend the living beings above and below.
As indeed He sucked Mary's milk,
He has given suck—life to the universe.
As again He dwelt in His mother's womb,
in His womb dwells all creation.
Mute He was as a babe, yet He gave
to all creation all His commands.

# Christmas

## CONSTANTIJN HUYGENS

Netherlands, 1596–1687. A man of many accomplishments, Huygens was a
diplomat, musician, and composer as well as a poet. On a diplomatic mission
to London, he met JOHN DONNE, whose poetry so intrigued him that he
translated nineteen of Donne's poems. Huygens' poetry is baroque as well in
its terse wit and ingenuity, as illustrated in "Christmas," which plays with para-
doxes of the Incarnation. "Christmas" is translated from the Dutch by Adriaan
J. Barnouw.

> Though crowded be the inn, although God's son
>   Is lying in the hay, my soul may enter.
>   There's need, on man of flesh, of thoughts that centre
> On fleshly things today: here cryeth one.
>
> Who'll cry one day for us, compared to whom
>   A queen's newborn is but a worthless plaything.
>   This child in manager will fulfil our waiting
> Whenas the times are full and ease our doom.
>
> God resteth in our flesh, here fatherless,
>   In heaven motherless, Word co-creative,
>   God, Father of the virgin and her native,
> Lies in the hay. Rest here and cease thy stress,
>
> My soul, cease rhyming without rhyme or reason.
> A mute humility is here in season.

# A Child in Starlight

ELMER DIKTONIUS

Finland, 1896–1961. Born in Helsinki, Diktonius studied literature and music (he originally hoped to be a composer) in England, France, and Czechoslovakia. A devoted Socialist from a working-class family, he founded two avant-garde magazines and as poet, translator, critic, and novelist he was an important influence on mid-twentieth-century Scandinavian literature. "A Child in Starlight" is translated from the Finnish by Martin S. Allwood.

> There is a child,
> A new-born child—
> A rosy, new-born child.
>
> The child whimpers—
> All children do.
> And the mother takes the child to her breast.
> Then it is quiet.
> So is every child.
>
> The roof is not over tight—
> Not all roofs are.
> And the star puts
> Its silver muzzle through the chink,
> And steals up to the little one's head.
> Stars like children.
>
> And the mother looks up at the star
> And understands—
> All mothers understand.
> And presses her frightened baby
> To her breast—
> But the child sucks quietly in starlight:
> All children suck in starlight.
>
> It knows nothing yet about the cross:
> No child does.

# An Abandoned Bundle

OSWALD MBUYOSENI MTSHALI

South Africa, 1940–. Raised under apartheid, Mtshali was denied a university education because he was black. Living in Soweto, he became the poet of apartheid's urban landscape, detailing its inhumanity with controlled irony. After achieving success as a poet, he did advanced study in the United States and returned to Soweto to teach college.

The morning mist
and chimney smoke
of White City Jabavu
flowed thick yellow
as pus oozing
from a gigantic sore.

It smothered our little houses
like fish caught in a net.

Scavenging dogs
draped in red bandanas of blood
fought fiercely
for a squirming bundle.

I threw a brick;
they bared fangs
flicked velvet tongues of scarlet
and scurried away,
leaving a mutilated corpse —
an infant dumped on a rubbish heap —
"Oh! Baby in the Manger
sleep well
on human dung."

Its mother
had melted into the rays of the rising sun,
her face glittering with innocence
her heart as pure as untrampled dew.

# The Nativity of Christ

LUIS DE GÓNGORA Y ARGOTE

Spain, 1561–1625. Attempting to ennoble the Spanish language by re-Latinizing it with intricate syntax and mythological allusion, Góngora invented an elaborate style that influenced all of seventeenth-century Spanish poetry. "The Nativity of Christ" is one of the more accessible samples, typical in its classical note (Aurora) and its changes rung on a single colorful image (the crimson blossom). "The Nativity of Christ" is translated from the Spanish by H. W. Longfellow.

Today from the Aurora's bosom
A pink has fallen—a crimson blossom—
And oh, how glorious rests the hay
On which the fallen blossom lay!

When silence gently had unfurled
Her mantle over all below,
And crowned with winter's frost and snow,
Night swayed the sceptre of the world,
Amid the gloom descending slow,
Upon the monarch's frozen bosom
A pink has fallen,—a crimson blossom.

The only flower the Virgin bore
(Aurora fair) within her breast,
She gave to earth, yet still possessed
Her virgin blossom as before;
That hay that colored drop caressed,—
Received upon its faithful bosom
That single flower,—a crimson blossom.
The manger, unto which 'twas given,
Even amid wintry snows and cold,
Within its fostering arms to fold
The blushing flower that fell from heaven,
Was as a canopy of gold,—
A downy couch,—where on its bosom
That flower had fallen,—that crimson blossom.

# The Lamb Baaed Gently

JUAN RAMÓN JIMÉNEZ

Spain, 1881–1958. Winner of the 1956 Nobel Prize for Literature, Jiménez wrote mystical poetry which is, like most of its genre, unbiblical; it expresses love for God unmediated by Scripture. Jiménez used poetry as his diary and confessional, recording (as in "The Lamb Baaed Gently," where the biblical moment does break in) his vision of the commonplace transformed by poetry's music. "The Lamb Baaed Gently" is translated from the Spanish by Eloise Roach.

The lamb baaed gently.
The tender donkey showed its joy
in lusty bray.
The dog barked playfully
almost talking to the stars.

I could not sleep. I went outdoors
and saw heavenly tracks upon the ground
all flower-decked
like a sky
turned upside down.

A warm and fragrant mist
hovered over the grove;
the moon was sinking low
in a soft golden west
of divine orbit.

My breast beat without a pause,
as if my heart had wined . . .

I opened wide the stable door to see
if He were there.
He was!

# Friend, This Is Your Christmas

RENÉ DEPESTRE

Haiti, 1926–. At age 19, abandoning his traditional education and Christianity, Depestre published inflammatory, Marxist-oriented poetry that brought about his banishment. Living first in France and then in Cuba, he has published many volumes of poetry, written in French. "Friend, This Is Your Christmas" is translated from the French by Norman Shapiro.

There is no
Baby Jesus Christmas-time
for dirty hands
for tattered clothes
for empty eyes
for gazes hanging on the baker's loaves.

For the sneering smile of poverty
on gaping lips
there is no
Baby Jesus Christmas-time
for the darkness of hovels
for the cold hard bed of pain
for the lack of blankets
for the paradox of slaving for your bread
for the crime of the salary-man
for all that underground humanity
that you would lighten with your firebrand words.

No, no my friend
the Christmas-time of gleaming shops
of pretty toys
of low-necked gowns
of dancing midnight revels
of cannon-shots
of stupid sermons
of starch-collared gentlemen
who wear away the future of your children
of merrymaking in the fine big houses
no, if the poor little child of Bethlehem

chose this day to be born
in the heady swirl of dizzying dances
Christmas-time is not for you.

Your Christmas-time, my friend
lies sleeping in your conscience
in your bitterness
in your hopes
in all your question-marks
that stand before the world they made for you
in the overflowing torrent of your hatreds long held back.

# The Shepherds

*Luke 2:8—14*

In that region there were shepherds living in the fields, keeping watch over their flock by night. Then an angel of the Lord stood before them, and the glory of the Lord shone around them, and they were terrified. But the angel said to them, "Do not be afraid; for see—I am bringing you good news of great joy for all the people: to you is born this day in the city of David a Savior, who is the Messiah, the Lord. This will be a sign for you: you will find a child wrapped in bands of cloth and lying in a manger." And suddenly there was with the angel a multitude of the heavenly host, praising God and saying,

> "Glory to God in the highest heaven,
>> and on earth peace among those whom he favors!"

# Snow in Paris

LÉOPOLD SÉDAR SENGHOR

Senegal, 1906–. Raised Catholic and trained as a priest in French colonial
Senegal, Senghor completed his studies in France. Choosing poetry rather than
priesthood as a career, he celebrated African culture without simply con-
demning the European. At Senegal's independence in 1960, Senghor was
elected President, which he remained until 1981. He kept writing poetry, how-
ever, and was honored for expanding the French language into a multicultural
medium by becoming, in 1983, the first African elected to the French Academy.
"Snow in Paris" is translated from the French by Melvin Dixon.


Lord, you have visited Paris on this day of your birth
Because it has become mean and evil,
You have purified it with incorruptible cold, with white death.
This morning, right up to the factory smokestacks
Singing in unison, draped in white flags–
"Peace to Men of Good Will!"
Lord, you have offered the snow of your Peace to a torn world,
To divided Europe and ravaged Spain
And the Catholic and Jewish Rebels have fired their fourteen hundred
Cannons upon the mountain of your Peace.
Lord, I have accepted your white cold, burning hotter than salt.
And now my heart melts like snow in the sun.


I forget
The white hands firing the rifles that crumbled our empires,
The hands that once whipped slaves, and that whipped you,
The snowy white hands that slapped you,
The powdery white hands that slapped me,
The firm hands that led me to loneliness and to hate,
The white hands that cut down the forests
Of straight, firm palmyra trees dominating Africa,
In the heart of Africa, like the Sara men,
Handsome as the first men born from your brown hands.
They tore down the black forest to build a railroad,
They cut down Africa's forests to save Civilization,
Because they needed human raw materials.

Lord, I know I'll never release this reserve of hatred
For diplomats who show their long canine teeth
And tomorrow trade in black flesh.
My heart, Lord, has melted like the snow on the roofs of Paris
In the sunshine of your gentleness.
It is kind even unto my enemies and unto my brothers
With hands white without snow
Because of these hands of dew, in the evening,
Upon my burning cheeks.

## Luke 2:15—19

When the angels had left them and gone into heaven, the shepherds said to one another, "Let us go now to Bethlehem and see this thing that has taken place, which the Lord has made known to us." So they went with haste and found Mary and Joseph, and the child lying in the manger. When they saw this, they made known what had been told them about this child; and all who heard it were amazed at what the shepherds told them. But Mary treasured all these words and pondered them in her heart.

# A Christmas Carol

SAMUEL TAYLOR COLERIDGE

England, 1772–1834. Philosopher, critic, poet, Coleridge is one of English literary history's greatest figures. In his early adult years, seeking a mean between atheism and what he saw as Anglican mystification, he proselytized for a Unitarianism merged with a radical politics of faith in human progress based on imitating Christ's good works. Later Coleridge developed a stronger sense of human sin and, disillusioned with Unitarianism as too rational and optimistic, gradually returned to the religious orthodoxy of the Church of England. "A Christmas Carol" (1799) belongs to his earlier period, when he was writing newspaper polemics embracing Napoleon's peace-making claims. The poem is historically significant for turning the Christmas story into an anti-war tract two decades before the newly founded European peace movement started popularizing such discourse.

> The shepherds went their hasty way,
>    And found the lowly stable-shed
> Where the virgin-mother lay:
>    And now they checked their eager tread,
> For to the babe, that at her bosom clung,
> A mother's song the virgin-mother sung.
>
> They told her how a glorious light,
>    Streaming from a heavenly throng,
> Around them shone, suspending night;
>    While sweeter than a mother's song,
> Blessed angels heralded the Saviour's birth,
> Glory to God on high! and peace on earth.
>
> She listened to the tale divine,
>    And closer still the babe she pressed;
> And while she cried, "The babe is mine!"
>    The milk rushed faster to her breast:
> Joy rose within her, like a summer's morn:
> Peace, peace on earth! the Prince of peace is born.
>
> Thou mother of the Prince of peace,
>    Poor, simple, and of low estate;
> That strife should vanish, battle cease,

Oh! why should this thy soul elate?
Sweet music's loudest note, the poet's story,
Didst thou ne'er love to hear of fame and glory?

And is not War a youthful king,
    A stately hero clad in mail?
Beneath his footsteps laurels spring;
    Him earth's majestic monarchs hail!
Their friend, their playmate! and his bold bright eye
Compels the maiden's love-confessing sigh.

"Tell this in some more courtly scene,
    To maids and youths in robes of state!
I am a woman poor and mean,
    And therefore is my soul elate.
War is a ruffian, all with guilt defiled,
That from the aged father tears his child!

"A murderous fiend, by fiends adored,
He kills the sire and starves the son,
The husband kills, and from her board
    Steals all his widow's toil had won;
Plunders God's world of beauty; rends away
All safety from the night, all comfort from the day.

"Then wisely is my soul elate,
    That strife should vanish, battle cease;
I'm poor, and of a low estate,
    The mother of the Prince of peace!
Joy rises in me, like a summer's morn;
Peace, peace on earth! the Prince of peace is born!"

# The Circumcision and Naming

*Luke 2:21*

After eight days had passed, it was time to circumcise the child; and he was called Jesus, the name given by the angel before he was conceived in the womb.

# The Circumcision

TERESA OF AVILA

Spain, 1515–1582. Founder of the reformed "discalced" branch of Carmelite nuns, Teresa travelled through Spain setting up convents. Her most famous writings are prose accounts of her life and mystical experiences. She composed poems for two purposes: either to express to God her love; or to instruct in Christian doctrine the nuns under her care, by delighting them with poetry's play of rhythm and sound. "The Circumcision" is translated from the Spanish by Adrian J. Cooney.

> He is shedding blood,
> *Dominguillo, eh!*
> *Why I know not!*
>
> I ask you why,
> Him they condemn,
> Innocent He is,
> And without evil?
> How ardent His desire,
> I know not why,
> To love me so ardently:
> *Oh, Dominguillo!*
>
> Then after He was born,
> Why did they torment Him?
>
> —Yes, for He is dying
> To cast out evil.
> Oh, what a great Shepherd
> He will surely be!
> *Oh, Dominguillo!*
>
> Certainly you have seen
> He is but a sinless child?
> —They have told me,
> Brasillo and Llorente;
> Great will be the loss
> Not to love Him
> *Oh, Dominguillo!*

# The Presentation in the Temple

*Luke 2:22—28*

When the time came for their purification according to the law of Moses, they brought him up to Jerusalem to present him to the Lord (as it is written in the law of the Lord, "Every firstborn male shall be designated as holy to the Lord"), and they offered a sacrifice according to what is stated in the law of the Lord, "a pair of turtledoves or two young pigeons."

Now there was a man in Jerusalem whose name was Simeon; this man was righteous and devout, looking forward to the consolation of Israel, and the Holy Spirit rested on him. It had been revealed to him by the Holy Spirit that he would not see death before he had seen the Lord's Messiah. Guided by the Spirit, Simeon came into the temple; and when the parents brought in the child Jesus, to do for him what was customary under the law, Simeon took him in his arms and praised God. . . .

# *from* Music of Harmonious Heaven
# in Reverent Thanks to the Lord of Heaven

WU LI

China, 1631–1718. Though Wu Li is renowned for his paintings of landscapes and bamboos, he was equally gifted as a poet. Converting to Christianity, Wu Li became a Jesuit priest in 1688. His effort to express his new faith poetically has earned him praise as the first Chinese to find a poetic vehicle for Christian doctrine. This selection from *Music of Harmonious Heaven* . . . is translated from the Chinese by Jonathan Chaves.

> Late in Han
> God's Son came down from Heaven
> to save us people
> and turn us towards the good.
> His grace goes wide!
> Taking flesh through the virginity
> > of the Holy Mother in a stable He was born.
> Joseph too came to present Him in the temple:
> there to offer praise was
> Simeon.
> They say He can
> save our souls from their destructiveness
> and sweep away the devil's wantonness.

# The Presentation of Christ in the Temple

CHRISTOPHER SMART

England, 1722–1771. His contemporaries institutionalized Smart for insanity
and saw his poetry as wild religious raving. But later generations recognized his
poetic gift, profuse in imagery while quite controlled in versification. Much of
Smart's poetry is inventive variations on the theme of praising God; in a famous
poem, "Jubilate Agno," the poet's cat Jeoffry joins in the praise.


Preserver of the church, thy spouse,
    From sacrilege and wrong,
To whom the myriads pay their vows,
Give ear, and in my heart arouse
    The spirit of a nobler song.

When Hiero built, from David's plan,
    The house of godlike style,
And Solomon, the prosp'rous man,
Whose reign with wealth and fame began,
    O 'erlaid with gold the glorious pile;

Great was the concourse of mankind
    The structure to review;
Such bulk with sweet proportion join'd
The labours of a vaster mind,
    In all directions grand and true.

And yet it was not true and grand
    The Godhead to contain;
By whom immensity is spann'd,
Which has eternal in his hand
    The globe of his supreme domain.

Tho' there the congregation knelt
    The daily debt to pay,
Tho' there superior glories dwelt,
Tho' there the host their blessings dealt,
    The highest GRACE was far away.

At length another fane arose,
        The fabrick of the poor;
And built by hardship midst her foes,
One hand for work and one for blows,
        Made this stupendous blessing sure.

That God should in the world appear
        Incarnate—as a child—
That he should be presented here,
At once our utmost doubts to clear,
        And make our hearts with wonder wild.

Present ye therefore, on your knees,
        Hearts, hands resign'd and clean;
Ye poor and mean of all degrees,
If he will condescend and please
        To take at least what orphans glean—

I speak for all—for them that fly,
        And for the race that swim;
For all that dwell in moist and dry,
Beasts, reptiles, flow'rs and gems to vie
        When gratitude begins her hymn.

Praise him ye doves, and ye that pipe
        Ere buds begin to stir;
Ev'n every finch of every stripe,
And thou of filial love the type,
        O stork! that sit'st upon the fir.

Praise him thou sea, to whom he gave
        The shoal of active mutes;
(Fit tenants of thy roaring wave)
Who comes to still the fiends, that rave
        In oracles and school disputes.

By Jesus number'd all and priz'd,
        Praise him in dale and hill;
Ye beasts for use and peace devis'd,

And thou which patient and despis'd,
        Yet shalt a prophecy fulfill.

Praise him ye family that weave
        The crimson to be spread
There, where communicants receive,
And ye, that form'd the eye to grieve,
        Hid in green bush or wat'ry bed.

Praise him ye flow'rs that serve the swarm
        With honey for their cells;
Ere yet the vernal day is warm,
To call out millions to perform
        Their gambols on your cups and bells.

Praise him ye gems of lively spark,
        And thou the pearl of price;
In that great depth or caverns dark,
Nor yet are wrested from the mark,
To serve the turns of pride and vice.

Praise him ye cherubs of his breast,
        The mercies of his love,
Ere yet from guile and hate profest,
The phenix makes his fragrant nest
        In his own paradise above.

# The Adoration of the Magi

## Matthew 2:1–3, 7–12

In the time of King Herod, after Jesus was born in Bethlehem of Judea, wise men from the East came to Jerusalem, asking, "Where is the child who has been born king of the Jews? For we observed his star at its rising, and have come to pay him homage." When King Herod heard this, he was frightened, and all Jerusalem with him.

Then Herod secretly called for the wise men and learned from them the exact time when the star had appeared. Then he sent them to Bethlehem, saying, "Go and search diligently for the child; and when you have found him, bring me word so that I may also go and pay him homage." When they had heard the king, they set out; and there, ahead of them, went the star that they had seen at its rising, until it stopped over the place where the child was. When they saw that the star had stopped, they were overwhelmed with joy. On entering the house, they saw the child with Mary his mother; and they knelt down and paid him homage. Then, opening their treasure chests, they offered him gifts of gold, frankincense, and myrrh. And having been warned in a dream not to return to Herod, they left for their own country by another road.

# Nativity

GLADYS MAY CASELY-HAYFORD

[Aquah Laluah] Gold Coast, 1904–1950. Born into the Fanti tribe, Aquah Laluah had, she writes, "singularly cultured parents": her mother was the daughter of a judge, her father a pioneer Ghanaian lawyer. Educated in England, she returned to Sierra Leone to teach school. "By twenty, I had the firm conviction that I was meant to write for Africa. The first thing to do was to imbue our own people with the idea of their own beauty. . . . "

Within a native hut, ere stirred the dawn,
Unto the Pure One was an Infant born,
Wrapped in blue lappah that His mother dyed,
Laid on His father's home-tanned deerskin hide,
The Babe still slept, by all things glorified.
Spirits of black bards burst their bonds and sang
'Peace upon earth' until the heavens rang.
All the black babies who from earth had fled
Peeped through the clouds—then gathered round His head,
Telling of things a baby needs to do,
When first he opes his eyes on wonder new;
Telling Him that sleep was sweetest rest,
All comfort came from His black mother's breast.
Their gift was Love, caught from the springing sod,
Whilst tears and laughter were the gifts of God.
Then all the Wise Men of the past stood forth,
Filling the air, East, West, and South and North,
And told Him of the joy that wisdom brings
To mortals in their earthly wanderings.
The children of the past shook down each bough,
Wreathed frangipani blossoms for His brow,
They put pink lilies in His mother's hand,
And heaped for both the first fruits of the land.
His father cut some palm fronds, that the air
Be coaxed to zephyrs while He rested there.
Birds trilled their hallelujahs; all the dew
Trembled with laughter, till the Babe laughed too.
Black women brought their love so wise,
And kissed their motherhood into His mother's eyes.

# The Magi in Europe

KHALĪL HĀWĪ

Lebanon, 1925–1982. Poet and scholar Hāwī was editing the *Encyclopedia of Arabic Poetry* at the time of his suicide, in protest of the Israeli invasion of Beirut in 1982. His poetry reflects a satiric pessimism about the Arab world's capacity to meet the challenge of Western scientific materialism—a pessimism evident in "The Magi in Europe." Hāwī claimed (perhaps defensively) that he used Christian symbols not for their doctrinal content but for their significance as archetypal images. "The Magi in Europe" is translated from the Arabic by Diana Der Hovanessian and Lena Jayyusi.

> "And it came to pass that the Magi, led by the Star
> of the East, found the Child, and fell on their
> knees before Him."

O Magi of the East, did you continue?
Did you follow the ocean flood and
civilization to the new lands?
Did you find what god reveals himself now
again in the cave? Come. The road starts here.
The star shines here. And here again
provisions for your travel.

Let the star of the adventurous lead
you to Paris where you can try the doors
of the laboratories of thought and where
you can discard thinking for celebrations
with buffoons. And in Rome you may watch
the star shroud itself and be
extinguished by the glow of censers
swung by eager priests.
Then in London it can disappear
and lose you in a fog of coal dust and in
ciphers of commerce. And now
it is Christmas night and you have
no star, and no hope left for
finding child or cave. It is midnight
and there is no child in sight. But
what is this tightness in the chest?

A street empties below you. And you follow
the sound of sad laughter past
corridors. Your eyes move from
door to door as you ask for the cave.
And you are told how to reach a door
with a sign, "Earthly Paradise." "A place
with no tempting serpent. And
no divine judge to cast stones.
Here roses have no thorns.
And nakedness is called purity."
You hear, "Now take off those
borrowed faces, those horrible masks
you formed out of chameleon skins."

"But these are our true faces.
They are not masks to put on and
peel off. We are from Beirut.
Don't you know? We are born with
borrowed faces. We are born with
borrowed minds. We are a tragedy.
Thinking is born a whore in our markets
and spends its life inventing virginity."
"Come on. Take off those borrowed faces."

And you enter as those who enter
a graveyard night. A fire is lit.
And you see bodies undulating
in a dance to the tune of some
sorcerer. Suddenly the dark ceiling
becomes blue crystal hung with
chandeliers. And the decaying putrid
walls have spigots of pure wine.
And the mud of the street is gold.
The writhing bodies are purified
and no longer clay but merged
into each other as nerve, blood, heart.

"This is earthly paradise. Now pray.
Heaven is on earth here."

You kneel to worship chemistry
and the magician who fashioned
paradise from burial and grave.
Yes, worship him,
the god who reveals himself in the cave.
Hailing him:
"God of the weary and lost,
god fleeing from the sun's madness
and the terror of certainty, who
conceals himself in the underground
cavern in the land of civilization."

# The Flight into Egypt

*Matthew 2:13 – 14*

Now after they had left, an angel of the Lord appeared to Joseph in a dream and said, "Get up, take the child and his mother, and flee to Egypt, and remain there until I tell you; for Herod is about to search for the child, to destroy him." Then Joseph got up, took the child and his mother by night, and went to Egypt.

# The Flight of the Holy Family

JOSEPH FREIHERR VON EICHENDORFF

Germany, 1788–1857. Eichendorff's strong Catholic Christian faith and his Romantic love of the countryside, especially that of the family estate of Ludowitz in Silesia, from which he was dispossessed as a result of the Napoleonic wars, underlie his lyric poetry. The meadow which the Holy Family crosses in "The Flight of the Holy Family" is much more likely to be found in Germany, for example, than in the deserts of Egypt. "The Flight of the Holy Family" is translated from the German by George Dardess.

> The shadows have been ready, falling
> Through cool evening air.
> Then from the cleft comes Joseph, striding
> Across the hush of meadow. There,
> Ahead, the trees.
> He points the donkey toward them
> And feels a lightly fanning breeze.
> It's from angels' wings—
> The child sees them in his dream.
> Mary, gazing down at him in love and pain, sings
> Silent cradle songs. The quiet has no seam.
> Crisscrossing glowworms light her way,
> Eager to show each step and stay;
> Sweet shudders bend the grasses—
> They stroke her cloak's hem as she passes;
> The brooklet ceases its chatter,
> The forest whispers scatter
> That they might not betray the flight.
> The child raised his hand,
> And for their kindness on this night,
> He blessed the silent land,
> So that the earth, each flower and tree,
> From then on to eternity
> Must dream of heaven each night.
> O happy time and bright!

# Christmas Sonnet

RUBÉN DARÍO

Nicaragua, 1867–1916. Considered in his lifetime Latin America's greatest poet, Darío inspired the Modernist movement, which revitalized Spanish poetry with a revolutionary aesthetic. His poems on Gospel themes express what is still Modernism's strained relation to Christianity: unable to believe in a supernatural world that he yet longs for faith in, the poet regrets that "I, on my poor donkey, ride toward Egypt, with no star any longer, and far from Bethlehem" ("Christmas Sonnet"). "Christmas Sonnet" is translated from the Spanish by Lysander Kemp.

Mary was pale, and Joseph the carpenter also:
they saw in the eyes of that pure and lovely face
the heavenly miracle which the star announced
and the martyrdom that was waiting for the lamb.

The shepherds sang very softly, and at the last
a car of archangels left a shining track;
the light of Aldebaran could hardly be seen,
and even the morning star was late to appear.

This vision rises within me, and multiplies
in gorgeous details, in a thousand rich marvels,
because of the sure hope of most divine good

of the Virgin, the Child, and outlawed Saint Joseph;
and I, on my poor donkey, ride toward Egypt,
with no star any longer, and far from Bethlehem.

# The Slaughter of the Innocents

*Matthew 2:16−18*

When Herod saw that he had been tricked by the wise men, he was in-
furiated, and he sent and killed all the children in and around Beth-
lehem who were two years old or under, according to the time that he
had learned from the wise men. Then was fulfilled what had been
spoken through the prophet Jeremiah:

> "A voice was heard in Ramah,
>> wailing and loud lamentation,
>
> Rachel weeping for her children;
>> she refused to be consoled, because they are no more."

# Christmas Night

JOOST VAN DEN VONDEL

Netherlands, 1587–1679. Raised in the Mennonite faith, Vondel felt starved by its aesthetic spareness, and became a Roman Catholic in 1641. His lushly sculptured poetic style has been compared to the art of his countryman Rubens. The Amstersdam arts world honored Vondel as its leading poet in 1653. "Christmas Night" is translated from the Dutch by Adriaan J. Barnouw.

O Christmas Night whose star outblazeth
The brilliance of the days and dazeth
   King Herod, who can scarce abide
Such light, Thou art adored in wonder!
But he, although thy message thunder
   Into his ears, is deaf with pride.

To kill one Innocent he dreadeth
He murders innocents, and spreadeth
   A wail through countryside and town
In Bethlehem, in field and meadow,
And wakens Rachel's ghostly shadow,
   Who goes awandering up and down,

Now to the west, then eastward turning.
Who'll quench the fire that is burning
   Her heart for loss of her dear wards,
Now that she sees them bleeding, smothered,
When they had hardly yet been mothered,
   And sees so many bloodstained swords?

She sees the milk drops still adripping
From pale, dead lips that still were sipping
   When they were torn from mother's breast,
She sees the tears that leave their traces
In pearls of dew upon their faces,
   She sees them stained and foully messed.

The eyebrows' arches now are bending
O'er tearful eyes that once were sending

Their rays into the mother's heart,
Like shining stars by which their faces
   Turned into heavens ere all traces
      Of light did in a mist depart.

O who can name the woes and horrors
And count so many tender flowers
   That wilted ere their petals blew
And could unfold upon the morning
Their first sweet fragrance, ere the dawning
   Could slake their thirst with its first dew?

Thus fells the sickle of the mower
The ripened ears, thus shakes a shower
   The green leaves in the storm-swept wood.
What havoc's wrought by blind ambition,
When whipped to fury by suspicion
   And raving in remorseless mood!

O Rachel, cease thy wandering sorrow.
Thy martyred children are tomorrow
   The first seeds of that blood-sown sod
Whose crop shall grow and reach fruition
And, tyrant-proof, complete Christ's mission:
   The imperishable Church of God.

# Black Yule

ERIK AXEL KARLFELDT

Sweden, 1864–1931. One of the few literary figures ever to decline the Nobel
Prize, Karlfeldt was awarded it posthumously in 1931. A poet of provincial life
and rural traditions—his work is rooted in his native Dalarna—he wrote with a
mastery of meter and rhyme. Some of his best known poems were inspired by
popular Dalarna wall painting depicting Old Testament tales in local peasant
settings. "Black Yule" is translated from the Swedish by C. D. Locock.


Kindle no lamp on this black night—the air
Stifles us, like a tight-closed register.
No Michael comes with flaming sword to cleave
A path for souls to heaven this Christmas Eve.
No psalms of hope befit this night of woe,
No choral strain *in dulci jubilo.*
"Dark, and passed by"—
That is our Yule-tide's dismal melody.

Like to a foolish virgin hath the world
Wasted its oil—see the wick's smoke upcurled
The bridegroom tarrieth—no sound of bells
Visit of Kings nor Eastern Star foretells.
On such a night no God may come to birth,
The angel-dreams of children sink to earth:
Till Yule be o'er,
Black imps stand lurking by the garden door.

Hardly the wretched mother may keep warm
'Gainst her thin breast the child upon her arm;
Her dream this Yule-time is of Mary's need—
No room within the inn, no food nor bed.
Minions of Herod go from door to door—
Wrap up thy child in haste, nor tarry more!
"Farewell, depart,"
That be thy matin-song, O weary heart!

But Christ's day dawns: mid trembling grove and sky
Earth wakens from her dreams of misery;

Earth wakens to the vision of her pain,
As on her forehead strikes the thaw-fed rain,
With wet tears dripping from the icy hand
That waves Good-tidings o'er the dreary land:—
Nay, waves good-bye
To many a mother's son now risen to die.

# The Holy Innocents

ROBERT LOWELL

U.S., 1917–1977. Scion of a famous Boston literary family, Lowell studied with
some of the best teachers and poets of his time and became himself a major in-
fluence on other poets. Converting to Roman Catholicism in 1940, Lowell in
his early poetry used Christian symbolism to satirize contemporary events —
"The Holy Innocents" is an example. Lowell moved away from this public
stance to a personal, confessional style for which he became famous. Lowell
was much troubled by manic depression from 1949 to the end of his life. He
left the Church in the 1950s.

Listen, the hay-bells tinkle as the cart
Wavers on rubber tires along the tar
And cindered ice below the burlap mill
And ale-wife run. The oxen drool and start
In wonder at the fenders of a car,
And blunder hugely up St. Peter's hill.
These are the undefiled by woman — their
Sorrow is not the sorrow of this world:
King Herod shrieking vengeance at the curled
Up knees of Jesus choking in the air,

A king of speechless clods and infants. Still
The world out-Herods Herod; and the year,
The nineteen-hundred forty-fifth of grace,
Lumbers with losses up the clinkered hill
Of our purgation; and the oxen near
The worn foundations of their resting-place,
The holy manger where their bed is corn
And holly torn for Christmas. If they die,
As Jesus, in the harness, who will mourn?
Lamb of the shepherds, Child, how still you lie.

# The Return to Nazareth

*Luke 2:39–40*

When they had finished everything required by the law of the Lord, they returned to Galilee, to their own town of Nazareth. The child grew and became strong, filled with wisdom; and the favor of God was upon him.

# The Blessed Virgin and the Infant Jesus

(attrib.) GIOVANNI DOMINICI

Italy, 1357–1419. A Florentine, Giovanni Dominici was a leading anti-Humanist theologian. He became Archbishop of Ragusa, Sicily, and at the time of his death was a Cardinal in Hungary. "The Blessed Virgin and the Infant Jesus" is attributed to him; as with many medieval poems, authorship is uncertain. "The Blessed Virgin and the Infant Jesus" is translated from the Italian by Joseph Tusiani.

> Say, O sweet Mary, with how much desire
> you gazed upon your son, my Christ, my Sire.
>
> When without labor you to him gave birth,
> I am quite certain the first thing you did
> was to adore him, full of grace and mirth;
> then on the hay you laid him in the crib,
> and wrapped him round in humble raiments few,
> and wonderment and joy, I know, you knew.
>
> Oh, what great bliss, what ecstasy was yours
> when you could hold him in your arms so tight!
> O Mary, tell me (out of mercy you
> should not perhaps deny me such a grace):
> and did you then not kiss him on the face?
> I know you did, and called him, "O my babe!"
>
> You called him Son, and Father, and my Lord,
> you called him Jesus, and you called him God.
> Oh, what warm love within your heart you felt
> when on your lap you suckled him at breast!
> Oh, what caresses and what tender love
> whene'er you were with him—your baby blest!
>
> I do believe you suffered very much
> when Jesus in the morn you had to dress,
> for but in touching him your bliss was such,
> you would not let him go from you away;
> how you could bear all this, I fail to guess,
> and how your heart did not desert you then.

If in the day he fell asleep awhile,
and you desired to waken paradise,
softly you went to him, who could not hear,
and bent your face upon his holy face,
and whispered then with your maternal smile:
"Oh, too much sleep can hurt you; sleep no more!"

Often, when he with other children was,
in haste, I think, you called your Jesus home,
to yourself saying, "You enjoy your playing,
but it takes something from my happiness."
And you would kiss him with so great a bliss,
no one felt ever such a love as you.

I have said nothing, nothing great or new,
in mentioning the least of all your joys;
but now a thought seems from my heart to rise
about your first and most sublime delight
(I do not know how in so great a bliss
your heart did not burst open and soon cease):

Oh, when you heard yourself called *Mamma*, how
did you not die of sweetness at that name?
How could you then withstand love's burning flame,
and soon not perish in its happiness?
Great your endurance must have truly been
if your existence did not finish then.

Our high Eternal Father called her, Daughter,
and with unending tenderness our Lord
called on this earth his humble handmaid Mother!
This thought alone makes my heart melt away.
Who wants to feel some sweet and tender spark
of this high love to which I ever aspire,
must place in my good Jesus all desire.

# Jesus Among the Doctors

*Luke 2:41–49*

Now every year his parents went to Jerusalem for the festival of the Passover. And when he was twelve years old, they went up as usual for the festival. When the festival was ended and they started to return, the boy Jesus stayed behind in Jerusalem, but his parents did not know it. Assuming that he was in the group of travelers, they went a day's journey. Then they started to look for him among their relatives and friends. When they did not find him, they returned to Jerusalem to search for him. After three days they found him in the temple, sitting among the teachers, listening to them and asking them questions. And all who heard him were amazed at his understanding and his answers. When his parents saw him they were astonished; and his mother said to him, "Child, why have you treated us like this? Look, your father and I have been searching for you in great anxiety." He said to them, "Why were you searching for me? Did you not know that I must be in my Father's house?"

# from *A Woman Wrapped in Silence*

JOHN W. LYNCH

U.S. 1904–1990. When first published in 1941, Lynch's A *Woman Wrapped in Silence* was praised in both the secular and religious press for drawing on "the modern instruments of psychology" for insights into Mary's trials (*New York Times*). The poem is a book-length blank verse meditation on the Gospels, imagined from Mary's point of view. John Lynch was a Catholic priest in the diocese of Syracuse, New York.

> Joseph was remembering the fall
> Of quiet accent on the word He'd said
> About His Father, and he'd marked the sure
> Inclusion of himself and of his heart
> When she'd said first they had been searching Him.
> It was the only bliss he'd ever hoped,
> This name, and strength, and head he was for them.
> And when at Nazareth they'd come to him
> And gave precedence and had asked decisions
> For his home, when she'd deferred to him,
> And He had raised His eyes and asked consent,
> Joseph was not dull nor uninformed
> Of what his honor was. This was a name
> That gave his arms good strength and warmed his mind
> To prayer. It was his life to be for Him
> A father. Joseph swore then he would break
> Two hands in labor, wear them to the stumps
> Of hands if He would ask or ever breathe
> One whispered wish. But He had gone from him,
> And said it was His Father's business here
> That took Him, and He'd be alone. The words
> Said that, and he had heard them all. His Father's . . .
>
> Joseph spoke again and said they might
> Attain so far as Beeroth while the day
> Was holding if they were not wearied now.
>
> The words that moved again across his mind,
> The sight of masters standing, and the air

They had of reverence, these are the sum
For him of miracles. This was to be
The end of all he'd see of signs and wonders
And the growth of Him; he is to have
No seat at Cana's table, and the place
Of resurrection shall not find him glad.

This is the end. His fingers will not close
Upon the thorns, nor will the wounds be scarred
Upon his eyes. This is the end, and after
This we shall not find him on the page
That tells of her. Joseph walks a road
And brings them home; he will be waiting there
A while, and for a little he will speak
Directions and be heard, and he will guide
Young hands in building scaffolds and the beams
And doors much smaller than He'd builded once
Of space. But he will see no more than this.
And walking now, his gospel has been heard.

# PART TWO

# PREPARATION FOR PUBLIC MINISTRY

# The Preaching of John the Baptist

*Mark 1:4—8*

John the baptizer appeared in the wilderness, proclaiming a baptism of repentance for the forgiveness of sins. And people from the whole Judean countryside and all the people of Jerusalem were going out to him, and were baptized by him in the river Jordan, confessing their sins. Now John was clothed with camel's hair, with a leather belt around his waist, and he ate locusts and wild honey. He proclaimed, "The one who is more powerful than I is coming after me; I am not worthy to stoop down and untie the thong of his sandals. I have baptized you with water; but he will baptize you with the Holy Spirit."

# Ut Queant

(attrib.) PAULUS DIACONUS

[Paul the Deacon] Italy, c. 730–799. A monk of Monte Cassino in Italy, Paulus is best known as a grammarian and historian. Much of his poetry was written for the Carolingian court; epitaphs make up the rest. While the ascription of the ardent "Ut Queant" ("That They Might Be Able [to Pass Through]") to him is uncertain, the poem itself is a notable example of the effort many Christian poets of the time made to imitate Latin models, in this case the Sapphic meter of a number of Horace's odes. The poet's admiration of Horace also explains the transformation of heaven into "Olympus" in stanza 2. "Ut Queant" is translated from the Latin by George Dardess.

O blessed Saint John,
Clean my stained lips,
That your great deeds
Pass through my mouth
  A pure song.

Lo! the angel, come down from Olympus,
Tells your father how it will be:
A great one born, his name,
  And life history.

But doubting the heavenly promise,
He lost his voice,
Which you regained,
Fathering your father's speech
  In your own.

In that hidden nest of Mary's womb
You saw a king waiting
In a bridal chamber.
Your leap brought both mothers to unfold
  Secret joys.

Little more than a boy, you sought desert caves,
Fleeing the crowds of town,
That you might not take one stain, speak
  One false word.

A camel covered your shoulders
With his skin.
A goat became a belt for your waist.
You shared their water, their food,
        The locusts and honey.

True, other prophets saw and sang from afar
The approaching light.
But your very forefinger
Picked out
        The Lamb Himself.

Go, circle the immensity of space—
Never was a holier one born than John.
Who but he worthy to bathe the one
        Who bathes the world?

How high you stand above us—
Your soul a peak of snowy whiteness!
Greatest of martyrs,
Who taught the desert to bloom,
        And prince of prophets.

On some heroes they lay thirty crowns,
On others thirty more,
While on your head
They lay three hundred crowns
        Flowing with fruit.

These heavy stones that crush our chest—
Sweep them away, O mighty one!
Smooth and sweeten our road,
And lay it straight to the goal,
        No more retreating.

And do so, not only for our sake,
But that the tender savior of the world

Finding us free of fault,
Will joy
      To approach us.

All this in praise of you,
Unity in three.
We beg you spare us,
      Your redeemed.

# Unemployed

ANDERS JOHAN ÖSTERLING

Sweden, 1884–1979. Influenced by a combination of the French Symbolists
and William Wordsworth, Österling wrote idyllic poetry based on the rural life
of his native Skane. Known also for his translations and journalism, he was a
member of the Swedish Academy and its secretary from 1941 to 1964. "Unem-
ployed" is translated from the Swedish by Martin S. Allwood.

> The August sun beats down on endless stone.
> A jobless fellow on the road alone.
> Against the city's smoke, a cloud of thrift,
> The churches' granite angels spires lift.
> A cardboard box contains his poor wares,
> Show lace, the trade of helplessness. He stares.
> The roadside grass turns yellow—early fall.
> Now feasts the hawk on dove-breasts, white and small.
> A bloody wing lay in the bush beside
> His resting-place last night: it could not hide
> The signs. The unimportant spoils abide.
> The cars roll by. But only those who walk
> Have need of shoes to walk in. His are gone.
> Shoe lace and shoes. His thoughts revolve upon
> A feverish vision of the flaming red
> Gas station tabernacles there ahead.
> The flies are buzzing. Here's the city limit.
> His license? Will the city cops just skim it?
> He meets school children. Pass them quickly—see!
> But who was it that once said: "After me
> Shall come a man whose dusty lace I may
> Not even loosen?" . . . Where is He today?

## Luke 3:7–9

John said to the crowds that came out to be baptized by him, "You brood of vipers! Who warned you to flee from the wrath to come? Bear fruits worthy of repentance. Do not begin to say to yourselves, 'We have Abraham as our ancestor'; for I tell you, God is able from these stones to raise up children to Abraham. Even now the ax is lying at the root of the trees; every tree therefore that does not bear good fruit is cut down and thrown into the fire."

# Bitter Winter

FRANCO FORTINI

Italy, 1917–. The Florentine-born Franco Lattes assumed his mother's name to escape persecution as a Jew. An intellectual and poet, Fortini, who was deeply influenced by Brecht, is one of Italy's most influential Marxist literary critics. He edited several prominent magazines, including *Politecnico* and *Avanti*. "Bitter Winter" is translated from the Italian by Lawrence R. Smith.

Bitter winter, you crackle your fire
winter, you consume the woods, the roofs
winter, you slash and burn.

Whoever mourns, let him mourn; whoever suffers, let him suffer more
whoever hates, let him hate more; whoever deceives, let him triumph:
this is the ultimate text and decree of our winter.

We didn't know what to do with
green life and the loving flowers.
That's why the ax is at the root of our hearts

and like writhing twigs we shall be burnt.

# Christianity Was Once an Eagle Message

NILS BOLANDER

Sweden, 1902–1959. Bolander studied theology at Uppsala and in 1947 began serving as a parish vicar. "Christianity Was Once an Eagle Message" is translated from the Swedish by Martin S. Allwood.

Christianity was once an eagle message
Sprung from the nest on the highest mountain peak
On diving wings that glittered.
But we chastened its bold feathers,
Competently straightened its cutting beak
And lo!—it was a black bird,
A tame loquacious raven.

Christianity was once a lion gospel
Always seeking a warm and living prey,
A young lion of Judah.
But we clipped its sharp, crooked claws,
Stilled its thirst for the blood of the heart
And turned it into a purring cottage cat.

Christianity was once a desert sermon,
Mean and sharp as the terrible africus,
Burning as the desert sand.
But we turned it into a garden idyll,
Mignonettes, asters and pious roses,
A romantic mood in Gethsemane.

Lord, take care of our pious cowardice!
Give it swift eagle wings and sharp lion's claws!
Give it scent of wild honey and simoom
And then say with the Baptist's voice:
This is the victory that conquers the world.
This is Christianity.

# I Am Too Loud When You Are Gone

LEONARD COHEN

Canada, 1934–. Born in Montreal, Cohen was educated at McGill University and published his first book of poetry in 1956, a year after graduation. A popular novelist, poet, and recording star, Cohen learned guitar as a teenager at a socialist camp (he later abandoned socialism) and some of his poems became internationally bestselling songs. Both Old and New Testament themes figure prominently in his lyric poetry.

> I am too loud when you are gone
> I am John the Baptist, cheated by mere water
> and merciful love, wild but over-known
> John of honey, of time, longing not for
> music, longing, longing to be Him
> I am diminished, I peddle versions of Word
> that don't survive the tablets broken stone
> I am alone when you are gone.

# The Baptism of Jesus

## *Mark 1:9−11*

In those days Jesus came from Nazareth of Galilee and was baptized by John in the Jordan. And just as he was coming up out of the water, he saw the heavens torn apart and the Spirit descending like a dove on him. And a voice came from heaven, "You are my Son, the Beloved; with you I am well pleased."

# Christ Our Lord Came to the Jordan

MARTIN LUTHER

Germany, 1483?–1546. Though not thought of as a poet, Luther wrote hymn verses of great and lasting power. Ulrich S. Leupold, editor of *Luther's Works*, points out that the verses derive from the German folk song. As such, says Leupold, "to the modern ear the verses sound awkward, if not uncouth. They lack the rich emotional overtones, the mellow flow of words, and the metric regularity that we commonly associate with poetry. . . . But Luther's hymns were meant not to create a mood, but to convey a message. They were a confession of faith, not of personal feelings." The present translation strives for the "ruggedness" Leupold says has been lost in most English versions. "Christ Our Lord Came to the Jordan" is translated from the German by George Dardess.

Christ our Lord came to the Jordan
heeding his Father's will.
From John he received baptism
to fulfil his work and mission.
He wanted to appoint for us a bath
to wash away our sins
and drown that bitter death
in his own blood and wounds
to give us all new life.

So hear and mark well, all of you,
what God himself calls baptism,
and what a Christian should believe
to escape the mobs in schism.
God speaks and wills, Let water be,
yet not just plain water.
His holy Word is also there,
with the Spirit's gifts past measure.
He is the true baptizer.

All this he has shown us clearly
in picture and in word,
the Father's voice
at Jordan plainly heard.
He said, This is my beloved son,
in Him I am well pleased.

Him have I sent to you
that all of you might hear
and do as he tells you.

And so the Son himself stands here
in vulnerable humanity.
Then down descends the Holy Ghost
clothed in the likeness of a dove.
So that we should suffer no doubts
when we approach baptism,
all three persons gather at our side,
making themselves known
by dwelling with flesh and bone.

Christ spoke to his disciples,
Go forth, teach all the world
that it is lost in sin
and that it must turn, repent.
He who believes and seeks baptism,
he will be blessed thereby.
Twice-born he will be called
who can no longer die
but shall inherit heaven.

But he who rejects this bliss,
he stays mired in sin,
damning himself to eternal death
deep in Hell's abyss.
His own goodness cannot help him.
All his striving is lost.
Original sin annihilates him.
In it he is born.
He cannot pay his own cost.

The eye sees only water
as when men pour it.
Belief in the Spirit reveals
the power of Christ's blood,
where the water becomes a red fountain

dyed by the blood of Christ:
blood which makes all wounds whole,
those inherited from Adam
and those self-inflicted on the soul.

# Stream—Fountain
## from *The Christ of Velasquez*

MIGUEL DE UNAMUNO

Spain, 1864–1936. Professor of Greek and Director of the University of Sala-
manca, Unamuno became a national hero for protesting his government's poli-
cies and suffering temporary exile. A prolific writer in many genres, a Catholic
who struggled with his faith, he always carried with him the New Testament in
the original Greek. *The Christ of Velasquez*, a series of 89 poems on this
painting, is in the Spanish tradition of intense focus on the image of the
bleeding, crucified Christ. "Stream—Fountain" is translated from the Spanish
by Y. R. Pérez.

Like a stream against the sun your body glistens,
a vein of silver alive in the gloom
of the rocks which encircle its gorge;
the waters run, they flood as one
over the soul of the channel enduring.

We bathe in You, Jordan of the flesh,
and in You from water and from spirit we are born.
From your image in the crystal—ripples of silver—
we see the white flight of the dove;

Its wings merge with the ripples,
as it seems to fly in the depth
of the bed of your waters. You baptize
with the Holy Spirit and dip us
in the uncreated ocean, pure light.
On your chest the apparition of the spirit
is reflected, and its dove,
white tongue of fire, we see as a snowflake
that floats down from your breast.

Jesus, you are as a living fount
which, in the thick of the forest,
sings ever new songs of eternal love.

# The Temptation of Jesus

*Luke 4:1—2*

Jesus, full of the Holy Spirit, returned from the Jordan and was led by
the Spirit in the wilderness, where for forty days he was tempted by the
devil. He ate nothing at all during those days, and when they were
over, he was famished.

# from *Paradise Regained*

JOHN MILTON

England, 1608–1674. From his first major poem to his last, Milton turned to the Bible for literary themes and inspiration. Educated at Cambridge, fluent in Hebrew and classical languages, Milton began his great epic on the fall of man, *Paradise Lost*, only after he had devoted himself to the Commonwealth's political cause and produced in magnificent prose some of the finest defences of human liberty in English. His "brief epic" of Christian heroism, *Paradise Regained*, recreates the story of Christ's temptation in the wilderness as told in Luke 4:1–13. The passage reprinted represents one of the earliest attempts in literature to enter imaginatively the consciousness of Jesus.

> Meanwhile the Son of God, who yet some days
> Lodg'd in *Bethabara*, where *John* baptiz'd,
> Musing and much revolving in his breast,
> How best the mighty work he might begin
> Of Savior to mankind, and which way first
> Publish his Godlike office now mature,
> One day forth walk'd alone, the Spirit leading,
> And his deep thoughts, the better to converse
> With solitude, till far from track of men,
> Thought following thought, and step by step led on,
> He enter'd now the bordering Desert wild,
> And with dark shades and rocks environ'd round,
> His holy Meditations thus pursu'd.
>
>   O what a multitude of thoughts at once
> Awak'n'd in me swarm, while I consider
> What from within I feel myself, and hear
> What from without comes often to my ears,
> Ill sorting with my present state compar'd.
> When I was yet a child, no childish play
> To me was pleasing, all my mind was set
> Serious to learn and know, and thence to do
> What might be public good; myself I thought
> Born to that end, born to promote all truth,
> All righteous things: therefore above my years,
> The Law of God I read, and found it sweet,
> Made it my whole delight, and in it grew
> To such perfection that, ere yet my age

Had measur'd twice six years, at our great Feast
I went into the Temple, there to hear
The Teachers of our Law, and to propose
What might improve my knowledge or their own;
And was admir'd by all: yet this not all
To which my Spirit aspir'd; victorious deeds
Flam'd in my heart, heroic acts; one while
To rescue *Israel* from the *Roman* yoke,
Then to subdue and quell o'er all the earth
Brute violence and proud Tyrannic pow'r,
Till truth were freed, and equity restor'd:
Yet held it more humane, more heavenly, first
By winning words to conquer willing hearts,
And make persuasion do the work of fear;
At least to try, and teach the erring Soul
Not wilfully misdoing, but unware
Misled: the stubborn only to subdue.
These growing thoughts my Mother soon perceiving
By words at times cast forth, inly rejoic'd,
And said to me apart: High are thy thoughts
O Son, but nourish them and let them soar
To what height sacred virtue and true worth
Can raise them, though above example high;
By matchless Deeds express thy matchless Sire.
For know, thou art no Son of mortal man;
Though men esteem thee low of Parentage,
Thy Father is th'Eternal King, who rules
All Heaven and Earth, Angels and Sons of men.
A messenger from God foretold thy birth
Conceiv'd in me a Virgin; he foretold
Thou shouldst be great and sit on *David's* Throne,
And of thy Kingdom there should be no end.
At thy Nativity a glorious Choir
Of Angels in the fields of *Bethlehem* sung
To Shepherds watching at their folds by night,
And told them the Messiah now was born,
Where they might see him, and to thee they came,
Directed to the Manger where thou lay'st,
For in the Inn was left no better room.

A Star, not seen before in Heaven appearing
Guided the Wise Men thither from the East,
To honor thee with Incense, Myrrh, and Gold,
By whose bright course led on they found the place,
Affirming it thy Star new-grav'n in Heaven,
By which they knew thee King of *Israel* born.
Just *Simeon* and Prophetic *Anna*, warn'd
By Vision, found thee in the Temple, and spake,
Before the Altar and the vested Priest,
Like things of thee to all that present stood.
This having heard, straight I again revolv'd
The Law and Prophets, searching what was writ
Concerning the Messiah, to our Scribes
Known partly, and soon found of whom they spake
I am; this chiefly, that my way must lie
Through many a hard assay even to the death,
Ere I the promis'd Kingdom can attain,
Or work Redemption for mankind, whose sins'
Full weight must be transferr'd upon my head.
Yet neither thus dishearten'd or dismay'd,
The time prefixt I waited, when behold
The Baptist (of whose birth I oft had heard,
Not knew by sight) now come, who was to come
Before Messiah and his way prepare.
I as all others to his Baptism came,
Which I believ'd was from above; but hee
Straight knew me, and with loudest voice proclaim'd
Mee him (for it was shown him so from Heaven)
Mee him whose Harbinger he was; and first
Refus'd on me his Baptism to confer,
As much his greater, and was hardly won.
But as I rose out of the laving stream,
Heaven open'd her eternal doors, from whence
The Spirit descended on me like a Dove;
And last the sum of all, my Father's voice,
Audibly heard from Heav'n, pronounc'd me his,
Mee his beloved Son, in whom alone
He was well pleas'd; by which I knew the time
Now full, that I no more should live obscure,

But openly begin, as best becomes
The Authority which I deriv'd from Heaven.
And now by some strong motion I am led
Into this Wilderness, to what intent
I learn not yet; perhaps I need not know;
For what concerns my knowledge God reveals.
   So spake our Morning Star then in his rise,
And looking round on every side beheld
A pathless Desert, dusk with horrid shades;
The way he came not having mark'd, return
Was difficult, by human steps untrod;
And he still on was led, but with such thoughts
Accompanied of things past and to come
Lodg'd in his breast, as well might recommend
Such Solitude before choicest Society.

## Matthew 4:3–11

The tempter came and said to him, "If you are the Son of God, command these stones to become loaves of bread." But he answered, "It is written,

'One does not live by bread alone,
   but by every word that comes from the mouth of God.'"

Then the devil took him to the holy city and placed him on the pinnacle of the temple, saying to him, "If you are the Son of God, throw yourself down; for it is written,

'He will command his angels concerning you,'
   and 'On their hands they will bear you up,
so that you will not dash your foot against a stone.'"

Jesus said to him, "Again it is written, 'Do not put the Lord your God to the test.'"

Again, the devil took him to a very high mountain and showed him all the kingdoms of the world and their splendor; and he said to him, "All these I will give you, if you will fall down and worship me." Jesus said to him, "Away with you, Satan! for it is written,

'Worship the Lord your God,
   and serve only him.'"

Then the devil left him, and suddenly angels came and waited on him.

# Christ Meets Lucifer

BERTIL MALMBERG

Sweden, 1889–1958. Born into an educated family, Malmberg studied philosophy and German literature. His early writings were influenced by the aesthetic movements of *fin de siecle* European culture. Later, as he grew more disenchanted with European civilization following the collapse of Germany after World War I, he became connected with the Oxford Group Movement. A translator of Thomas Mann, Stefan George, and Friedrich von Schiller, Malmberg was elected to the Swedish Academy in 1953. "Christ Meets Lucifer" is translated from the Swedish by Thorild Fredenholm and Martin S. Allwood.

Who set the stage? Who chose the time, the place,
That suddenly they stood there, face to face?

High on a lonely cliff they chanced to meet,
The azure valley's castles at their feet,

A city named Evasion far below
Shining through the tree-trunks, pale as snow

And Christ saw to the bottom of his soul,
Saw lust and sadness and their ghastly toll.

And Christ thought: "Here is one who must
Know that all living things are transient dust,

And deep within his being I surmise
A sympathy with everything that dies."

And Christ's stern love could clearly see
A love of charming, drug-like quality,

Yes, like a drug, a powerful witch's brew,
But lacking strength to heal and build anew,

A mildness, different from his own,
Which hesitated, flickered, as it shone.

Christ thought: "But to the sating of desires
And self-glorification he aspires.

He wants to change all things, make them dissolve
And watch an eerie shadowland evolve.

And even though his heart may cry
For all that withers and is bound to die,

His actions, governed by an arrant mind,
Cannot be merciful or kind.

Yes, in his love, ethereal and unreal,
There is a hardness as of ice and steel.

And if he had the power to bestow
The balm of truth upon a world of woe

That power would remain unspent.
Only with dampened cloth and liniment,

Ambiguous magic tricks, a weird refrain,
Secretive, moonlike he approaches pain.

No, not damnation's fearful scourge,
The wail of tortured souls, a hellish dirge

In an eternal chorus, would
He stay or baffle even if he could.

For only upon treacherous ground
Are his illusive gardens to be found.

Seductive, specular is his domain,
Full of futility and sex and pain,

Where asphodels in silvery meadows sway
And stone-blind herons, shadow fountains play,

And limbs, hypnotically blue and sheer,
Flit through the mist and disappear."

And Christ saw to the bottom of his need,
Saw disillusionment, deception, greed.

With judgelike clarity his eyes looked straight
Into the depths of Satan's dreamlike fate,

And all was muteness. Christ was still,
But for his breast, which rose and rose, until

There glowed upon his forehead, where he stood,
The word "Awaken," like a cross of blood.

Immutable and cold and grim,
His cloak already gathered around him,

Before Reality's great son,
The duke of Shadowland, the Evil One,

Stood there transfixed by his own ban—
The wrath of God, embodied in this man.

And presently, with a disdainful frown,
His eyes were lowered, and he started down

A stairway lined with sphinxes,—down into
His beckoning gardens, tropically blue.

But having reached the city's gate, he found
Himself compelled to turn around.

He glanced along the stairway once again,
Up to the cliff, anxious to ascertain

If he, up there, had left his lofty stand
And wandered back to his own land.

Then this uneasiness would be allowed
To leave his mind and vanish like a cloud,

And to the slightest remnant be diffused.
–That pair of eyes, which soberly accused

Would then forever leave his soul. On wings
Of filmy silver they would soar
To dwell amongst forgotten things.

*But Christ stood on the mountain as before.*

# from *The Divine Narcissus*

JUANA INÉS DE LA CRUZ

[Juana de Asbaje] Mexico, 1651–1695. Sor Juana is the greatest poet of colonial Spanish America. Raised at the Mexican court, she chose at age 18 to become a nun, probably to give herself the intellectual freedom that marriage would have prohibited. Her voluminous poetry sparkles with the wit and wordplay of Spanish baroque. Among the genres of her time in which she excelled are *villancicos* (popular dance-songs for interludes during religious festivals) and *autos sacramentales* (verse-plays for the feast of Corpus Christi). *The Divine Narcissus* stands out among *autos* for its ingenious blending of classical myth with Catholic sacramental theology. In the tableau below, Echo (Satan) speaks to Narcissus (Christ). This selection from *The Divine Narcissus* is translated from the Spanish by Alan S. Trueblood.

> Most beautiful Narcissus,
> from your mountain of glory,
> you bring loftiness down
> to these human valleys:
> hear my unhappy tale,
> though such is my distress
> that even in the telling
> my pain will not lessen.
> I am Echo, the richest
> shepherd maid of these dales;
> for the gift of my beauty
> in unhappiness I pay.
> For you met this beauty
> with a look of contempt.
> That I now find it ugly
> is my song's lament.
> You are surely aware
> that those bright-shining lodestars
> of your eyes can allure
> the freest of lovers.
> Thus it will not surprise you
> to find Echo on bended knee,
> for your heavenly endowments
> place the world at your feet.
> Listen then to my plea:

Since my station and name
have proved unavailing
to soften your disdain,
    won't you stop and consider
your own welfare? Don't ignore
the riches I offer,
the ease they afford.
    I propose to enrich you.
To support my petition,
to strengthen my plea,
I bring a proposition.
    Now, since time began,
self-interest—it's well known—
has been love's surest means
to drive his darts home,
    so let your gaze take in
all the land it surveys
from this lofty summit
that leaves Atlas in the shade.
    See, into the valleys
those streams of cattle pour
to graze on the emeralds
that stud each valley floor.
    See, like drifts of snow,
the curdled milk in jars
puts the jasmine to shame
with which dawn snuffs out stars.
    See red-gold ears of grain
sending billows everywhere
like waves of watered silk
stirred by waves of the air.
    Behold the rich ores
those swelling mountains hold:
how they teem with diamonds,
glow with rubies and gold.
    See in the leaping ocean
how the dawn's welling tears
are congealed in conch shells
and turn into pearls.

See, in those gardens,
how the fruit trees flourish;
behold the broad range
of rich fruits they nourish.
   See how green crowns of pine
on high summits endeavor
to repeat the exploit
of the giants storming heaven.
   Listen to the music
of all those singing birds.
In all of their choirs
sweet descants are heard.
   See from pole to pole
realms spread far and wide.
Behold the many regions
which arms of sea divide,
   and see the ambitious prows
of those swift-sailing ships—
how they cleave in their passage
the azure's crystal drift.
   See amid those grottos
creatures of every sort,
some timidly fleeing,
some bursting fiercely forth.

   All this, fair Narcissus,
is mine to dispose of;
these are my possessions,
they accompany my love.
   All is yours to enjoy
if you cease to be cold,
put severity aside
and love me heart and soul.

# Stones and Bread

GYÖRGY RÓNAY

Hungary, 1913–1978. Poet, essayist, and translator, Rónay became after World War II a symbol of Catholic literature in Hungary. He edited the Catholic journal *Vigilia*, one of the few religious publications which managed to operate openly under Communist rule. "Stones and Bread" is translated from the Hungarian by Dalma Hunyadi Brunauer.

Stop here stop here stop here they kept yelling
the blind the deaf the lame the epileptic
stop here stop here stop! they stood by the roadside yelling
beat the earth with sticks waving their crutches
for Jesus came on the road before Him shift-clad
children were buzzing at His side softly
the Twelve walked along and behind Him the people.
Stop here stop here! cried all the wretched the sea
of filthy cripples foamed two panting
servants were dragging onto the flat roof of his house
the paralytic
        stop here
            the palms'
lacy leaves were writhing
              stop here
                the paralytic
beat his servants with a stick his eyes
bloodshot Do not pass before I get upstairs Do not
pass until I get upstairs! he screamed
and beat the servants he saw the people already  the servants
sweated he saw already the shift-clad running
kids and yelled O do not pass until
I get upstairs! and he saw already the blind eyes
saw already the beggars the lame and the wildly
undulating mob
        Look on us and we will see
look on us and we'll walk look on us and our ears
will hear!
      Jostling each other they ran forward
Jesus came on the road

Stop here stop here stop here!
And Jesus stopped
            and looked at them
                        and they were healed.
O what is this radiance said the blind o what is this sweet
music this soft rustling this heavenly melody
said the deaf Sound! said the blind Light!
said the deaf Sound Light Radiance Music
                        Light Light
cried the blind and laughed and sparkled
                        O Sound Sound
Sound laughed the deaf
            and the lame groping spread
his hands out in front Earth Earth Earth he stammered and
watched the earth as it with elastic thumping
thumped under his step
            On the roof the paralytic
threw himself down on the stone O I'm walking I live!


                        Jesus
stood in the midst of the crowd the midst of the joy
sadly
looked at the distant mount on the peak a soft breeze stirred
the leaves of the blue-green olives
                        Peace unto you
He said and the folk fell silent Peace unto you
blessed ones
            Then He waved and all gathered unto Him
and the blind lame deaf limping demented
the paralytic stood up lifted his hand to his ears
so he may hear better.
                        And Jesus Peace unto you
He said for the third time.  But I woe beyond the peace already
see the strife Death comes
slowly over the hills it comes over the hills comes
slowly the blood Death comes suffering the cross behold I say
unto you agony of agonies comes near agony
of agonies comes near
            The people stood mute

O men o you
happy ones here you who see hear run if only one drop
of blood would be taken on by you just one drop of blood by you
who
see hear and
walk if just one of the thorns which tears my forehead ragged if just
one sigh just one of the whips'
brutal lashes
And they all stubbornly suspiciously
backed away
if just one tear if just one drop
of blood or bile and vinegar
And stealthily they among the houses
slunk away the limping and deaf and blind and demented
lame and stuttering and none remained
near Him the paralytic ran down from the roof
slinking in his cellar and behind the lush
green of an opulent thicket jostling and knavish
cowered the Twelve
The eyes of Jesus were tear-filled
His arms fell down
He looked around and noticed the Man    The others
ran away this single one stood there this one who knew
that He was god but did not want Him to be God
this single one stood there sternly
Behold said he
the lame walk the paralytic arises
lepers are whole he sees who was blind and hears who was deaf and
no longer thirst the thirsty the hungry does not perish
Behold
laughing he showed the denuded road
the blessed
people your people!
And stealthily there under
the gardens all the tawdry small thieves were slinking
hungry
are you and who gives you food you would eat their hearts and behold
stone stone
they say look at our hearts stone only stone no

hearts have we our hearts are stone do not bite it just stone
you spit it out no taste our blood o our blood
is lye do not taste it this blood will blister your mouth
it's lye and behold here is your people stone only stone stone
eat the stone
                     he laughed
                           well eat the stone only stone stone
STONE STONE STONE
                    you may be the son of God
                                 only STONE STONE
so change the stones to bread!
change the stones to bread!!!
No
                  said Jesus wearily
                           What for
said Jesus discouraged
                      Depart from me Satan
said Jesus sadly
              I WILL NOT CHANGE
THE STONES TO BREAD.

# The Call of the Disciples

*Matthew 4:18—21*

As [Jesus] walked by the Sea of Galilee, he saw two brothers, Simon, who is called Peter, and Andrew his brother, casting a net into the sea —for they were fishermen. And he said to them, "Follow me, and I will make you fish for people." Immediately they left their nets and followed him. As he went from there, he saw two other brothers, James son of Zebedee and his brother John, in the boat with their father Zebedee, mending their nets, and he called them. Immediately they left the boat and their father, and followed him.

# Song of the Fisherman

WU LI

China, 1631–1718. See page 38 for biographical information on this poet.
"Song of the Fisherman" is translated from the Chinese by Jonathan Chavez.


From patching rips in tattered nets
    his eyes have gotten blurred;

he scours the river, does not disdain
    the tiniest fish and shrimp.

Selecting the freshest, he has supplied
    the feasts of sovereigns;

all four limbs exhausted now,
    dare he refuse the work?

Spreading nets he gets confused
    by water just like sky;

song lingering, still drunk, approaches
    dragons as they sleep.

Now hair and whiskers are all white,
    his face has aged with time;

he's startled by the wind and waves
    and fears an early autumn.

Some friends of his have changed their job:
    they now are fishers of men;

he hears, compared to fishing fish,
    this task is tougher still.

Of late he finds the Heavenly Learning
    has come into the city:

to customers now happily add families that fast.

## John 1:35–39

The next day John again was standing with two of his disciples, and as he watched Jesus walk by, he exclaimed, "Look, here is the Lamb of God!" The two disciples heard him say this, and they followed Jesus. When Jesus turned and saw them following, he said to them, "What are you looking for?" They said to him, "Rabbi" (which translated means Teacher), "where are you staying?" He said to them, "Come and see." They came and saw where he was staying, and they remained with him that day. It was about four o'clock in the afternoon.

# The Dwelling-Place

## HENRY VAUGHAN

Wales, 1622–1695. Vaughan studied at Oxford and was preparing for the law in London when the Civil War interrupted his plans. Returning to Wales, whose countryside he loved, he practiced medicine and began writing poetry. Though influenced by GEORGE HERBERT, Vaughan was less interested than his mentor in religious institutions, and Vaughan's spiritual impulses were a response more to his natural surroundings than to Anglican services. He is considered one of English literature's first nature poets.

> What happy, secret fountain,
>   Fair shade, or mountain,
> Whose undiscover'd virgin glory
> Boasts it this day, though not in story,
> Was then thy dwelling? did some cloud
> Fix'd to a Tent, descend and shrowd
> My distrest Lord? or did a star
> Becken'd by thee, though high and far,
> In sparkling smiles haste gladly down
> To lodge light, and increase her own?
> My dear, dear God! I do not know
> What lodgd thee then, nor where, nor how;
> But I am sure, thou dost now come
> Oft to a narrow, homely room,
> Where thou too hast but the least part,
> My God, I mean *my sinful heart.*

# The Maori Jesus

JAMES KEIR BAXTER

New Zealand, 1926–1972. Baxter's poetry expresses a deeply felt Catholic
Christianity, seen especially in his identification with the poor. In 1968 Baxter,
living comfortably in Auckland, heard a voice in a dream say, "Go to
Jerusalem"—"Jerusalem" is the name of a small settlement of Maori, the in-
digenous people of New Zealand. Baxter left immediately with a change of
clothes and a bible in Maori, calling himself "a Christian guru, a barefooted
and bearded eccentric, a bad smell in the noses of many good citizens."

I saw the Maori Jesus
Walking on Wellington Harbour.
He wore blue dungarees.
His beard and hair were long.
His breath smelt of mussels and paraoa.
When he smiled it looked like the dawn.
When he broke wind the little fishes trembled.
When he frowned the ground shook.
When he laughed everybody got drunk.

The Maori Jesus came on shore
And picked out his twelve disciples.
One cleaned toilets in the Railway Station;
His hands were scrubbed red to get the shit out of the pores.
One was a call-girl who turned it up for nothing.
One was a housewife who'd forgotten the Pill
And stuck her TV set in the rubbish can.
One was a little office clerk
Who'd tried to set fire to the Government Buildings.
Yes, and there were several others;
One was an old sad quean;
One was an alcoholic priest
Going slowly mad in a respectable parish.

The Maori Jesus said, 'Man,
From now on the sun will shine.'

He did no miracles;
He played the guitar sitting on the ground.

The first day he was arrested
For having no lawful means of support.
The second day he was beaten up by the cops
For telling a dee his house was not in order.
The third day he was charged with being a Maori
And given a month in Mount Crawford.
The fourth day he was sent to Porirua
For telling a screw the sun would stop rising.
The fifth day lasted seven years
While he worked in the asylum laundry
Never out of the steam.
The sixth day he told the head doctor,
'I am the Light in the Void;
I am who I am.'
The seventh day he was lobotomized;
The brain of God was cut in half.

On the eighth day the sun did not rise.
It didn't rise the day after.
God was neither alive nor dead.
The darkness of the Void,
Mountainous, mile-deep, civilized darkness
Sat on the earth from then till now.

# Jesus Rejected at Nazareth

*Mark 6:1–6*

He left that place and came to his hometown, and his disciples followed him. On the sabbath he began to teach in the synagogue, and many who heard him were astounded. They said, "Where did this man get all this? What is this wisdom that has been given to him? What deeds of power are being done by his hands! Is not this the carpenter, the son of Mary and brother of James and Joses and Judas and Simon, and are not his sisters here with us?" And they took offense at him. Then Jesus said to them, "Prophets are not without honor, except in their hometown, and among their own kin, and in their own house." And he could do no deed of power there, except that he laid his hands on a few sick people and cured them. And he was amazed at their unbelief.

Then he went about among the villages teaching.

# Jesus Leaves Nazareth Forever

ISTVÁN SINKA

Hungary, 1897–1967. A shepherd's son, Sinka achieved literary recognition during a 1930s movement celebrating "writers of the folk." After the Soviet occupation of Hungary, his passionate belief in his country's destiny earned him the official status of "nonperson," whose name it was unlawful to mention. After the 1956 revolution, he was permitted to publish again. "Jesus Leaves Nazareth Forever" is translated from the Hungarian by Dalma Hunyadi Brunauer.


Cobalt-blue
was the sky
and on the fence, on the latticed slats
the scarlet runner blossomed out in red.
Mourning doves cooing
and on the hillside
among the bushes, goats
were grazing, and from the fig-trees honeyed dewdrops dripped.
In the inner courtyard
bearded folks were sitting
stubborn, unappeasable, none of them weeping;
vineyard-workers, hewers of skillets, sellers of oddments
sons of the Law each one;
loitering among the roses
waiting for "The Raving One,"
The Astounding One, the carpenter with the lightning eyes
who swirls in mirrors of skies and seas,
dreams dreams and among little bread-snatchers, youthful harlots,
tattered orphans, abandoned, sad widows,
and sinners, sits down in the square
and shares their dried-out pancake and green onions
there where glassine gnats cry and green flies
buzz on the remnants of a crimson drop of blood.
Oh, it was because of him that the family
became targets of gossip in
Nazareth, but he must leave now
like the wind which rises on the Hermon,
on this cool golden ladder,

and comes and sweeps through Galilee
and then is no more, is gone forever.

And Jesus came
from the workshop, across
the rose-trees in the courtyard
among the kinsfolk;
with a mild smile he said goodbye to each one,
and stepped out the gate.

And music rose from every zither on earth
and long-dead flowers burst to bloom anew,
birds trilled, and every bird
and every wanderer was called home to gentle Capernaum.
That was where Jesus was going: Capernaum.
He was shadowed by midnight-colored doves:
the scorn of the kinsmen,
where will there be a bench or bank
for him in this world, room enough
for him to lay down his head, to close his eyes and sleep;
they looked at each other, the hewers of skillets,
dressers of vine, for whom there is only: workshop in the corner,
vineyard on the hillside,
multitudes of rugs, from far off, from Perzas;
each of them lasting five lifetimes
and copper dishes and clinging silver vessels
and earthly values, weighed with reality and facts;
they looked after him and were watching with amazement
the otherworldly radiance of Jesus.

# Jesus

JAMES MCAULEY

Australia, 1912–1981. A convert to Catholicism, McCauley was a professor of English at the University of Tasmania and a founder of the prestigious literary journal, *Quadrant*. Along with another poet, McCauley invented the fictitious bard "Ern Malley," one of modern literature's most successful and sensational hoaxes. Like the English poet John Dryden, to whom he addressed a major poem, McCauley was often intellectually engaged with the problem of faith in a skeptical age.

> Touching Ezekiel his workman's hand
> Kindled the thick and thorny characters;
> And seraphim that seemed a thousand eyes,
> Flying leopards, wheels and basilisks,
> Creatures of power and of judgment, soared
> From his finger-point, emblazoning the skies.
>
> Then turning from the book he rose and walked
> Among the stones and beasts and flowers of earth;
> They turned their muted faces to their Lord,
> Their real faces, seen by God alone;
> And people moved before him undisguised;
> He thrust his speech among them like a sword.
>
> And when a dove came to his hand he knew
> That hell was opening behind its wings.
> He thanked the messenger and let it go;
> Spoke to the dust, the fishes and the twelve
> As if they understood him equally,
> And told them nothing that they wished to know.

# PART THREE

# HEALINGS AND MIRACLES

# The Wedding at Cana

## John 2:1—10

There was a wedding in Cana of Galilee, and the mother of Jesus was there. Jesus and his disciples had also been invited to the wedding. When the wine gave out, the mother of Jesus said to him, "They have no wine." And Jesus said to her, "Woman, what concern is that to you and to me? My hour has not yet come." His mother said to the servants, "Do whatever he tells you." Now standing there were six stone water jars for the Jewish rites of purification, each holding twenty or thirty gallons. Jesus said to them, "Fill the jars with water." And they filled them up to the brim. He said to them, "Now draw some out, and take it to the chief steward." So they took it. When the steward tasted the water that had become wine, and did not know where it came from (though the servants who had drawn the water knew), the steward called the bridegroom and said to him, "Everyone serves the good wine first, and then the inferior wine after the guests have become drunk. But you have kept the good wine until now." Jesus did this, the first of his signs, in Cana of Galilee, and revealed his glory; and his disciples believed in him.

# On the Marriage at Cana

RAINER MARIA RILKE

Germany, 1875–1926. The most well-known of twentieth-century poets writing
in German, Rilke was noted for the exquisite workmanship of his verse and for
his effort to achieve self-transcendence through poetry. Though he rejected his
mother's pious Roman Catholicism, he wrote frequently about Jesus, seeing
him in his struggling human dimension. He wrote also a poem-cycle, *The Life
of Mary*. "On the Marriage at Cana" is translated from the German by David
Curzon and Will Alexander Washburn.

> How could she not take pride in him since he
> could make (to her) the plainest things adorned?
> Wasn't even the large and lofty night
> all in disarray when he appeared?
>
> And didn't that time he got lost
> end up, amazingly, a glory of his?
> Hadn't the wisest then exchanged
> their tongues for ears? Didn't the house
>
> become fresh at his voice? She had
> repressed, surely a hundred times,
> the display of her delight in him.
> She followed him with astonishment.
>
> But at that wedding-feast, there when
> unexpectedly the wine ran out,—
> she begged him for a gesture with her look
> and didn't grasp that he resisted her.
>
> And then he did it. Later she understood
> how she had pressured him into his course:
> for now he really was a wonder-worker,
> and the whole sacrifice was now ordained,
>
> irrevocably. Yes, it was written.
> But had it, at the time, as yet been readied?
> She: she had driven it forth
> in the blindness of her vanity.

At the table piled with fruits and vegetables,
she shared everybody's joy and didn't know
that the water of her own tear ducts
had turned to blood with this wine.

# Footnote to John ii.4

R. A. K. MASON

New Zealand, 1905–1971. Mason was one of New Zealand's first poets to break away from derivative, sentimental verse and portray honestly the harshness of antipodean life. His Christ refuses to offer simple comfort. Mason's poems on the Gospels can be bitterly cynical ("Nails and a Cross"); or they can express faith-filled hope ("Oils and Ointments").

> Don't throw your arms around me in that way:
>   I know that what you tell me is the truth—
>   yes I suppose I loved you in my youth
>   as boys do love their mothers, so they say,
>   but all that's gone from me this many a day:
>   I am a merciless cactus an uncouth
>   wild goat a jagged old spear the grim tooth
>   of a lone crag . . . Woman I cannot stay.
>
> Each one of us must do his work of doom
>   and I shall do it even in despite
>   of her who brought me in pain from her womb,
>   whose blood made me, who used to bring the light
>   and sit on the bed up in my little room
>   and tell me stories and tuck me up at night.

# Hymn on Faith: The Wedding Feast

EPHREM

Syria, d.373. See page 21 for biographical information on this poet. "Hymn on
Faith: The Wedding Feast" is translated from the Syriac by Sebastian Brock.


I have invited You, Lord, to a wedding-feast of song,
but the wine—the utterance of praise—at our feast has failed.
You are the guest who filled the jars with good wine,
fill my mouth with Your praise.

The wine that was in the jars was akin and related to
this eloquent wine that gives birth to praise,
seeing that that wine too gave birth to praise
from those who drank it and beheld the wonder.

You who are so just, if at a wedding-feast not Your own
You filled six jars with good wine,
do You, at this wedding-feast, fill, not the jars,
but the ten thousand ears with its sweetness.

Jesus, You were invited to the wedding-feast of others,
here is Your own pure and fair wedding-feast: gladden Your
            rejuvenated people,
for Your guests too, O Lord, need
Your songs; let Your harp utter!

The soul is Your bride, the body Your bridal chamber,
Your guests are the senses and the thoughts.
And if a single body is a wedding-feast for You,
how great is Your banquet for the whole church!

The holy Moses took the synagogue up on Sinai:
he made her body shine with garments of white, but her heart
            was dark;
she played the harlot with the calf, she despised the Exalted one,
and so he broke the tablets, the book of her covenant.

Who has ever seen the turmoil and insult
of a bride who played false in her own bridal chamber, raising
        her voice?
When she dwelt in Egypt she learnt it from
the mistress of Joseph, who cried out and played false.

The light of the pillar of fire and of the cloud
drew into itself its rays
like the sun that was eclipsed
on the day that she cried out, demanding the King, a further crime.

How can my harp, o Lord, ever rest from Your praise?
How could I ever teach my tongue infidelity?
Your love has given confidence to my shamefacedness,
—yet my will is ungrateful.

It is right that man should acknowledge Your divinity,
it is right for heavenly beings to worship Your humanity;
the heavenly beings were amazed to see how small You became,
and earthly ones to see how exalted!

*Refrain:* Praise to You from all who perceive Your truth.

# Sunday

CARLOS PELLICER

Mexico, 1899–1997. Author of many volumes of poems, Pellicer was one of the initiators of the Mexican new poetry and belonged to the loosely knit literary group known as the Contemporáneos. Pellicer arranges his images in a kind of formal mural, and his tone tends to be one of classical detachment. "Sunday" is translated from the Spanish by Dudley Fitts.

The table is imposing
like a monument to the heroes
of any land.
I revere the fish,
gleaming mediaeval knight.
I adore the small roast deer, so delicate
that it died simply from existing.
I smile at the orange, nearly peeled.
I am saddened by the freshly ravished cake.
And the dazzling fruits, fit for badges
to be worn at tropical garden-parties.
Raving pomegranates. Virgin apples—
Dutch, naturally—
and my eyes like X-rays,
piercing, relentless, in an auspicious relishing
that makes the lips glisten and the teeth acid
with a sure magnificent animal culmination.
And divine Poetry,
as at the marriage feast of Cana,
casts a spell on the water: and wine shimmers
in a tall crystal goblet.

# A Wedding Toast

## RICHARD WILBUR

U.S., 1921–. After serving in Italy and France during World War II, Wilbur finished his education at Harvard where he taught for several years before moving on to positions at Wesleyan and Smith. His first volume of poetry, *The Beautiful Changes* (1947), instantly established Wilbur as one of the most accomplished poets of his generation. His poetry is known for its light-hearted optimism. "I feel that the universe is full of glorious energy," he has said, "and that the ultimate character of things is comely and good." An Episcopalian, Wilbur often alludes to the meditative verse of seventeenth century England. He was the 1987–88 Poet Laureate of the U.S.

St. John tells how, at Cana's wedding-feast,
The water-pots poured wine in such amount
That by his sober count
There were a hundred gallons at the least.

It made no earthly sense, unless to show
How whatsoever love elects to bless
Brims to a sweet excess
That can without depletion overflow.

Which is to say that what love sees is true;
That the world's fullness is not made but found.
Life hungers to abound
And pour its plenty out for such as you.

Now, if your loves will lend an ear to mine,
I toast you both, good son and dear new daughter.
May you not lack for water,
And may that water smack of Cana's wine.

# The Pool at Bethesda

*John 5:2—9*

Now in Jerusalem by the Sheep Gate there is a pool, called in Hebrew Beth-zatha, which has five porticoes. In these lay many invalids — blind, lame, and paralyzed. One man was there who had been ill for thirty-eight years. When Jesus saw him lying there and knew that he had been there a long time, he said to him, "Do you want to be made well?" The sick man answered him, "Sir, I have no one to put me into the pool when the water is stirred up; and while I am making my way, someone else steps down ahead of me." Jesus said to him, "Stand up, take your mat and walk." At once the man was made well, and he took up his mat and began to walk.

# Bethesda: A Sequel

ARTHUR HUGH CLOUGH

England, 1819–1861. Born in Liverpool, Clough spent much of his childhood in
Charleston, South Carolina, where his father was a cotton merchant. After a
spectacular career at Rugby, Clough won a scholarship to Oxford, but was
unable to live up to his early expectations. Troubled in faith and fortune, he re-
turned to America and, encouraged by Emerson, Longfellow, and Lowell, tried
to earn a living writing and tutoring, but eventually found a secure position back
in England with the Education Office. As the poem on Bethesda illustrates,
Clough's religious belief is shaped by an awesome sense of human duty.


I saw again the spirits on a day,
Where on the earth in mournful case they lay;
Five porches were there, and a pool, and round,
Huddling in blankets, strewn upon the ground,
Tied-up and bandaged, weary, sore and spent,
The maimed and halt, diseased and impotent.

For a great angel came, 'twas said, and stirred
The pool at certain seasons, and the word
Was, with this people of the sick, that they
Who in the waters here their limbs should lay
Before the motion on the surface ceased
Should of their torment straightway be released.

So with shrunk bodies and with heads down-dropt,
Stretched on the steps, and at the pillars propt,
Watching by day and listening through the night,
They filled the place, a miserable sight.

And I beheld that on the stony floor
He too, that spoke of duty once before,
No otherwise than others here to-day
Foredone and sick and sadly muttering lay.
'I know not, I will do—what is it I would say?
'What was that word which once sufficed alone for all,
'Which now I seek in vain, and never can recall?'
'I know not, I will do the work the world requires

'Asking no reason why, but serving its desires;
'Will do for daily bread, for wealth, respect, good
'The business of the day—alas, is that the same?'
And then, as weary of in vain renewing
His question, thus his mournful thought pursuing,
'I know not, I must do as other men are doing.'

But what the waters of that pool might be,
Of Lethe were they, or Philosophy;
And whether he, long waiting, did attain
Deliverance from the burden of his pain
There with the rest; or whether, yet before,
Some more diviner stranger passed the door
With his small company into that sad place,
And breathing hope into the sick man's face,
Bade him take up his bed, and rise and go,
What the end were, and whether it were so,
Further than this I saw not, neither know.

# The Man Brought in Through the Roof

*Mark 2:3—12*

Then some people came, bringing to him a paralyzed man, carried by four of them. And when they could not bring him to Jesus because of the crowd, they removed the roof above him; and after having dug through it, they let down the mat on which the paralytic lay. When Jesus saw their faith, he said to the paralytic, "Son, your sins are forgiven." Now some of the scribes were sitting there, questioning in their hearts, "Why does this fellow speak in this way? It is blasphemy! Who can forgive sins but God alone?" At once Jesus perceived in his spirit that they were discussing these questions among themselves; and he said to them, "Why do you raise such questions in your hearts? Which is easier, to say to the paralytic, 'Your sins are forgiven,' or to say, 'Stand up and take your mat and walk'? But so that you may know that the Son of Man has authority on earth to forgive sins "—he said to the paralytic—"I say to you, stand up, take your mat and go to your home." And he stood up, and immediately took the mat and went out before all of them; so that they were all amazed and glorified God, saying, "We have never seen anything like this!"

# The Risk

MARCELLA MARIE HOLLOWAY

U.S., 1913–. Prizewinning playwright and poet, Holloway did her doctoral thesis on GERARD MANLEY HOPKINS, who remained the focus of her scholarly publications. Professor of English at various colleges, she has been a Roman Catholic nun of the Sisters of St. Joseph since 1932.

> You take a risk when you invite the Lord
> Whether to dine or talk the afternoon
> Away, for always the unexpected soon
> Turns up: a woman breaks her precious nard,
> A sinner does the task you should assume,
> A leper who is cleansed must show his proof:
> Suddenly you see your very roof removed
> And a cripple clutters up your living room.
>
> There's no telling what to expect when Christ
> Walks in your door. The table set for four
> Must often be enlarged and decorum
> Thrown to the wind. It's His voice that calls them
> And it's no use to bolt and bar the door:
> His kingdom knows no bounds of roof, or wall, or floor.

# At Seven O'Clock

DOM MORAES

India, 1938–. A prizewinning poet and prolific writer, Moraes has also written nonfiction travel and autobiographical prose works.

The masseur from Ceylon, whose balding head
Gives him a curious look of tenderness,
Uncurls his long crushed hands above my bed
As though he were about to preach or bless.

His poulterer's fingers pluck my queasy skin,
Shuffle along my side, and reach the thigh.
I note however that he keeps his thin
Fastidious nostrils safely turned away.

But sometimes the antarctic eyes glance down,
And the lids drop to hood a scornful flash:
A deep ironic knowledge of the thin
Or gross (but always ugly) human flesh.

Hernia, goitre and the flowering boil
Lie bare beneath his hands, for ever bare.
His fingers touch the skin: they reach the soul.
I know him in the morning for a seer.

Within my mind he is reborn as Christ:
For each blind dawn he kneads my prostrate thighs,
Thumps on my buttocks with his fist
And breathes, Arise.

# The Blind Man at Bethsaida

*Mark 8:22–25*

They came to Bethsaida. Some people brought a blind man to him and begged him to touch him. He took the blind man by the hand and led him out of the village; and when he had put saliva on his eyes and laid his hands on him, he asked him, "Can you see anything?" And the man looked up and said, "I can see people, but they look like trees, walking." Then Jesus laid his hands on his eyes again; and he looked intently and his sight was restored, and he saw everything clearly.

# Resurrection

MARGARET ATWOOD

Canada, 1939–. Born in Ottawa and educated at the University of Toronto and Radcliffe College, Atwood is considered one of North America's preeminent literary figures. Her poetry and fiction often boldly explore themes of sexual identity and self-fragmentation. Her first important volume of poetry, *The Circle Game* (1966), won the prestigious General's Medal, as did her 1985 novel, *The Handmaid's Tale*.

I see now I see
now I cannot see

earth is a blizzard in my eyes

I hear now

    the rustle of the snow

the angels listening above me

    thistles bright with sleet
    gathering

waiting for the time
to reach me
up to the pillared
sun, the final city

    or living towers

unrisen yet
whose dormant stones lie folding
their holy fire around me

    (but the land shifts with frost
    and those who have become the stone
    voices of the land
    shift also to say

god is not
the voice in the whirlwind

god is the whirlwind

at the last
judgement we will all be trees

# House with a Sanguine Roof

MIGUEL DE UNAMUNO

Spain, 1864–1936. See page 77 for biographical information on this poet. "House with a Sanguine Roof" is from his diary of morning poetic meditations on Scripture. It is translated from the Spanish by Edita Mas-López.

House with a sanguine roof
whereto the ivy clings,
the smoke like the breathing
of some meek ox is rising.

Next to the pen a youthful donkey
effortlessly grazes,
and, far away, the country road
smells of pestiferous petroleum.

In the silence of the greenness
the coming hours are heard
as they tread with steps of doves
upon the earth.

The roots of every tree
dream of the water of heaven,
and, just like trees, men, too,
go for a stroll in the field.

# The Widow's Son at Nain

## Luke 7:11—15

Soon afterwards he went to a town called Nain, and his disciples and a large crowd went with him. As he approached the gate of the town, a man who had died was being carried out. He was his mother's only son, and she was a widow; and with her was a large crowd from the town. When the Lord saw her, he had compassion for her and said to her, "Do not weep." Then he came forward and touched the bier, and the bearers stood still. And he said, "Young man, I say to you, rise!" The dead man sat up and began to speak, and Jesus gave him to his mother.

# The Widow of Naim

THOMAS MERTON

U.S., 1915–1968. Writer (most famous for his autobiography, *The Seven Storey Mountain*), peace activist, bridge between Christianity and the world's other great religions, Trappist monk, and priest, Merton was also a poet for whom poetry and prayer were allied. "To the true Christian poet," he wrote, "the whole world and all the incidents of life tend to be sacraments—signs of God, signs of His love working in the world."

The men that cut their graves in the grey rocks
Go down more slowly than the sun upon their dusty country:
White as the wall, the weepers leave the town,
To be the friends of grief, and follow
To the new tomb a widow's sorrow.

The men with hands as hard as rope,
(Some smell of harvests, some of nets,) the strangers,
Come up the hill more slowly than the seasons of the year.

"Why do you walk in funerals, you men of Naim,
Why go you down to graves, with eyes like winters,
And your cold faces clean as cliffs?
See how we come, our brows are full of sun,
Our smiles are fairer than the wheat and hay,
Our eyes are saner than the sea.
Lay down your burden at our four-roads' crossing,
And learn a wonder from the Christ, our Traveller."

(Oh, you will say that those old times
Are all dried up like water,
Since the great God went walking on a road to Naim,
How many hundred years has slept again in death
That widow's son, after the marvel of his miracle:
He did not rise for long, and sleeps forever.
And what of the men of the town?
What have the desert winds done to the dust
Of the poor weepers, and the widow's friends?)

The men that cut their graves in the grey rocks
Spoke to the sons of God upon the four cross roads:
"Men of Genesareth, who climb our hill as slow as spring or summer,
Christ is your Master, and we see His eyes are Jordans,
His hands and feet are wounded, and His words are wine.
He has let death baptize the one who stirs and wakens
In the bier we carry,
That we may read the Cross and Easter in this rising,
And learn the endless heaven
Promised to all the widow-Church's risen children."

# Spes

RUBÉN DARÍO

Nicaragua, 1867–1916. See page 49 for biographical information on this poet.
"Spes" is translated from the Spanish by Lysander Kemp.

Jesus, incomparable pardoner of wrongs,
hear me. Sower of wheat, give me the tender
bread of the Mass. Protect me from Hell's power
with the grace that washes away all wrath and lust.

Tell me that this horrible dread of agony
which possesses me is my own wicked fault;
that, dead, I will see the light of a new day,
and then will hear you say, "Arise and walk!"

# The Calming of the Storm

## Mark 4:35–41

When evening had come, he said to them, "Let us go across to the other side." And leaving the crowd behind, they took him with them in the boat, just as he was. Other boats were with him. A great windstorm arose, and the waves beat into the boat, so that the boat was already being swamped. But he was in the stern, asleep on the cushion; and they woke him up and said to him, "Teacher, do you not care that we are perishing?" He woke up and rebuked the wind, and said to the sea, "Peace! Be still!" Then the wind ceased, and there was a dead calm. He said to them, "Why are you afraid? Have you still no faith?" And they were filled with great awe and said to one another, "Who then is this, that even the wind and the sea obey him?"

# On Christ Calming the Storm

ANATOLIUS

Alexandria/Constantinople, c.400–458. Anatolius was patriarch of the Byzantine Church and played an active part in the disputes of his day between the Roman Pope and Constantinople. His poetic compositions, according to his nineteenth century English translator, J. M. Neale, "are almost all short, but they are usually very spirited." "On Christ Calming the Storm" is translated from the Greek by J. M. Neale.

Fierce was the wild billow;
  Dark was the night;
Oars labour'd heavily;
  Foam glimmer'd white;
Trembled the mariners;
  Peril was nigh;
Then said the GOD OF GOD,
  —'Peace! It is I!'

Ridge of the mountain-wave,
  Lower thy crest!
Wail of Euroclydon,
  Be thou at rest!
Sorrow can never be,—
  Darkness must fly,—
Where saith the Light of Light
  —'Peace! It is I!'

JESU, Deliverer!
  Come Thou to me:
Soothe Thou my voyaging
  Over Life's sea!
Thou, when the storm of Death
  Roars, sweeping by,
Whisper, O Truth of Truth!
  —'Peace! It is I!'

# Miracles

JULIA RANDALL

U.S., 1923–. Former college teacher Randall has published poetry for adults and children. Randall's ability to bend conversational diction to poetic form, and to suggest at the same time the subtle traps into which the possession of power leads us, is evident in "Miracles."

I said to the stream, Be still, and it was still.
I walked across the water like a fool.
Such ease—you'd think a man had never tried
The simple miracles, but lived and died
Sweating at wood and steel: chop, forge, bend, bind,
Get up the armory, don't trust humankind,
They were damned from the start.

                      I said to the mineral hill,
Lie down, and the hanging rocks and the canyons fell
As soft as smoke. It was quiet. I called out
Some friends to look. For a while they walked about
Uncomfortably, I thought, and one picked up
A fragment for the Museum. Envy? Fear?
I don't know what. I kept on all that year.
Wherever I went, the trees bowed down; the fruit
Rolled like obedient coins to my feet,
And so on. Late one night I tried to command—
How shall I say?—my holy spell to end,
Break, blast, unmagic me here in the dark
Tower I'd built. I wanted a horn to knock
The cullis in, and the crazy ditch to rise.
Oh god, for the need of nails, for the wild eyes
Of Noah with creation in his hold
Stampeding. But I'd sold
My Ararat for meadows. Oh, the flowers!
Too deep, too deep.
I said, accept my tears.

# The Gadarene Swine

*Matthew 8:28–33*

When he came to the other side, to the country of the Gadarenes, two demoniacs coming out of the tombs met him. They were so fierce that no one could pass that way. Suddenly they shouted, "What have you to do with us, Son of God? Have you come here to torment us before the time?" Now a large herd of swine was feeding at some distance from them. The demons begged him, "If you cast us out, send us into the herd of swine." And he said to them, "Go!" So they came out and entered the swine; and suddenly, the whole herd rushed down the steep bank into the sea and perished in the water. The swineherds ran off, and on going into the town, they told the whole story about what had happened to the demoniacs.

# Readings

## CZESLAW MILOSZ

Lithuania/Poland, 1911–. Winner of the Nobel Prize in Literature for 1980, Milosz was born in Lithuania and educated at the University in Wilno (Vilnius). A leader of the Polish avant garde literary movement in the 1930s, Milosz served in the Resistance during the Nazi occupation and after the war spent several years in diplomatic service. Disillusioned by communism, he left Poland in 1951, eventually settling in California, where he became a professor at Berkeley. Raised a Catholic, Milosz has often written on religion and has worked on a Polish translation of the Bible. "Readings" is translated from the Polish by Czeslaw Milosz and Lillian Vallee.

You asked me what is the good of reading the Gospels in Greek.
I answer that it is proper that we move our finger
Along letters more enduring than those carved in stone,
And that, slowly pronouncing each syllable,
We discover the true dignity of speech.
Compelled to be attentive we shall think of that epoch
No more distant than yesterday, though the heads of Caesars
On coins are different today. Yet still it is the same eon.
Fear and desire are the same, oil and wine
And bread mean the same. So does the fickleness of the throng
Avid for miracles as in the past. Even mores,
Wedding festivities, drugs, laments for the dead
Only seem to differ. Then, too, for example,
There were plenty of persons whom the text calls
*Daimonizomenoi*, that is, the demonized
Or, if you prefer, the bedeviled (as for "the possessed"
It's no more than the whim of a dictionary).
Convulsions, foam at the mouth, the gnashing of teeth
Were not considered signs of talent.
The demonized had no access to print and screens,
Rarely engaging in arts and literature.
But the Gospel parable remains in force:
That the spirit mastering them may enter swine,
Which, exasperated by such a sudden clash
Between two natures, theirs and the Luciferic,
Jump into water and drown (which occurs repeatedly).
And thus on every page a persistent reader
Sees twenty centuries as twenty days
In a world which one day will come to its end.

# The Cure of the Nobleman's Son

*John 4:46 – 53*

Then he came again to Cana in Galilee where he had changed the water into wine. Now there was a royal official whose son lay ill in Capernaum. When he heard that Jesus had come from Judea to Galilee, he went and begged him to come down and heal his son, for he was at the point of death. Then Jesus said to him, "Unless you see signs and wonders you will not believe." The official said to him, "Sir, come down before my little boy dies." Jesus said to him, "Go; your son will live." The man believed the word that Jesus spoke to him and started on his way. As he was going down, his slaves met him and told him that his child was alive. So he asked them the hour when he began to recover, and they said to him, "Yesterday at one in the afternoon the fever left him." The father realized that this was the hour when Jesus had said to him, "Your son will live." So he himself believed, along with his whole household.

# Good Friday, 1993: Heading East

ROBERT ATWAN

U.S., 1940–. Born in Paterson, New Jersey, Atwan, whose grandfather came from Aleppo, was raised in a Syrian-Catholic household and educated at Seton Hall and Rutgers University. The founder and series editor of *The Best American Essays*, Atwan has published essays, poetry, reviews, and criticism in a wide range of periodicals, as well as numerous college anthologies. He is coeditor of the two-volume *Chapters into Verse: Poetry in English Inspired by the Bible*.

> *Unless you see signs and*
> *wonders you will not believe.*

Low on gas, I pull into Grady's Gulf.
Barney's at the pump, wire-rimmed glasses
taped together, reciting the opening lines
of "The Pardoner's Tale," still preparing
for the exams he missed because of Nam.
It's unsettling to hear.

My stomach's growling. Grady's inside cursing
one of the candy machines. He still wears coveralls,
though there's no repair business left.
Customers come only to fill up on gas & oil,
smokes & cokes. "It's a full time job," he says,
"keeping this damned vending crap from breaking down."
He points to a small bag of peanuts dangling
at the end of its coil.

"Half the time they won't goddamn drop."
He kicks the machine, slams it with the heel of his hand.
I hope the nuts will fall—but they hang there,
stuck in their coil. Barney comes in with advice,
says he learned it from an old drill sergeant,
and leans his head against the machine gently,
the way a school girl at the movies might rest
her head on a boyfriend's shoulder. I can't hear
what Barney whispers but the spell works:
the nuts tumble softly from the coiled wire.

He hands me the bag. "Must've loosened them,"
Grady says, taking the credit card.

I savor the nuts as I drive home,
my busted radio miraculously
filling the air.

# Jairus's Daughter

## Luke 8:41−42a, 49−55

Just then there came a man named Jairus, a leader of the synagogue. He fell at Jesus' feet and begged him to come to his house, for he had an only daughter, about twelve years old, who was dying. . . . While he was still speaking, someone came from the leader's house to say, "Your daughter is dead; do not trouble the teacher any longer." When Jesus heard this, he replied, "Do not fear. Only believe, and she will be saved." When he came to the house, he did not allow anyone to enter with him, except Peter, John, and James, and the child's father and mother. They were all weeping and wailing for her; but he said, "Do not weep; for she is not dead but sleeping." And they laughed at him, knowing that she was dead. But he took her by the hand and called out, "Child, get up!" Her spirit returned, and she got up at once. Then he directed them to give her something to eat.

# Jesus with the Daughter of Jairus

ERNST LUDWIG SCHELLENBERG

Germany, 1883–1964. An unaffiliated scholar and free lance writer, Schellenberg published more than thirty books between 1902 and 1942. His work is varied, comprising lyric poetry, a novel, literary criticism, poetry anthologies, books on music, on landscape, and on the Bible. "Jesus with the Daughter of Jairus" is translated from the German by George Dardess.

Child—child! Your narrow cheeks are white
which once a mother's love caressed
and the red of youth once blessed.
Your limbs are stiff. At this sight
the mourners wail.
Sweet child, your lips so pale—
My eyes flinch
from them. I know you sleep.
Your eyelids close on bedtime prayer.
Dream on—don't stop—all hinges on your choice.
I echo your silenced voice.
"Give me, father, give me a brother's strength to share.
I'm lost and can't get back.
It's all black
in my eyes, like a forest a long way off and deep—
I'm shivering—a night without a day or name
where everything is just the same . . .
If only I had a brother! He'd stand,
he'd hold tight my shadowy hand!"

Then, to meet your prayer,
A light sleep began to inch . . .
Your father rushed to me in terror,
Begging me come to your bed. I ache.
Give me your hand, my sister: Awake!

# The Hemorrhaging Woman

## Luke 8:42b–48

As he went, the crowds pressed in on him. Now there was a woman who had been suffering from hemorrhages for twelve years; and though she had spent all she had on physicians, no one could cure her. She came up behind him and touched the fringe of his clothes, and immediately her hemorrhage stopped. Then Jesus asked, "Who touched me?" When all denied it, Peter said, "Master, the crowds surround you and press in on you." But Jesus said, "Someone touched me; for I noticed that power had gone out from me." When the woman saw that she could not remain hidden, she came trembling; and falling down before him, she declared in the presence of all the people why she had touched him, and how she had been immediately healed. He said to her, "Daughter, your faith has made you well; go in peace."

# On the Woman with an Issue of Blood

ROMANOS

Constantinople, 6th c. Romanos was a deacon in the Byzantine church. His poeticized sermons on biblical texts are in the genre later called *kontakia*, considered the great achievement of Byzantine literature. Homiletic dramatic dialogues, they were written to be sung, and they follow a strict poetic form. "On the Woman with an Issue of Blood" is translated from the Greek by Marjorie Carpenter.

Like the woman with the issue of blood, I fall down before Thee, Lord,
    So that Thou wilt deliver me from distress, O Lover of man,
    And grant to me forgiveness for my failures,
      In order that I may cry out to Thee with contrition of heart,
        "Savior, save me."

I hymn Thee in odes, O exalted King, since Thou dost not deprive
  me of Thy glory;
For Thou dost overlook my sins, wishing to find me repentant,
Thou who art in Thy nature sinless; hence I beg that Thy long
  suffering
Produce in me conversion
And not presumption, for I cry:
        "Savior, save me."

Now Thou didst walk upon the earth with feet of incorruption,
    dispensing healing to all;
For Thou didst give sight to the blind,
    muscular control to the weakened
By the touch of Thy hand, and by a word, by Thy will alone;
    and this the woman with the issue of blood had heard.
She came to Thee to be saved, silent in speech,
But crying out earnestly to Thee with her hand:
        "Savior, save me."

Unnoticed she came to Thee, Savior, for indeed she considered
  Thee only a man,
But when she was cured, she was taught that Thou art God and man;
Secretly she touched the hem of Thy garment,

laying hold on it with her hand, fearful in spirit.
She thought that she would rob Thee with her hand;
By Thee she was robbed as she cried to Thee:
"Savior, save me."

Listener, do you wish to know clearly how the Savior was robbed and
    also robbed?
The woman knew what she had to do, and because of the theft kept
    silence;
For if she had made herself known, the enemy would have found out
        about the deliverance of the young woman
And cast her into despair;
Hence Christ heard her say silently:
        "Savior, save me."

The woman with the issue of blood, it seems to me,
        not only reasoned in this way, but said to herself:

WOMAN: "How shall I be seen by the All-seeing One, as I come
    bearing the shame of my sins?
If the blameless One sees the issue of blood, He will cast me away
    as impure,
And this will be more terrible than my disease,
If He turns away from me as I cry to Him:
            'Savior, save me.'

"On seeing me, all the people pushed me away,
        'Now where are you going?' they cried to me;
'Just consider, woman, your shame,
        know who you are and whom you now wish to approach,
The impure to the pure! Go away and purify yourself of your filth,
And when you have rubbed off your stain,
Then you will run to Him crying out:
            "Savior, save me".'

"Do you men, perhaps, wish to be harder on me than my misfortune?
Am I, then, acting as thou ruled by ignorance? I know that He is pure,
It is for this reason that I have come to Him
        in order to be relieved of the shame of the stain,

Do not then prevent me from gathering strength for myself.
I beg you allow me to cry out:
            'Savior, save me'."

CROWD: "You do not know what you ask, woman, go away
            so that we shall not all come under blame;
If we allow you to go, we shall all be considered guilty of His dishonor;
If the ones who accompany Him see you again going near Him,
They will blame us as scorning Him,
And they will consider us foolish, when you cry out:
            'Savior, save me'."

WOMAN: "It is you, wretches, who have been ruled by jealousy;
            and that is why you do not wish me to be saved,
The spring gushes forth for all;
            for what reason do you block it?
See, I go to my Creator,
            and if He is made angry, He will not be under reproach;
But if He saves me from my disease,
You will feel shame when I cry out:
            'Savior, save me.'

"You are witnesses of His healings; and why do you forbid those who
    approach?
Each day He calls out and begs:
            'Come unto me all who are weary and heavy laden
For I shall give you rest.' He rejoices in giving the gift of health to all,
And why do you bully me, preventing me,
As though under pretext of respect, from crying out to Him:
            'Savior, save me.'

"Why did I appear before you:
            Because I shall receive healing, as you know not.
Are you the initiated followers of Christ?
            Why do you follow Him gloomily?
You tread on the heels of the Immaculate One; hence, withdraw,
            and even then He is not alone?
You breathe forth a breath of jealousy, of murder;
That is why you prevent me from crying out:
            'Savior, save me'."

These, I think, were the words of the woman with the issue of blood
        to those who wanted to scare her away.
Secretly she touched the hem of His garment;
        she tried to rob Him as though He were a man,
He who in His divinity knows no sleep. However, Christ bore being
   robbed —
He who of old stole the side of Adam in Eden,
He who formed the woman now crying out to Him,
        "Savior, save me."

He who knows all things before their origin,
        who was not unaware before this of what she suffered,
Turning to His disciples, said:

CHRIST: "Who has just now touched the hem of my garment?
Who has taken whatever she desired? How, then, do you guard my
   treasure?
While you, my disciples, were watchful
Lest I be robbed, despoiled by a hand crying out
        'Savior, save me.'

"By whom was this done? You ought to know, my friends;
I just now revealed to you the dramatic act,
        and now I shall disclose how the one who stole
Made use of my power; without words she came to me crying,
And clinging to my robe like a message,
She took possession of healing as she cried to me,
        'Savior, save me.'

"She who came near me received the healing,
        for she plundered the power from me.
Why do you say to me, Simon Bar-Jonah,
        that crowds of people were pressing me?
They do not touch my divinity
        but she, in touching my visible robe,
Clearly grasped my divine nature,
And took possession of health as she cried to me,
        'Savior, save me'."

When she saw that she was not unobserved, the woman reasoned as
   follows
And said

WOMAN: "Now that I am purified of my stain,
      I shall be seen by my Savior, Jesus,
For I am no longer afraid,
      for it is by His will that I have accomplished this.
What He willed, this I did;
For, in faith I came crying out to Him,
            'Savior, save me.'

"Surely the Creator was not ignorant of what I did,
      for He supported me, as He is indeed merciful,
Merely by touching Him, I reaped healing, since really He was gladly
   despoiled.
Therefore I am not afraid now of being seen as I announce to my God
That He is the Healer of the sick and the Savior of souls,
And the Master of nature to whom I cry,
            'Savior, save me.'

"I fled for refuge to Thee, a good physician,
      casting aside my shame.
Do not stir up Thy anger against me
      and do not be annoyed by Thy servant,
For I have accomplished what Thou didst will;
      for before I considered doing this deed,
Thou wert preparing me for it.
Thou didst know my heart as I cried to Thee:
            'Savior, save me'."

CHRIST: Now, O woman, be strengthened in your faith;
      since you despoiled me of my own will, henceforth take
   courage;
For it was not for the sake of shaming you
      that I brought you into the midst of all these people,
But in order that I might assure them
      that I rejoice in being despoiled; I did not reproach you.

Henceforth, then, be in good health,
You who up until the end of your malady cried out to me,
                'Savior, save me.'

"This is not the work of my hand,
        but the accomplishment of your faith;
For many have touched my garment,
        but they did not gain the power,
Since they did not bring faith;
        but you, when you touched me with much faith,
Gained for yourself health; and hence I have brought you
Before all, that you might cry out,
              'Savior, save me'."

O incomprehensible Son of God, incarnate for us as Lover of man,

As Thou hast delivered her just now from the issue of blood,
        do deliver me from my sins,
Thou who alone art free from sin.
        By prayers and intercessions of the saints,
O Thou who alone art powerful, incline my heart
Always to meditate on Thy words
            In order to save me.

# The Multiplication of the Loaves and Fishes

## Mark 6:34–44

As he went ashore, he saw a great crowd; and he had compassion for them, because they were like sheep without a shepherd; and he began to teach them many things. When it grew late, his disciples came to him and said, "This is a deserted place, and the hour is now very late; send them away so that they may go into the surrounding country and villages and buy something for themselves to eat." But he answered them, "You give them something to eat." They said to him, "Are we to go and buy two hundred denarii worth of bread, and give it to them to eat?" And he said to them, "How many loaves have you? Go and see." When they had found out, they said, "Five, and two fish." Then he ordered them to get all the people to sit down in groups on the green grass. So they sat down in groups of hundreds and of fifties. Taking the five loaves and the two fish, he looked up to heaven, and blessed and broke the loaves, and gave them to his disciples to set before the people; and he divided the two fish among them all. And all ate and were filled; and they took up twelve baskets full of broken pieces and of the fish. Those who had eaten the loaves numbered five thousand men.

# Oblation

## VASSAR MILLER

U.S., 1924–. The unashamedly Christian voice in Miller's poetry startled the secular literary world with its sure yet unsentimental faith when she began publishing in the 1950s. Her continuous output of poems has remained fundamentally religious. Handicapped by cerebral palsy since birth, Miller focuses often in her poems on the Word become flesh. "Poetry is always religious," she has said; like all art, it "has a trinitarian function: creative, redemptive, and sanctifying." A lifelong resident of Houston, Texas, Miller was raised a Presbyterian, but chose later to worship as an Episcopalian and more recently with the Covenant Baptist Church.

I kneel,
my heart in my hands—
a cold fish,
a stale loaf.

What are
these among so many?
Lord, Your business
is to know.

I rise,
my body a shell
heavy with
emptiness,

You whom
worlds cannot contain
not disturbing
one pulse beat.

My bones
being boughs aflame
with Thy glory,
Lord, suffices.

# Remembrance of Five Loaves

MIKHAIL POZDNYAYEV

Russia, 1953–. A Moscow journalist, whose father was a distinguished literary critic, Pozdnyayev was formerly the editor in chief of the newspaper *Literaturnaia Rossiia*. In his journalism and poetry he has attacked the entrenched ecclesiastical authority of the Russian Orthodox Church, while insisting on greater individual freedom for the clergy. "Remembrance of Five Loaves" is translated from the Russian by Vladimir Lunis and Albert C. Todd

*To V. Ch.*

Man, for whom everything is past,
                              with man
for whom everything is ahead, on his chest—
stands in the middle of a bread store with a
                              cashier's receipt
at the end of the line.
Judge for yourself—

how is it for him at this moment, when
before the face of the saleswoman by the name of Sveta
all his hungers and grievances receded somewhere—
far, far away, where sometime yet he will have to appear
                              in order to answer.

It is there that all will be accounted for and imputed—
to man,
        fortunately or unfortunately, in our world,
                              calculating and absurd,
who has experienced everything,
even, by the way, atomic war,
so that now
        finally he could get into this line for bread.

Yes, not by bread alone . . . and nevertheless, you know, my
                              love,
I see us so often
        not in the stormy waves of daily life,

but in the desert, among those more than five thousand,
              who were filled by five loaves of bread—
and yet, they say, twelve baskets full of fragments remained.

Yes, "fragments that remained twelve baskets full" . . .
                                                    and when
it happened, imagine! All victuals do not diminish.
Know, verily:
              if the lords have already sat at the table—
then even the dogs are given something from their meal.

Thus I see
       how these stale fragments float over the multitude,
                                            as if circles
are spreading on water, and, passing along a chain,
fingers lock on them, from one, then the other hand . . .
and below, as if on the bottom, can be seen
now the border of a great empire, now a crooked pale of
                                            settlement,
now a village fence, now a front-line position.

. . . Beaten, hardened, threatened, shot, radiated—
who would dare to justify him or forgive?—
behold man stands at the end of the line, doomed
thus to stand until the time
       when he won't be frightened onto the earth
                            his progeny to lower . . .

And if in truth beauty alone saves this earth
or at least
       is still able to save—
man, for whom everything is ahead,
                            afraid of nothing, falls asleep
on the chest of man,
              for whom everything is past.

# Jesus Walks on the Sea

*Matthew 14:22–27*

Immediately he made the disciples get into the boat and go on ahead to the other side, while he dismissed the crowds. And after he had dismissed the crowds, he went up the mountain by himself to pray. When evening came, he was there alone, but by this time the boat, battered by the waves, was far from the land, for the wind was against them. And early in the morning he came walking toward them on the sea. But when the disciples saw him walking on the sea, they were terrified, saying, "It is a ghost!" And they cried out in fear. But immediately Jesus spoke to them and said, "Take heart, it is I; do not be afraid."

# Jesus Walks on the Water

HANS BENZMANN

Germany, 1869–1926. Benzmann was able to combine two seemingly anti-
thetical gifts, one for law and public life, the other for lyric poetry. Rising to
the position of Secretary of the Reichstag, he also published several volumes
of his own poetry as well as studies of the German ballad and of German evan-
gelical verse. "Jesus Walks on the Water" is translated from the German by
George Dardess.

Slowly scattering, that crowd which just today
Sat in a press at his feet, on the homeward way
Thoughtfully wandering, through the darkening day—
He sees them, old and young—
What peace thrills that throng! . . .
The sea takes deep red from the peach-colored skies,
And on its back the band of disciples tries
Their skiff, now venturing far out . . .
Not a sound or shout
As man and oar through redness ease their way,
Jet black like shadows, like ghosts at play! . . .
Listen—that's their song drifting back to him,
Catchy, festive, a thanksgiving hymn.
Blissfully, hidden in the thickets,
He attends their singing, while crickets
And other nighttime creatures, dreamy, shy,
Stretch, chirp, whistle, fiddle, seek a reply,
Then hush in longing, then renew their cry . . .
And suddenly, on the horizon right behind him,
The moon blazes up, almost terrifies him . . .
Yet the quiet weaves its charm around,
Some force moves even the Holy One to shift his ground—
It lifts his feet, almost pulls him in a ring . . .
What a spellbound night! . . . the crickets sing—
Golden absorption—a round is danced
Somewhere near—invisible forms, still entranced,
Climb lightly down from hidden flowers
And stretch their wings in secret bowers—
What a circle! Both here and there and on the sea—

. . . O dance of souls all around me,
Beloved Nature, a longing seizes me,
Not to be this sacred circle's guest
But to join the play with all the rest! . . .
So he whispers, hastening through moonbeams
Down to the sea's silent streams—
And upon the weaving of the light
His feet hover and take flight—
And Jesus walks—walks on the water!—
And under his feet the waves in silver flutter—
What a dance!—his clothing and his soul aglow . . .
What gliding, what magical to and fro . . .
Oh may the moment last forever so . . .
Then the wind lifts the sea's cool wings.
The waters surge in hills. One rise brings
To Jesus' sight the disciples' little boat—
On flames of white moonlight it seems to float—
And he sees their eyes, shocked, staring,
Sucking him from the waves—the arms reaching—
Then his blood is flowing, warming,
A gripping, a seizing, and he is with them . . .
And while, still fearful, they hug and tend him,
He speaks, as if just awake:
"Peace—it is I. The wind . . . be careful for my sake!"

# Miracle

SUSAN GRIFFEN

U.S., 1943 –. Poet, editor, and teacher, Griffen has written extensively, in prose
and verse, about women's identification with nature and about the larger cul-
ture's revolt against both women and nature by attempting to separate and sup-
press them. "Miracle" expresses a more positive vision—how a divine action re-
stores nature to us, by allowing us to appreciate its ordinariness.

It all happened on the water
Jesus' walking
the fishermen watching
from their boats.
When they picked up their nets
they half expected
a miraculous catch
but it was as ordinary
as the rest of the day.
Only some of them understood.
This is how it always is
with a vision.
Jesus walked on the water
only once.
This wasn't science.
What was it the fishermen were
supposed to see.
A man moving over the surface
of the sea as if it were
some other substance like ground.
Was this all there was?
Picture yourself
you are out there on the water
you look at the horizon.
You are so used to seeing that part
of the sky it's become
part of your eyes.
Then you blink, staring
you turn to shake your companion.
This was not what you expected to see.

Not even what you wished for.
What difference does it make
a man walking on the water?
But even so the day
going on as it usually does
is cut with a certain clarity
and you, you feel an inexplicable
happiness, the water
beneath you, the
bright air above.

# Does a Mirror Forget?

JOSÉ GARCIA VILLA

Phillipines, 1911–. The best known Filipino poet who writes in English, Villa
crafted a formalist, experimental verse in the 1930s. Villa uses his poetry to
wrestle at once with language and with his anguished relation to God. "Does
a Mirror Forget?" expresses a rare moment of peace in a poetry of tormented
mysticism.

> Does a mirror forget?
> I believe it does not.
> I believe a mirror will not forget
> If you come to it superb.
>
> Clear gaze of mirrors
> Towards the gaze of God:
> As the waters of Galilee
> Upholding the superb Feet.

# Peter Tries and Fails

*Matthew 14:28–32*

Peter answered him, "Lord, if it is you, command me to come to you on the water." He said, "Come." So Peter got out of the boat, started walking on the water, and came toward Jesus. But when he noticed the strong wind, he became frightened, and beginning to sink, he cried out, "Lord, save me!" Jesus immediately reached out his hand and caught him, saying to him, "You of little faith, why did you doubt?" When they got into the boat, the wind ceased.

# A Prayer to Saint Peter

## (I was caught in a storm while returning from Rome)

FRANCISCO DE MEDRANO

Spain, 1570?–1607?. A Jesuit who left the order, Medrano was a classical and
Horatian poet. His poems were published posthumously. "A Prayer to Saint
Peter" is translated by Y. R. Pérez.

> Fisherman most mighty, in whose net
> powerful monarchs have been caught
> to their great good luck, and taught
> to exchange their prisons for the glory of benevolence,
>
> with mighty key you lock up heaven, or let
> its gate swing open to your flock,
> and on earth you've attained a palace wrought
> of walls and columns all porphyry, yet
>
> deign to fix your eyes upon this boiling sea,
> and if once it dared to wet your foot
> when trod by your fortitude and faith,
>
> now break its swells, calm this calamity;
> as you once were taught, with mighty hand now put
> daring in my feet, and in my faith.

# The Transfiguration

*Mark 9:2—9*

Six days later, Jesus took with him Peter and James and John, and led them up a high mountain apart, by themselves. And he was transfigured before them, and his clothes became dazzling white, such as no one on earth could bleach them. And there appeared to them Elijah with Moses, who were talking with Jesus. Then Peter said to Jesus, "Rabbi, it is good for us to be here; let us make three dwellings, one for you, one for Moses, and one for Elijah." He did not know what to say, for they were terrified. Then a cloud overshadowed them, and from the cloud there came a voice, "This is my Son, the Beloved; listen to him!" Suddenly when they looked around, they saw no one with them any more, but only Jesus.

As they were coming down the mountain, he ordered them to tell no one about what they had seen, until after the Son of Man had risen from the dead.

# Cloud–Music

## from *The Christ of Velázquez*

MIGUEL DE UNAMUNO

Spain, 1864–1936. See page 77 for biographical information on this poet.
"Cloud–Music" is translated from the Spanish by Anthony Kerrigan.

A white cloud You are, white as the one
that across the desert guided
the children of Israel; cloud of whiteness,
like a pearl in the limitless black
opacity of the infinite shell
which is Your Father. White cloud stained
by the blood of the sun piercing the earth
to be born again in another world
of its kingdom. White as the clouds,
the spray of the heavens, celestial
cumulus which waters the earth.
The tunic of Your exhausted soul, Nazarene,
is white as the snow; no fuller on earth
could wash it so white: it shines
like the snow, mirror of light. It invites us
to remain on the mountain, to pitch camp there
and drink in its whiteness. But suddenly
see: another cloud casts the shadow of sadness
across Your livid forehead, and the voice
of its depths resounds: "This is my beloved Son,
in whom I am well pleased; hear ye Him!"
And the snow-thick dawn of Your divine body
sings of resurrection from among the dead, sings
—not says—for Your divine body
is music, and this silent song
(its whiteness music for the eyes)
gives refreshment like the harp of David
to our souls when the spirit of the Evil
One is upon them, and at the sounds
of Your heavenly breast's harmony
our pain is laid to sleep,

in the nests of our hearts inhumed
by enchantment. And then our poor soul
which has cowered before the Stygian
hand of the Tempter, who paws
and crushes it, straightens like a wilted
shoot to which the sap returns
when it hears the symphony of Your body,
and assumes a martial stance.
   You are the song without end or confine,
Lord, the sonorous solitude,
and in the concert which links all beings
the epiphany. The spheres sing
through Your body, harp of the universe.

# Jesus and the Carrion Path

FRANZ WERFEL

Germany, 1890–1945. Though born a Jew in Prague and loyal to Judaism throughout his life, poet, novelist, and playwright Werfel was also strongly attracted to Roman Catholicism, writing his best-known novel, *The Song of Bernadette,* in answer to a vow he made at Lourdes in 1940. His "Jesus and the Carrion Path" expresses in part his own struggle to maintain his idealistic belief in the fellowship of humankind after his military service in World War I on the Russian front. "Jesus and the Carrion Path" is translated from the German by George Dardess.

And when we'd put the dead dog behind—
Upon its teeth the Lord had lectured lightly—,
He spurred us from this ocean-sound up
The mountain. Gasping, we crawled after.

And once he'd reached the peak
And we'd come up some steps in back,
He pointed out the paths at our feet
That shot in a storm to the plain below.

We each thought one of them especially soft.
Didn't it fly down the fastest?
So when Jesus turned around to ask us,
We all shouted, "Take that!"

He only nodded. Then off he went.
We shivered with joy to be alive,
To be touched by air melting green into green,
In eddies of olive and almond.

Suddenly crumbling walls loomed in our path.
In the middle, a dark tower.
The Savior pushed open the gate.
He waited while we stepped through.

And then something happened that slammed our eyes shut,
That stuck us like trees to the spot.
Before us was a flood of dead stuff.
The sun danced on its sucking surge.

Half-chewed rats swam in a tangle
Of snakes, themselves half gnawed away—
Putrid deer and donkeys and a shiny cloud
Of plague and flies.

Such a sulphurous stink
Bubbled up from the stew
That we heaved forward on the yellow grass
To vomit in fear and disgust.

But the Savior straightened up,
Crying to heaven again and again,
"My God and father, hear me. Save me
From my loathing. Bless this horror!

"I call myself Love.
Then why does my stomach turn too?
Oh, I'm emptier than a used-up whore,
More packed with sterile nonsense than a fool.

"My father—if you are my father—you—
Let me somehow love these rotten things.
Let me read your mercy in this carrion.
Can there be love where there's still disgust?"

And see! Suddenly his face exploded
In those familiar surges,
And then light on light tangled at the top of his head
So that dazzled, we turned away.

Then—kneeling he buried his hands
In the reeking slop of rats and mice.
Then—from his whiteness
We smelt something deeper than roses.

He wove his hair with rotten pieces
And crowned himself with crawling things.
He hung a hundred little corpses from his belt
And from his shoulders draped dead bats.

The day was dark. But as he stood,
The mountains split,
Lions wept at his feet,
And wild geese swooped down to him in streams.

Four dark suns danced above.
From behind, a steady, broader ray.
The heavens opened. God's dove hovered,
Lifted by the blue universal breeze.

# Christ of Calcutta

## NIRENDRA NATH CHAKRABARTI

India, 1924–. Journalist and editor, Chakrabarti is also the author of several
books of poems in Bengali. "Christ of Calcutta" is translated from Bengali by
Provat Guha.

There was no restriction of red lights.
Yet the city of Calcutta rushing at hurricane speed
      came to a sudden stop;
somehow avoiding crashes stood still
        taxies and private cars, tempos, tiger-crested
                          double-deckers.

All those who came running with frightened cries
      from both sides of the road—
      porters, hawkers, shopkeepers and shoppers—
they, too, like a painted still life on an artist's easel
      were now immobile.
Silently watch all:
      in toddling steps
      from one side of the road to the other walks
      a completely naked child.

It had rained in Chowringhee a little while ago.
The sun now like a very long lance
      piercing the heart of the clouds
      has come down.
In a magical glow floats the city of Calcutta.

From the state-bus window
      I look at the sky and I look at you,
      child of a beggar-mother,
      Christ of Calcutta.

You've stopped all traffic as if with a mesmeric *mantra.*
At the crowd's agony, the impatient driver's gnashing of teeth,
      you don't deign to lift a single eyebrow;
stalled death all around, and through its midst
      you toddle on.

Like a symbol of humanity, in the sheer joy of
                              learning the first steps,

        you want the whole universe
        within your grip.
                        As if that is why
on unsteady steps
from one end of the world you proceed to the other.

# The Man Born Blind

## *John 9:1—7*

As he walked along, he saw a man blind from birth. His disciples asked him, "Rabbi, who sinned, this man or his parents, that he was born blind?" Jesus answered, "Neither this man nor his parents sinned; he was born blind so that God's works might be revealed in him. We must work the works of him who sent me while it is day; night is coming when no one can work. As long as I am in the world, I am the light of the world." When he had said this, he spat on the ground and made mud with the saliva and spread the mud on the man's eyes, saying to him, "Go, wash in the pool of Siloam" (which means Sent). Then he went and washed and came back able to see.

# I Feel More Precious

## MICHELANGELO

Italy, 1475–1564. Throughout his illustrious career as a painter, Michelangelo was influenced by both classical mythology and biblical subjects, and his ceiling frescoes in the Sistine Chapel represent our civilization's most impressive attempt to visualize scriptural characters and events. Though less known as a poet, Michelangelo wrote some of the most memorable and impassioned sonnets of the Italian Renaissance. "I Feel More Precious" is translated from the Italian by Joseph Tusiani.

> I feel more precious, I am more than one,
> For, since you held my heart, my worth grew more:
> A marble block, when carving has been done,
> Is not the rough, cheap stone it was before.
>
> As paper painted or just written on
> No longer is a rag one can ignore,
> So, since you looked at me, and I was won,
> My value has increased for evermore.
>
> Now, with your splendor printed on my face,
> I go like one who, dressed with every kind
> Of amulets and arms, can dare all wars.
> I can walk on the ocean, brave all blaze,
> Give in your name the light to all the blind,
> And my saliva heals all poisonous sores.

# Christian's Poem

## JORGE DE LIMA

Brazil, 1893–1953. After early work bemoaning civilization's lack of spiritual values, de Lima converted to Catholicism in 1937. Thereafter his poetry was often biblical; "Christian's Poem" is a Whitmanesque tour de force of Christian identity. He was one of the initiators of the renaissance of poetry in contemporary Brazil. "Christian's Poem" is translated from the Portuguese by Dudley Poore.

Because the blood of Christ
spurted upon my eyes
I see all things
and so profoundly that none may know.
Centuries past and yet to come
dismay me not, for I am born and shall be born again,
for I am one with all creatures,
with all beings, and with all things;
all of them I dissolve and take in again with my senses
and embrace with a mind
transfigured in Christ.
My reach is throughout space.
I am everywhere: I am in God and in matter;
I am older than time and yet was born yesterday,
I drip with primeval slime,
and at the same time I blow the last trumpet.
I understand all tongues, all acts, all signs,
I contain within me the blood of races utterly opposed.
I can dry, with a mere nod,
the weeping of all distant brothers.
I can spread over all heads one all-embracing and starry sky.
I invite all beggars to dine with me,
and I walk on the waters like the prophets of the Bible.
For me there is no darkness.
I imbue the blind with light,
I can mutilate myself and grow my limbs anew like the starfish,
because I believe in the resurrection of the flesh and because I
        believe in Christ,
and in the life eternal, amen.

And possessing eternal life I am able to transgress the laws of nature:
my passing is looked for in the streets,
I come and go like a prophecy,
I come unbidden like knowledge and Faith.
I am ready like the Master's answer,
I am seamless like His garment,
I am manifold like His Church,
my arms are spread like the arms of His Cross, broken yet always
      restored,
at all hours, in all directions, to the four points of the compass;
and I bear His Cross on my shoulders
through all the darkness of the world, because the light eternal is in
      my eyes.
And having in my eyes the light eternal, I am the greatest worker of
      wonders:
I rise again from the mouth of tigers, I am clown, I am alpha and
      omega, I am fish, lamb, eater of locusts, I am ridiculous, I am
      tempted and pardoned, I am
cast down upon earth and uplifted in glory, I am clothed in mantles
      of purple and fine linen, I am ignorant like Saint Christopher
      and learned like Saint Thomas. And I am mad, mad, wholly
      mad forever, world without end, mad with God, Amen.
And being the madness of God I am the reason in all things, the
      order and the measure,
I am judgment, creation, obedience,
I am repentance, I am humility,
I am the author of the passion and death of Jesus,
I am the sin of all men,
I am nothing.
Miserere mei, Deus, secundum magnam misericordiam tuam!

# Two Blind Men

## *Matthew 9:27–30a*

As Jesus went on from there, two blind men followed him, crying loudly, "Have mercy on us, Son of David!" When he entered the house, the blind men came to him; and Jesus said to them, "Do you believe that I am able to do this?" They said to him, "Yes, Lord." Then he touched their eyes and said, "According to your faith let it be done to you." And their eyes were opened.

# Kyrie Eleison I
## (Nagasaki 1961)

THOMAS IMMOOS

Switzerland, 1919–. A priest in the Swiss order of Bethlehem Fathers, Thomas Immoos began his career as a missionary in post-War Japan, where he still resides as professor at Sophia University in Tokyo. His *Missa Mundi*, or *Mass of the World*, from which "Kyrie" is taken, is the result of fifty years of meditation on his roles as priest, poet, and citizen of the world. "Kyrie Eleison I" is translated from the German by Dalma Hunyadi Brunauer.

>Lord, have mercy on us!
>Have mercy on your children
>in the firestorm of Nagasaki.
>Lord, was it really your hand
>which guided the iron death-bird
>over the Vale of Martyrs
>and their Dom, which praised the trust
>of the abandoned children?
>See they had stayed true to you
>from generation to generation
>in the glow-oven of the persecution.
>They died on the cross, on the stake,
>in the slime-crater of Unzen,
>they suffocated in stinking pits.
>They ate the bitter bread
>of being exiled
>without priests, without sacrament.
>
>But their faithfulness broke not
>over hundreds of years.
>Have mercy on us, O Lord!
>Hadn't they been, long before then,
>annealed in the fire which proves?
>
>Why, O Lord, did the blinding flash
>have to break in over your children
>in the Vale of Oura,

why did the atom-mushroom have to hover
over their huts and gardens
their tortured bodies
exactly over the spot
where once the killing fields had lain
and then rose the victory-rejoicing Dom?

Lord, have mercy on us!
Are you really a consuming fire, O God?
Were you in the white glow
in the heat that followed,
in the black rain of ashes,
in the deadly rays?
O, Hill of Oura!
Killing fields and God's House!
Were you the altar, on which, like a
Peace offering, was scorched
the holiest community
of this realm of islands,
spotless Lamb,
that over the blasphemous world
may once more arise
a rainbow of a
morning filled with peace?
A terrible God are you indeed,
tremendous in your love!
Is there no other means
to melt the icy cold of the age
than the spirit-dove in the
atom-mushroom?
Do you speak to us now only
in the fiery tongues
of atoms that are split?

# The Raising of Lazarus

## John 11:1—6, 17—44

Now a certain man was ill, Lazarus of Bethany, the village of Mary and her sister Martha. Mary was the one who anointed the Lord with perfume and wiped his feet with her hair; her brother Lazarus was ill. So the sisters sent a message to Jesus, "Lord, he whom you love is ill." But when Jesus heard it, he said, "This illness does not lead to death; rather it is for God's glory, so that the Son of God may be glorified through it." Accordingly, though Jesus loved Martha and her sister and Lazarus, after having heard that Lazarus was ill, he stayed two days longer in the place where he was. . . .

When Jesus arrived, he found that Lazarus had already been in the tomb four days. Now Bethany was near Jerusalem, some two miles away, and many of the Jews had come to Martha and Mary to console them about their brother. When Martha heard that Jesus was coming, she went and met him, while Mary stayed at home. Martha said to Jesus, "Lord, if you had been here, my brother would not have died. But even now I know that God will give you whatever you ask of him." Jesus said to her, "Your brother will rise again." Martha said to him, "I know that he will rise again in the resurrection on the last day." Jesus said to her, "I am the resurrection and the life. Those who believe in me, even though they die, will live, and everyone who lives and believes in me will never die. Do you believe this?" She said to him, "Yes, Lord, I believe that you are the Messiah, the Son of God, the one coming into the world."

When she had said this, she went back and called her sister Mary, and told her privately, "The Teacher is here and is calling for you." And when she heard it, she got up quickly and went to him. Now Jesus had not yet come to the village, but was still at the place where Martha had met him. The Jews who were with her in the house, consoling her, saw Mary get up quickly and go out. They followed her because they thought that she was going to the tomb to weep there. When Mary came where Jesus was and saw him, she knelt at his feet and said to him, "Lord, if you had been here, my brother would not have died." When Jesus saw her weeping, and the Jews who came with her also weeping, he was greatly disturbed in spirit and deeply moved. He said, "Where have you laid him?" They said to him, "Lord, come and see." Jesus began to weep. So the Jews said, "See how he loved him!" But some of them said, "Could not he who opened the eyes of the blind man have kept this man from dying?"

Then Jesus, again greatly disturbed, came to the tomb. It was a cave, and a stone was lying against it. Jesus said, "Take away the stone." Martha, the sister of the dead man, said to him, "Lord, already there is a stench because he has been dead four days." Jesus said to her, "Did I not tell you that if you believed, you would see the glory of God?" So they took away the stone. And Jesus looked upward and said, "Father, I thank you for having heard me. I knew that you always hear me, but I have said this for the sake of the crowd standing here, so that they may believe that you sent me." When he had said this, he cried with a loud voice, "Lazarus, come out!" The dead man came out, his hands and feet bound with strips of cloth, and his face wrapped in a cloth. Jesus said to them, "Unbind him, and let him go."

# Lazarus

JAMES KEIR BAXTER

New Zealand, 1926–1972. See page 99 for biographical information on this poet.

After the wake and speeches, when the guests in black
Had with the charm of ordinariness
Dispelled the gross terror of a fellow dead
(Eyelids grown waxen, the body like a sack
Bundled into the tomb) and the women with their mindless
Ritual of grief had murmured abroad all that could be said—

Then, as the world resumed its customary
Mask of civil day, he came, too late to mend
The broken vase (a cracked one could have been mended)
God's image blackened by causality.
And the woman said, 'Since he was called your friend,
Why did you not come then? Now it is ended.'

And when, the army blanket of grey earth
Put off, Lazarus from the cave mouth stumbled
(Hand, foot and mouth yet bound in mummy cloth)
To the sun's arrow, furnace of rebirth—
What could they do but weep? infirm and humbled
By Love not their love, more to be feared than wrath.

# Autobiography of Mr. X

JASBIR SINGH AHLUWALIA

India, 1935–. A pioneer poet-critic in Punjabi literature, Ahluwalia edits *Panj Darya*, a Punjabi literary journal. "Autobiography of Mr. X" is translated from the Punjabi by the poet.

I did not hit the jackpot this time even
prices spiral
unbearable is the tax burden
groans the common man.
There's a new arrival,
how can I turn my back on this gift of God?

Appearing grief stricken
for woes of common man
leaders went round
collecting subscriptions.
They announced,
"Where the Government has retired,
some light is required.
With gleaming torches in our hands
we'll present a charter of demands."

Sensing some gain
I followed the leaders in train.
(And for the last time
made use of my brain).
An A was the standard bearer
and B the slogan monger.

Next day the newspapers
announced in bold letters:
'Hundreds and thousands of common people
in their zeal
in their anger
thronged from four corners
in the Long March'.

There was another news item
printed at an obscure place:
'The man crushed by the crowd
has passed away.'

It was I
who was milled by the mob;
it was I
in the din of slogans
who lost his sob;
it was I
who rose from the tomb
and laughed like Lazarus.

# *from* City of Sinbad

## BADR SHĀKIR AL-SAYYĀB

Iraq, 1926–1964. Dismissed from his post as a teacher because of his member-
ship in Iraq's Communist party, al-Sayyāb lived and died in exile. His poetry,
much influenced by T. S. Eliot and Edith Sitwell, increasingly took up the
theme of protest against Iraq's oppressive regimes. Though al-Sayyāb was a
Muslim, Christ's death and resurrection attracted him as a way of expressing
the need for sacrifice to bring about the rebirth of his people. "City of Sinbad"
is set in Iraq under the bloody revolutionary rule of General Qasim in the
1950s. Lazarus is the Iraqi people, revived by Qasim only then to be incited to
violence themselves. Christ, representing hope for genuine political renewal, is
conflated with Adonis in the fertility myth made famous by T. S. Eliot's "The
Waste Land." The selection from "City of Sinbad" is translated from the Arabic
by Mounah A. Khouri and Hamid Algar.

### 1

Hungry in the tomb without food,
Naked in the snow without a cloak,
I cried out in winter:
Bestir, o rain,
The beds of bones and snow and particles of dust,
The beds of stone,
Make the seeds grow, let the flowers open,
And set the sterile threshing floors
On fire with lightning,
Make the roots break through,
And burden down the trees.
And you came, o rain,
The sky and the clouds broke forth to anoint you,
And the rocks were split open,
And, flowing over with your gifts,
The Euphrates muddy turned
The tombs moved, their dead
Were shaken and they arose
And their bones cried out:
Blessed be the god who grants us
Blood in the form of rain
And alas, o rain,
We should like to sleep again,

We should like to die again,
And with our sleep will be buds of awareness,
And our death will conceal life;
We wish the god would take us back
To the heart of his deep, many-layered mystery;
We wish he would lead us backward on the road
To where it has its far beginning.
Who awakened Lazarus from his long sleep?
That he might know the morning and evening,
And summer and winter,
That he might be hungry, or feel
The burning coal of thirst,
And shun death,
And count the heavy, swift minutes
And praise the rabble
And shed blood!
Who revived us?
Did he revive too what we fear?
Who is the god in our dwelling place?
His fire takes life upon our wax candles,
His malice takes life on our tears.

. . .

3

There is death in the streets,
And barrenness in the fields,
And all that we love is dying.
They have bound up the water in the houses
And brooks are panting in the drought.
Behold, the Tatars have advanced,
Their knives are bleeding,
And our sun is blood, our food
Is blood upon the platter.
They have burned Muhammad, the orphan,
And the evening glows from his fire,
The blood boiled up in his feet,
In his hands and in his eyes,
And in his eyelids the god was burned.

They have bound up Muhammad,
The prophet, on Mt. Hirā´
And the day was nailed down
Where they nailed him.
Tomorrow, Christ will be crucified
In Iraq, and the dogs will feast
On the blood of Burāq.


4

Oh Spring
Oh Spring, what has afflicted you?
You have come without rain
You have come without flowers,
You have come without fruit,
And your end was like your beginning
Wrapped round in gore; Now Summer
Is upon us with black clouds
Its days full of cares
And its nights
We spend wakefully, counting the stars;
Until that time when the ears of grain
Will be ripe for harvest
And the sickles will sing
And the threshing floors
Will cover up crevices
Then will it seem to the hungry that Ishtar,
The goddess of flowers, has brought back the captive
To mankind, and crowned his lush forehead with fruit?
Then will it seem to the hungry that the shoulder
Of Christ has rolled back the stone from the tomb
Has set out to resurrect life from the grave
And cure the leper or make the blind to see?
Who is this that let loose the wolves from their bonds?
Who is this that gave us to drink from a mirage,
And concealed the plague in the rain?
Death is being born in houses,
Cain is being born in order to tear out life
From the womb of earth and from the wellsprings of water,
And it will soon be dark.

Women are aborting in slaughterhouses,
And the flame is dancing along the threshing floors,
And Christ will perish before Lazarus.
Let him sleep
Let him, for Christ did not call him!
What do you want? His flesh cut into strips and dried
To be sold in the city of sinners,
The city of rope and blood and wine,
The city of bullets and boulders!
Yesterday they took from its place the copper horseman,
Yesterday they took the stone horseman,
Lethargy reigned in the heavens
And discontent stepped in
And a human horseman pranced through the streets
Slaughtering women
Dyeing the cradles with blood
Cursing divine decree and fate!

# Unrecorded

## ÁNGELOS SIKELIANÓS

Greece, 1884–1951. One of the preeminent Greek poets of the early twentieth century, Sikelianós was related on his father's side to a number of Ionian patriots and on his mother's to Saint Dionysios. With epic ambitions in verse and in life, Sikelianós tried, with his wealthy American wife's help, to revive the Delphic Festivals in the 1920s, hoping to bring nations together religiously in a spirit of peace and justice. During the Nazi occupation of Greece, he made a valiant effort to save Jewish lives, often risking his own. "Unrecorded" is set in the terrible winter of 1941; the dog's carcass that Christ gazes upon symbolizes Greece devastated by war. "Unrecorded" is translated from the modern Greek by Kimon Friar.

A little beyond the walls of Zion walking
one day somewhat before the set of sun,
Jesus and his disciples came by chance
to that place where for years the town had cast
its rubbish: burnt mattresses of the diseased,
rags, broken crockery, refuse and filth.

And there upon the highest mound of all,
bloated, its legs turned upward toward the sky,
the carcass of a dog lay stretched, from which
at once, as vultures thickly piled on it
took fright at steps approaching, so foul a stench
broke forth, that the disciples as one man,
holding their breath within their hands, drew back.

But Jesus paced his way alone and paused
serenely awhile before that mound of filth,
and gazed upon that carcass, until one
of the disciples, unable to restrain himself,
spoke from afar: "Rabbi, can you not smell
that horrid stench and stand so closely by?"

And he, his eyes not swerving from that sign
on which he gazed, replied: "This horrid stench
does he whose breath is pure breathe even in that
same town from which we came . . . But now with all

my soul do I most marvel at that thing
which issues here from this decay . . . For see
how in the sun the teeth of this dog shine,
now like the hailstone, now like the lily, far
beyond the decay, like a tremendous vow,
reflection of the Eternal, but still more,
the lightning bolt and the harsh hope of Justice."

Thus did he speak; and if they understood
these words or not, together the disciples
followed once more as he went on his silent way.

And now, my Lord, the last of all indeed,
how I do turn my mind on these Thy words,
and wholly in one thought consumed, do stand
before Thee. O grant, even to me, my Lord,
that when I walk beyond the walls of Zion,
and all, from the one end to the other end
of earth are ruins, all are sweepings, all
unburied corpses that choke up the sacred spring
of breath, that in the city or beyond the city,
amid this horrible stench through which I pass,
grant me, my Lord, of only for a moment,
Thine own sublime serenity, that I may pause
unterrified within the midst of carrion
until I also may be given to see
some white spot, like the hailstone, like the lily,
something that suddenly may glow deep in me
out of decay, beyond the world's decay,
as shone the teeth of that dog, O my Lord,
on which Thou gazed at in the setting sun,
and stood and marveled, a tremendous vow,
reflection of the Eternal, but still more,
the lightning bolt and the harsh hope of Justice.

# Lazarus

## Anglo-Saxon, A.D. 1000 Chichester Cathedral

MAY SARTON

U.S., 1912–1995. Born Eléanore Marie Sarton in Belgium of a Belgian mother and English father, Sarton moved with her parents to England at the outbreak of World War I and then to Cambridge, Massachusetts, where her father taught philosophy. Sarton published her first work at age 17 in *Poetry* magazine. Throughout her celebrated career, she demonstrated her skill in using a variety of poetic forms as well as her cultivation of powers of inner growth and spontaneity.

1

From the rock and from the deep
The sculptor lifts him out aware.
This is the dead man's waking stare.
This is a man carved out of sleep.
The grave is hard; the walls are steep.

The sculptor lifts him out aware
From the rock and from the deep.
We watch with awe; we watch and keep
The heavy world he has to bear.
The sculptor lifts him out, aware.
Huge forlorn eyes open from sleep.
When morning comes, what do we keep?

The heavy world he has to bear.
He comes from the unconscious deep
With what to give and what to keep?
Lazarus lifts huge hands in prayer.
He turns the world round in his stare.

He sees his late death everywhere.
It hurts his eyes, he has to care.

Now broken from the rock of sleep,
He comes toward us from the deep

To face once more the morning star,
To see us desperate as we are.

And Lazarus relearns despair.
His look is grave; his gaze is deep
Upon us, men carved out of sleep
Who wish to pray but have no prayer.

2

A weightless traveler, I too come back
From miles of air, from distant and strange lands,
Put on my house again, my work, my lack,
And looking down at my own clumsy hands,
Feel courage crack.

How can I answer all these needs at once?
Letters and friends and work and flowers?
They sweep me back in their devouring glance
To carry off my calm and hoarded powers
In a huge pounce.

That heavy thickness as of new-mown hay
Flung down in heaps over a tentative fire —
How lift my smothered flame up to the day?
Have I come back depleted of desire,
To tire and fray?

At last I hear the silence in the room:
That buried self is breaking through to be,
And Lazarus is calling me by name.
At last I slowly lift the poem free,
One-pointed flame.

I hear, "to live as one already dead" —
A voice heard in Japan long months ago.
The sweat of *muga* starts on my forehead.
It is the sweat poets and dancers know,
In joy and dread.

Images flow together in that heat,
And confused numbers thread a single line.
Detached from all except the living beat,
I dance my way into complex design
On weightless feet.

# PART FOUR

# ENCOUNTERS

# Nicodemus at Night

## *John 3:1–21*

Now there was a Pharisee named Nicodemus, a leader of the Jews. He came to Jesus by night and said to him, "Rabbi, we know that you are a teacher who has come from God; for no one can do these signs that you do apart from the presence of God." Jesus answered him, "Very truly, I tell you, no one can see the kingdom of God without being born from above." Nicodemus said to him, "How can anyone be born after having grown old? Can one enter a second time into the mother's womb and be born?" Jesus answered, "Very truly, I tell you, no one can enter the kingdom of God without being born of water and Spirit. What is born of the flesh is flesh, and what is born of the Spirit is spirit. Do not be astonished that I said to you, 'You must be born from above.' The wind blows where it chooses, and you hear the sound of it, but you do not know where it comes from or where it goes. So it is with everyone who is born of the Spirit." Nicodemus said to him, "How can these things be?" Jesus answered him, "Are you a teacher of Israel, and yet you do not understand these things?

"Very truly, I tell you, we speak of what we know and testify to what we have seen; yet you do not receive our testimony. If I have told you about earthly things and you do not believe, how can you believe if I tell you about heavenly things? No one has ascended into heaven except the one who descended from heaven, the Son of Man. And just as Moses lifted up the serpent in the wilderness, so must the Son of Man be lifted up, that whoever believes in him may have eternal life.

"For God so loved the world that he gave his only Son, so that everyone who believes in him may not perish but may have eternal life.

"Indeed, God did not send the Son into the world to condemn the world, but in order that the world might be saved through him. Those who believe in him are not condemned; but those who do not believe are condemned already, because they have not believed in the name of the only Son of God. And this is the judgment, that the light has come into the world, and people loved darkness rather than light because their deeds were evil. For all who do evil hate the light and do not come to the light, so that their deeds may not be exposed. But those who do what is true come to the light, so that it may be clearly seen that their deeds have been done in God."

# The Night

HENRY VAUGHAN

Wales, 1622–1695. See page 98 for biographical information on this poet.

Through that pure Virgin-shrine,
That sacred veil drawn o'er thy glorious noon
That men might look and live as glow-worms shine,
      And face the moon:
      Wise Nicodemus saw such light
      As made him know his God by night.

Most blessed believer he!
Who in that land of darkness and blind eyes
Thy long expected healing wings could see,
      When thou didst rise,
      And what more can be done,
      Did at midnight speak with the sun!

O who will tell me, where
He found thee at that dead and silent hour!
What hallowed solitary ground did bear
      So rare a flower
      Within whose sacred leafs did lie
      The fulness of the Deity.

No mercy-seat of gold,
No dead and dusty cherub, nor carved stone,
But his own living works did my Lord hold
      And lodge alone;
      Where trees and herbs did watch and peep
      And wonder, while the Jews did sleep.

Dear night! this worlds defeat;
The stop to busy fools; cares check and curb;
The day of spirits; my souls calm retreat

Which none disturb!
Christ's° progress, and his prayer time;
The hours to which high Heaven doth chime.

Gods silent, searching flight:
When my Lords head is filled with dew, and all
His locks are wet with the clear drops of night;
His still, soft call;
His knocking time; The souls dumb watch,
When spirits their fair kindred catch.

Were all my loud, evil days
Calm and unhaunted as is thy dark tent,
Whose peace but by some angels wing or voice
Is seldom rent;
Then I in Heaven all the long year
Would keep, and never wander here.

But living where the sun
Doth all things wake, and where all mix and tire
Themselves and others, I consent and run
To every mire,
And by this worlds ill-guiding light,
Err more than I can do by night.

There is in God (some say)
A deep, but dazzling darkness; As men here
Say it is late and dusky, because they
See not all clear;
O for that night! where I in him
Might live invisible and dim.

°*Mark, chap.* 1. 35, *S. Luke, chap.* 21. 37. [Vaughan's note.]

# The Samaritan Woman at the Well

## John 4:5—7

He came to a Samaritan city called Sychar, near the plot of ground that Jacob had given to his son Joseph. Jacob's well was there, and Jesus, tired out by his journey, was sitting by the well. It was about noon.

A Samaritan woman came to draw water, and Jesus said to her, "Give me a drink."

# The Samaritan Woman

KAROL WOJTYLA (POPE JOHN PAUL II)

Poland, 1920 –. Until Karol Wojtyla became Pope John Paul II in 1978, few knew that the volumes of poetry published during the previous forty years under the name "Andrzej Jawien" were his. Written while he was a worker, student, priest, professor, and bishop, the poems reflect the concerns of a man of faith in a country dominated by Communism. "The Samaritan Woman" is translated from the Polish by Jerzy Peterkiewicz.

> It joined us together, the well;
> the well led me into you.
> No one between us but light
> deep in the well, the pupil of the eye
> set in an orbit of stones.
>
> Within your eyes, I,
> drawn by the well,
> am enclosed.

# Like the Samaritan Woman by the Well

HAE-IN LEE

[Sister Claudia Lee] Korea, 1945–. A Benedictine nun, Sister Claudia is one of Korea's most popular living poets. Her books of poems have sold nearly two million copies, a record in Korean literature. "Readers ask me if poets shouldn't complain about social injustices. As a Sister, my responsibility is meditation and prayer . . . I think the mission of the poet is to be a representative of the times by songs which help purify people's feelings." "Like the Samaritan Woman by the Well" is translated from the Korean by Brother Anthony of Taizé.

> Lord, won't you come and quietly speak
> as if asking me for one cup of water first
> like you did the Samaritan woman who came
> to draw water out of Jacob's Well?
> You know that since I'm a sinner
> I lack courage—
>
> Speak quickly, please,
> I want to hear directly from you today
> who I am
> and who you are
> and what our encounter means.
>
> I keep drawing water for you
> from the well of daily life
> in my small shabby bucket
> but won't you show me a way
> to draw water without any bucket at all?
>
> From the moment you took your place beside me,
> deep pure well of water that you are,
> every day has been a new festival for me.
> My long stagnant sorrow and thirst
> like drops of water in my jar
> have risen up to dance, all smiling now.
>
> The happiness of meeting you is such
> I may forget for a moment how sinful I am;

I hope you will forgive me?
Lord, the happiness of loving you
can really not be kept hidden.

Grant me now to go running farther
like that Samaritan woman beside the well
who left her pitcher and ran to the village.
To bring many others to you
and also
to tell about the living water—

# The Woman at Simon's House

## *Luke 7:36—50*

One of the Pharisees asked Jesus to eat with him, and he went into the Pharisee's house and took his place at the table. And a woman in the city, who was a sinner, having learned that he was eating in the Pharisee's house, brought an alabaster jar of ointment. She stood behind him at his feet, weeping, and began to bathe his feet with her tears and to dry them with her hair. Then she continued kissing his feet and anointing them with the ointment. Now when the Pharisee who had invited him saw it, he said to himself, "If this man were a prophet, he would have known who and what kind of woman this is who is touching him—that she is a sinner." Jesus spoke up and said to him, "Simon, I have something to say to you." "Teacher," he replied, "Speak." "A certain creditor had two debtors; one owed five hundred denarii, and the other fifty. When they could not pay, he canceled the debts for both of them. Now which of them will love him more?" Simon answered, "I suppose the one for whom he canceled the greater debt." And Jesus said to him, "You have judged rightly." Then turning toward the woman, he said to Simon, "Do you see this woman? I entered your house; you gave me no water for my feet, but she has bathed my feet with her tears and dried them with her hair. You gave me no kiss, but from the time I came in she has not stopped kissing my feet. You did not anoint my head with oil, but she has anointed my feet with ointment. Therefore, I tell you, her sins, which were many, have been forgiven; hence she has shown great love. But the one to whom little is forgiven, loves little." Then he said to her, "Your sins are forgiven." But those who were at the table with him began to say among themselves, "Who is this who even forgives sins?" And he said to the woman, "Your faith has saved you; go in peace."

# Marie Magdalene

GEORGE HERBERT

England, 1593–1633. One of England's foremost religious poets, Herbert served as Public Orator of Cambridge University before being ordained an Anglican priest and assuming the rectorship of a country parish. An accomplished musician, Herbert—whose metrical virtuosity is nearly unparalled in English poetry—set many of his sacred poems to music. Herbert cherished the Church as an institution, as is demonstrated by his magnificent volume of poems, *The Temple*, with its deep devotion to ritual, liturgy, and priestly vocation.

> When blessed Marie wiped her Savior's feet,
> (Whose precepts she had trampled on before)
> And wore them for a jewel on her head,
>   Showing his steps should be the street,
>   Wherin she thenceforth evermore
> With pensive humbleness would live and tread;
>
> She being stained herself, why did she strive
> To make him clean, who could not be defiled?
> Why kept she not her tears for her own faults,
>   And not his feet? Though we could dive
>   In tears like seas, our sins are piled
> Deeper than they, in words, and works, and thoughts.
>
> Dear soul, she knew who did vouchsafe and deign
> To bear her filth; and that her sins did dash
> Ev'n God himself; wherefore she was not loth,
>   As she had brought wherewith to stain,
>   So to bring in wherewith to wash:
> And yet in washing one, she washed both.

# The Travail of Passion

WILLIAM BUTLER YEATS

Ireland, 1865–1939. Born into an artistically prominent Anglo-Irish Protestant family, Yeats studied at the Dublin School of Art. Enamoured of Celtic legends and Irish politics, he combined these national preoccupations with the international influence of the symbolist movement to create one of the twentieth century's dominant literary voices. Though his religious disposition turned to mysticism and the occult, Yeats—who searched for "a tradition of belief older than any European Church"—often found inspiration in Christian scripture; some of his most cherished poems are meditations on New Testament passages. Yeats was awarded the Nobel Prize for Literature in 1923.

When the flaming lute-thronged angelic door is wide;
When an immortal passion breathes in mortal clay;
Our hearts endure the scourge, the plaited thorns, the way
Crowded with bitter faces, the wounds in palm and side,
The vinegar-heavy sponge, the flowers by Kedron stream;
We will bend down and loosen our hair over you,
That it may drop faint perfume, and be heavy with dew,
Lilies of death-pale hope, roses of passionate dream.

# A Scandal in the Suburbs

X. J. KENNEDY

U.S., 1929–. Winner of several awards for his poetry, X. J. Kennedy is also a
writer of children's books and the author of the college text *An Introduction to
Poetry*. His mischievous wit and ingenious rhyming are given full play in "A
Scandal in the Suburbs" and "Walking Through Walls. (p. 555)"

We had to have him put away,
For what if he'd grown vicious?
To play faith-healer, give away
Stale bread and stinking fishes!
His soapbox preaching set the tongues
Of all the neighbors going.
Odd stuff: how lilies never spin
And birds don't bother sowing.
Why, bums were coming to the door—
His pockets had no bottom—
And then—the footwash from that whore!
We signed. They came and got him.

# Mary Magdalene and the Birds

FLEUR ADCOCK

New Zealand, 1934–. Now residing in England, Adcock is the author of numerous books of poetry. Her first collection, *The Eye of the Hurricane*, appeared in 1964, and her *Selected Poems* was published in 1983.

1

Tricks and tumbles are my trade; I'm
all birds to all men.
I switch voices, adapt my features,
do whatever turn you fancy.
All that is constant is my hair:

plumage, darlings, beware of it.

2

Blackbird: that's the one to watch—
or he is, with his gloss and weapon.
Not a profession for a female,
his brown shadow. Thrush is better,
cunning rehearser among the leaves,
and speckle-breasted, maculate.

3

A wound of some kind. All that talk
of the pelican, self-wounding,
feeding his brood from an ever-bleeding
bosom turns me slightly sick.

But seriousness can light upon
the flightiest. This tingling ache,
nicer than pain, is a blade-stroke:
Not my own, but I let it happen.

4

What is balsam? What is nard?
Sweetnesses from the sweet life,
obsolete, fit only for wasting.

I groom you with this essence. Wash it
down the drain with tears and water.
We are too human. Let it pass.


5

*With my body I thee worship*:
breast on stone lies the rockdove
cold on that bare nest, cooing
its low call, unlulled,
restless for the calling to cease.


6

Mary Magdalene sang in the garden.
It was a swansong, said the women,
for his downdrift on the river.

It sounded more of the spring curlew
or a dawn sky full of larks,
watery trillings you could drown in.

# Oils and Ointments

R. A. K. MASON

New Zealand, 1905–1971. See page 109 for biographical information on this
poet.

Let me fall down about your feet oh Christ
   that have bruised and bled along the lonely way,
   wait here my bringing forth those highly priced
   treasures I have saved up this many a day.

The ointments I bring up to you my lord
   gleam jewels like a steel-flashing beetle shard
   lo! I shower down cascading the rich hoard
   frankincense aloes myrrh cassia spikenard,

Sluggish oil that glints oh look rainbows and gold
   gently assailing unguents the orient has spiced
   slow pouring balm smooth smearing calm behold
   and stretch out your soothful longing foot oh Christ.

# John the Baptist Beheaded

## Matthew 14:6–12

When Herod's birthday came, the daughter of Herodias danced before the company, and she pleased Herod so much that he promised on oath to grant her whatever she might ask. Prompted by her mother, she said, "Give me the head of John the Baptist here on a platter." The king was grieved, yet out of regard for his oaths and for the guests, he commanded it to be given; he sent and had John beheaded in the prison. The head was brought on a platter and given to the girl, who brought it to her mother. His disciples came and took the body and buried it; then they went and told Jesus.

# Salome

## MIKOLA ZEROV

Ukraine, 1890–1941. A classical scholar who assembled a two-volume collection of Roman poetry, Zerov was a professor of Ukrainian literature at the University of Kiev. His literary criticism supported Ukraine's "westernizing" movement, a position which put him dangerously at odds with the prevailing "socialist realism" demanded by the Soviet regime. Only one collection of his classically-formal sonnets and lyrics was published during his lifetime. He was arrested during the Purge of 1935 and died, along with many other Ukrainian writers and poets, in a concentration camp. "Salome" is translated from the Ukranian by C. H. Andrusyshen and Watson Kirkconnell.

There the Levantine moon works sorcery
And fluctuates the warm blood in the heart;
There a wild bloom of love has flowered apart
And all is blood—the scent of blood floats free.

From gathered streams and punishments foretold
Thunder the fulminations of wild speech . . .
Yokanaan! . . . No such voice the forests teach,—
But flames and wilderness his words enfold.

And then, Salome! Still a child (a child!)
She drinks the potion, horrible, defiled,
That summons up dark vengeance and the sword.

My soul! By ship fly quickly from such shocks
And seek the place where amid snow-white rocks
Nausicaa walks like sunlight on the sward.

# To the Art of the Impossible

GUNNAR EKELOF

Sweden, 1907–1968. One of Sweden's major modern poets, Ekelof was influ-
enced early in his career by both the 12th century mystical odes of Sufi Muhi'd
Din Ibn al-Arabi and French surrealism. His deeply contemplative poetry de-
rives in part from reclusive habits as well as from a life-long study of antiquity
and ancient religions, especially near-eastern cults of the goddess that domi-
nated his later works. "To the Art of the Impossible" is translated from the
Swedish by Muriel Rukeyser and Lief Sjoberg.

> To the art of the impossible
> I profess myself
> am thereof a believer
> but of a belief that they call disbelief.
>
> I know:
> They are concerned here with the possible
> Let me then be one of those unconcerned
> with what is possible and what is impossible.
>
> So on the icons John the Baptist bears his head
> partly on healed shoulders
> partly and at the same time before himself on a platter.
> The one offered presents himself as offering
> So I profess myself
> to the art of the impossible
> out of a thirst for life and for self-effacement
> simultaneously.

# The Woman Taken in Adultery

*John 8:2–11*

Early in the morning he came again to the temple. All the people came to him and he sat down and began to teach them. The scribes and the Pharisees brought a woman who had been caught in adultery; and making her stand before all of them, they said to him, "Teacher, this woman was caught in the very act of committing adultery. Now in the law Moses commanded us to stone such women. Now what do you say?" They said this to test him, so that they might have some charge to bring against him. Jesus bent down and wrote with his finger on the ground. When they kept on questioning him, he straightened up and said to them, "Let anyone among you who is without sin be the first to throw a stone at her." And once again he bent down and wrote on the ground. When they heard it, they went away, one by one, beginning with the elders; and Jesus was left alone with the woman standing before him. Jesus straightened up and said to her, "Woman, where are they? Has no one condemned you?" She said, "No one, sir." And Jesus said, "Neither do I condemn you. Go your way, and from now on do not sin again."

# Joanna: The Wife of Herod's Steward

KAHLIL GIBRAN

Lebanon, 1883–1931. Born a Maronite Catholic in the village of Bsharri, Gibran emigrated with his mother to the Boston slums in 1895. Though his early writing appeared in Arabic, he was influenced by Walt Whitman and Stephen Crane. In 1920 he joined other Syrian emigré writers in founding "The Pen League" in New York City, a group designed to reinvent and promote Arab literature. An early product of the movement, Gibran's *The Prophet* launched the publishing firm of Alfred A. Knopf and remains one of America's bestselling volumes of poetry. Gibran's lifelong preoccupation with Christ inspired one of his finest books of prose poems, *Jesus the Son of Man* (1928).

Jesus was never married but He was a friend of women, and He knew them as they would be known in sweet comradeship.

And He loved children as they would be loved in faith and understanding.

In the light of His eyes there was a father and a brother and a son.

He would hold a child upon His knees and say, "Of such is your might and your freedom; and of such is the kingdom of the spirit."

They say that Jesus heeded not the law of Moses, and that He was over-forgiving to the prostitutes of Jerusalem and the country side.

I myself at that time was deemed a prostitute, for I loved a man who was not my husband, and he was a Sadducee.

And on a day the Sadducees came upon me in my house when my lover was with me, and they seized me and held me, and my lover walked away and left me.

Then they led me to the market-place where Jesus was teaching.

It was their desire to hold me up before Him as a test and a trap for Him.

But Jesus judged me not. He laid shame upon those who would have had me shamed, and He reproached them.

And He bade me go my way.

And after that all the tasteless fruit of life turned sweet to my mouth, and the scentless blossoms breathed fragrance into my nostrils. I became a woman without a tainted memory, and I was free, and my head was no longer bowed down.

# Forefinger of the Right Hand

## from *The Christ of Velasquez*

MIGUEL DE UNAMUNO

Spain, 1864–1936. See page 77 for biographical information on this poet. "Fore-finger of the Right Hand" is translated from the Spanish by Y. R. Pérez.

The accusing finger of your right hand
from the wooden cross directs us
to what is written in the eternal book
of life. Only once, on earth,
did you write, Jesus, You, the Word,
on dust tread by men of mud,
without ink or reed but with finger bare,
gently touching the lids of the blind,
and healing. It was morning.
Doing it, humbling yourself, you bent
over the earth. The inscribing finger
was God's, was yours when you cast out
those demons.

In the insubstantial dust
let us read the lesson of conscience
traced by your finger as you bent over
the earth, your open book,
alive and sacred. In writing on her
you showed the humility of your ministry.

The adultress,
her gaze upon that dust, veiled eyes,
tears of sighs, was going, alone,
arms across her chest,
guarding there the pledge of your forgiveness,
a mother embracing her new babe.

O, may my pen reborn
write upon the earth of my homeland
the lesson of the pardon you have left us!

# Unknown Letter

## TADEUSZ RÓZEWICZ

Poland, 1921–. Born in the Radomsko district of Lodz, Rózewicz suffered through both the depression of the thirties and the Nazi invasion. He fought as a guerrilla against the Nazis, an experience which left a powerful mark on his poetry. A widely translated poet, Rózewicz is perhaps best known internationally as one of Europe's preeminent playwrights. "Unknown Letter" is translated from the Polish by Victor Contoski.

But Jesus bent over
and wrote with his finger
on the earth
and again bent over
and wrote on the earth

Mother they are so ignorant
and naive that I have to show
miracles I do such silly
and unnecessary things
but you understand
and forgive your son
I change water to wine
I revive the dead
I walk on the sea

they are like little children
it's always necessary
to show them something new
can you imagine

When
Matthew Mark Luke and John
approached him
he covered the letters
and erased them
forever

# Mary and Martha

## Luke 10:38–42

Now as they went on their way, he entered a certain village, where a woman named Martha welcomed him into her home. She had a sister named Mary, who sat at the Lord's feet and listened to what he was saying. But Martha was distracted by her many tasks; so she came to him and asked, "Lord, do you not care that my sister has left me to do all the work by myself? Tell her then to help me." But the Lord answered her, "Martha, Martha, you are worried and distracted by many things; there is need of only one thing. Mary has chosen the better part, which will not be taken away from her."

# Mary Sat

PATRICK HENRY RYAN

U.S., 1943–. A Trappist monk at the Abbey of the Genesee in Piffard, New York, Brother Patrick has published poetry in numerous periodicals, including *America*, *Christian Century*, and *The Bible Today*. He is also the author of frequent scholarly articles on Cistercian topics. In Cistercian spirituality, Martha and Mary are exemplars, respectively, of action and contemplation; "Mary Sat" is one reading of the interplay between these two figures.

Martha stood
but Mary sat
and the sitting
led within
the things
that need two feet
to love
so peaceful
Martha
could not leave
her sister
all alone.

# Martha and Magdalene

GIUSEPPE GIOACCHINO BELLI

Italy, 1791–1863. The author of over two thousand satirical sonnets in Roman dialect, Belli was born in Rome, where he served as a papal civil servant. Though a Roman Catholic with politically conservative ideas (he opposed the revolution of 1848), Belli nevertheless was critical of church injustices and ritualism. His sonnets offer a vivid portrait of everyday Roman life during the first half of the nineteenth century. "Martha and Magdalene" is translated from the Italian by Miller Williams.

"But, Jesus Christ," said Martha, "I've had it to here
with Mary Magdalene. I cannot take her
rosaries, her novenas anymore.
I open my mouth and she calls me a troublemaker.

I'm tied up day and night. I've never complained,
but I'm getting tired—I'm always on my feet;
you can't find this painted doll of a saint
except, of course, when there's something to eat."

"Look, Martha," the Savior said, "here's where it's at.
You don't deserve any explanation,
but her job's more important. It's as simple as that."

And Martha: "So says you, but I know better.
Listen, if I sat around on my salvation
the way she does, who'd keep this house together?"

# Martha and Mary

GABRIELA MISTRAL

[Lucila Godoy y Alcayaga] Chile, 1889–1957. The first Latin American to receive the Nobel Prize for Literature (1945), Mistral began her career as a provincial schoolteacher. Her anguished poetry of betrayed love and spiritual turmoil (like "Nocturne") made her famous in the Spanish American literary world. Subsequent more hopeful poems for children quickly entered the Latin American school curriculum and made Mistral a household name on her continent. "Martha and Mary" is translated from the Spanish by Doris Dana.

They were born together, lived together,
ate together—Martha and Mary.
They closed the same door,
drank from the same well,
were watched by one thicket,
clothed by one light.

Martha's cups and dishes clattered,
her kettles bubbled.
Her chickenyard teemed with roosters,
a whirr of plover and dove.
She bustled to and fro
lost in a cloud of feathers.

Martha cut the air, reigned
over meals and linen,
governed wine press and beehives,
ruled the minute, the hour, the day . . .

A wounded outcry sounded
wherever she came and went.
Dishes, doors, bolts clamored
as to a belled sheep.
But all grew hushed when her sister passed by,
thin keening and Hail Marys.

In a whitewashed corner,
Mary in blue majolica
wove some strange thing in the quiet air

though she never raised her hand.
What was this thing that never finished,
never altered or increased?

One golden-eyed noon
while Martha with ten hands
was busy reshaping old Judea,
without a word or sign, Mary *passed on.*

She merely grew more languid,
her cheeks indrawn;
the mark of her body and spirit
imprinted in the cold lime,
a trembling fern,
a slow stalactite;
no more than a great silence
that no cry or lightning bolt could shatter.

When Martha grew old,
oven and kitchen grew quiet,
the house gained its sleep,
the ladder lay supine;
and falling asleep,
her flesh shrivelling from ruddy to ash,
Martha went to crouch
in Mary's corner
where with wonder and silence
her mouth scarcely moved . . .

She asked to go to Mary
and toward her she went, she went
murmuring, "Mary!"—only that,
repeating, "Mary!"
And she called out with such fervor
that, without knowing, she departed,
letting loose the filament of breath
that her breast did not protect.
Now she left, ascending the air;
now she was no longer and did not know it . . .

# The Little Children Brought to Jesus

*Matthew 19:13–14*

Then little children were being brought to him in order that he might lay his hands on them and pray. The disciples spoke sternly to those who brought them; but Jesus said, "Let the little children come to me, and do not stop them; for it is to such as these that the kingdom of heaven belongs."

# Jesus

## GIOVANNI PASCOLI

Italy, 1855–1912. Born at San Mauro, Pascoli suffered bitterly after his father's assassination and was briefly imprisoned for participating in an anarchic movement. He later studied with the Nobel Prize-wining poet Giosue Carducci at Bologna, mastered Latin poetry, and had a distinguished university teaching career. His innovative and unassuming poetic style is indebted to William Wordsworth (whose poetry he translated), and it helped establish the tone for much twentieth century Italian poetry. "Jesus" is translated from the Italian by Joseph Tusiani.

And Jesus saw once more, beyond the Jordan,
fields that once more the harvesters had cut:
his day by now was not too far behind.

And women at the threshold of their homes
appeared and, "Hail, O Prophet!," said to him.
And he was thinking of his coming death.

He sat to rest upon a heap of wheat,
and said: "Unless the seed be buried in
the earth, there is no harvest to be reaped."

But he referred to granaries in Heaven:
and you, O children, soon surrounded him
with withered spears of wheat in your dark curls.

And those dark curls he fondled on his breast,
when Cephas spoke: "If you are sitting there,
something will happen to your seamless dress."

He was embracing all his little heirs.
Whispering quickly, Judas said: "The son
of a thief, Rabbi,—look!—is at your feet.

"His father is Barabbas, bound to die
upon a cross." The Prophet raised his eyes,
and murmured, "No," with sadness in his voice:

and took that very child upon his knees.

# Peter's Profession of Faith

## Matthew 16:13–19

Now when Jesus came into the district of Caesarea Philippi, he asked his disciples, "Who do people say that the Son of Man is?" And they said, "Some say John the Baptist, but others Elijah, and still others Jeremiah or one of the prophets." He said to them, "But who do you say that I am?" Simon Peter answered, "You are the Messiah, the Son of the living God." And Jesus answered him, "Blessed are you, Simon son of Jonah! For flesh and blood has not revealed this to you, but my Father in heaven. And I tell you, you are Peter, and on this rock I will build my church, and the gates of Hades will not prevail against it. I will give you the keys of the kingdom of heaven, and whatever you bind on earth will be bound in heaven, and whatever you loose on earth will be loosed in heaven."

# How Wonderful Was Peter

ZHANG XINGYAO

China, 1633–1715. Zhang Xingyao, a Chinese literatus baptized at the age of 45, wrote treatises presenting Christianity, called in seventeenth-century China "the Lord of Heaven Teaching," as a harmonious continuation of Confucianism. The manuscripts of his poems, including "How Wonderful Was Peter," which deliberately blends Confucian and Christian terminology, were rediscovered in Shanghai in 1986 by historian D. E. Mungello. "How Wonderful Was Peter" is translated from the Chinese by D. E. Mungello.

How wonderful was Peter,
a sage who was a great cornerstone for the Teaching.
A fisherman who was commanded,
to leave his family and follow the Lord.
His love for the Lord was so filled with reverence,
that he was a great wave hurling onward.
A massive mountain of shining light,
he swore an oath to totally commit his time,
and sincerely believed in complete self-cultivation.
He underwent all sorts of worldly suffering,
and the spiritual light illumined his mind.
He was a sage who spread the teaching throughout a wide area.
He elevated the Teaching to a supreme position.
He lived five lives in only one lifetime,
and sacrificed his life in hurling himself against Satan.
He had the keys to open Heaven's blessings.

# Villancico for St. Peter

JUANA INÉS DE LA CRUZ

Mexico, 1651–1695. See page 88 for biographical information on this poet. *Villancicos*, developed in fifteenth century Spain and carried to Mexico, were dance-song lyrics composed for popular performance during religious festivals. "Villancico for St. Peter" is translated from the Spanish by Y. R. Pérez.

REFRAIN

Come on, Christ's children, get to school,
and learn the teaching full of truth!
Look, the Master is waiting! Hurry! Hurry! Hurry!
Run! Let's go! Look out, you'll get the cane!

VERSES

Write, Peter, on the waters
all that you have accomplished,
and although the letters be dissolved,
still tongues will not remain hushed.

As paper, let the seas serve you,
the oar your quill shall be,
though for defining all your points
even that grandness lacks capacity.

Line, first of all, the page
and trace us the script,
and if your stylus* should fail you
there's no other for suitable print.

Indeed in the ABCs
you've gotten the rudiments,
so too by acknowledging Christ
you have proven yourself a Rock.

---

* In Spanish the word is *lápiz*, derived from the Latin for stone or rock, making a pun on the name Peter, meaning Rock.

Don't write in 'bastardo' script
which, should it come to your hand, its mother,
would lose its bastard name
by becoming the Church's daughter.

Leave be the antique script
let the Prophets have that style,
for you can, in a Credo,
write in letters really new. While

the Negro and the Italian scrolls
are known by their trappings, their chrome,
more for you the romanilla,
for you are the head of Rome.

And do write quite liberally,
loose the reins to your impulse,
for the heavens give for free
what from your hand now falls.

Your writing so eternal
will preserve its purity,
with the heretic never prevailing,
nor even one comma assailing.

And no less than your life
its defense will cost you. Unafraid
now take heart and write,
with blood are your entries made.

# Women Followers

## *Luke 8:1−3*

Soon afterwards he went on through cities and villages, proclaiming and bringing the good news of the kingdom of God. The twelve were with him, as well as some women who had been cured of evil spirits and infirmities: Mary, called Magdalene, from whom seven demons had gone out, and Joanna, the wife of Herod's steward Chuza, and Susanna, and many others, who provided for them out of their resources.

# Hymn to Gospel Women

EPHREM

Spain, d.373. See page 21 for biographical information on this poet. "Hymn to Gospel Women" is translated from the Syriac by Kathleen E. McVey.

The Gracious One Who coaxed me to speak the blessings
that His mouth announced opened my mouth
not to investigate but to confess
that One Who sprang forth from Mary to portray by her
the childlike daughters of Eve, the innocent Eve.
I shall sing for Your advent the blessings of chaste women
that I may be worthy of association with You.


REFRAIN: *To You be praises from all!*

Blessed are you, Martha, who without fear
served the One feared by all.[1]
You nourished the Storehouse Who freely gives
living bread to humankind,
Blessed is your sister whom He made tranquil and taught,
and your brother who was strengthened and revived.
By you He stirred up the divided, the disunited,
to be united in one love.
Blessed are you, Martha, to whom love gave
the confidence that opened your mouth.
By the fruit Eve's mouth was closed
while she was hidden among the trees.
Blessed is your mouth that sounded forth with love
at the table at which God reclined.
You are greater than Sarah who served the servants,
for you served the Lord of all.

Blessed are you, woman, most enviable of women,
who kissed the holy feet![2]
Your hands anointed the holy Anointed
Whose horn priests and kings had anointed.
Blessed are your sufferings that were healed by the Word
and your sins that were forgiven by a kiss.

1. Luke 10.38–42.
2. Luke 7.38, 45.

He taught His church to kiss in purity
His all-sanctifying body.

Blessed are you, woman, whose voice became
a trumpet among the silent.
A blessing you gave to the pure womb
that carried the Lord of blessings.[3]
Blessed are you to whom as the representative of others
He handed over the blessing He gave you in conversation.
The blessing that He gave you He made a part of the whole
so that all would pursue it.

Blessed are you, woman! The flow of mercy
met you and healed the flow of your blood.[4]
That Sun Who dispelled from souls
the frost of the hidden death —
its hidden flash radiated and dried up
every fresh anger the mind perceives.
With the tip of your finger, you tasted the healing of the springs
of the Sea of benefits.

Blessed are you, woman, living in poverty,
who put two treasures on High.[5]
It is a wonder on which Greatness gazed.
His eye reached out to the contemptible thing.
The two obols were weighed and they surpassed
a talent on God's scale.
Her life depended on the obols she lent,
and, impoverished, she stood there.
Who is not reproved by greed?
And in whom is not hidden a foul manner of life?
Who has not stored up and set aside too much,
so that it reproaches him that he has not been purified?
Let one who resembles you, O widow, praise you,
for my mind is too poor to gaze at you.
By your poverty is convicted and exposed
the provision of our greed.

3. Luke 11.27.
4. Mark 5.25–34 et par.
5. Mark 12.41–44 et par.

You, too, daughter of Canaan, for righteousness
conquered the Unconquerable One by boldness.[6]
The Just One set a boundary on the land of the Gentiles
that the gospel might not cross over.
Blessed are you who broke through the obstacle fearlessly.
The Lord of boundaries praised you for the strength
of your faith. From afar He healed
your daughter in your house.

Blessed are you, too, O widow,
for the world was dead, and your son was dead.[7]
But your son revived without entreaty,
and without prayer the creation was saved.
Your wailing did not summon the Physician,
nor did our prayer make our Savior bend down.
Mercy made Him condescend—the One Who came down and
          gave life
to the world and to the youth.

Blessed are you, too, young girl,[8]
you who are like a mirror of simplicity.
He brought you to life and nourished you,
for childhood is in need of learning.
The girl who was dead is a symbol of the innocent flock.
Our Lord brought to life from the dead Jewish people
a sleeping corpse as a symbol of the youthful soul.
He summoned them and she was revived.

Blessed are you, woman, who, seeing
the Son seated, did not hesitate.
Doubtless His seat was contemptible and insignificant,
but you were not confused as the daughter of a woman.
Blessed are you who saw in your understanding the glorious
          judgment seat
and you saw places for your beloved sons.[9]
Like you are the mothers who join
their sons to our Savior.

6. Matt. 15.21–28. et par.
7. Luke 7.11–17.
8. Mark 5.21–43 et par.
9. Matt. 20.20–28.

Blessed are you, woman, who while our Lord
was on earth, saw Him on high.
Your love was exalted and broke through heaven
and saw the Son on the right hand.
Blessed is your gaze! How great its range
that it measured that immeasurable mountain.
From within His smallness your faith
saw His greatness.

That woman also, wife of the just man
who sat in judgment of the Judge of all—
dreams tormented her, visions upset her.[10]
A beckoning Watcher in her dream took pity on her;
he found faith in her and increased it.
To the shame of the Jewish people the daughter of Gentiles
        shouted out.
Jerusalem cried out against the Good One, "Let Him be crucified!"
But she cried out, "Let Him be spared!"
A wonder are you, woman, and also your spouse,
who washed his hands upon his judgment seat.
Waves of a pure dream
purified and cleansed you, too, in sleep.
The Gentiles were gleaming and purified and cleansed,
but the Jewish people were blackened and defiled by that
blood . . . the lamb put on light,
but the kid put on darkness.

Blessed, then, are all of you, O chaste women,
the church that was joined in marriage to the Son.
It is a wonder how much the Holy One condescended
so that women might be joined in marriage with honor.
They received from His bounty, and they gave to Him and
        nourished Him.
From His gift they reached out to Him and satisfied Him.
He gave us a refined symbol in His intimacy.
Glory to His purity!

10. Matt. 27.19.

# Zacchaeus

*Luke 19:1—10*

He entered Jericho and was passing through it. A man was there named Zacchaeus; he was a chief tax collector and was rich. He was trying to see who Jesus was, but on account of the crowd he could not, because he was short in stature. So he ran ahead and climbed a sycamore tree to see him, because he was going to pass that way. When Jesus came to the place, he looked up and said to him, "Zacchaeus, hurry and come down; for I must stay at your house today." So he hurried down and was happy to welcome him. All who saw it began to grumble and said, "He has gone to be the guest of one who is a sinner." Zacchaeus stood there and said to the Lord, "Look, half of my possessions, Lord, I will give to the poor; and if I have defrauded anyone of anything, I will pay back four times as much." Then Jesus said to him, "Today salvation has come to this house, because he too is a son of Abraham. For the Son of Man came to seek out and to save the lost."

# The Story of Zaccheus

CHRISTOPHER SMART

England, 1722–1771. See page 39 for biographical information on this poet. In "The Story of Zaccheus," Smart's genius as a poet shines best in the place where we would today least expect to find it: in the concluding moral statement.

Through Jericho as Jesus came
A man (Zaccheus was his name)
Chief of the Publicans for gold
And pow'r, sought Jesus to behold;
But could not for the press his eyes
Indulge by reason of his size.
He therefore hasty ran before,
And climb'd upon a sycamore,
That he his passing Lord might see.
Who when he came beside the tree,
Look'd up, and saw him o'er his head,
'Zaccheus, haste, come down, he said;
For in thy house this very day
Thy Lord has purposed to stay.'
He therefore coming down in haste,
With joy his holy Guest embrac'd:
Which when observ'd by all the rest,
They murmur'd, that he went a guest
With one so much immers'd in sin.
Mean time Zaccheus stood within,
And said unto the Lord, 'Behold,
The half of my ill-gotten gold
I give the poor; and if by theft,
Or falsehood, any I've bereft,
Four-fold the same I will replace.'
Then answer'd Jesus, This day grace
Is come upon this house; for he
Is also Abraham's progeny.

*Praise-worthy in a high degree*
*Is godly curiosity;*
*To search the Lord, above, around,*

*If haply he may yet be found.*
*Short-sighted reason, dwarf desire,*
*Are faith and zeal when lifted high'r.*
*Then on the Tree of Life sublime*
*With hands and knees devoutly climb;*
*Catch mercy's moments as they fly,*
*Behold! the Lord is passing by.*

# Christmas Lament

KU SANG

Korea, 1919 –. See page 4 for biographical information on this poet. "Christmas Lament" is translated from the Korean by Brother Anthony of Taizé.

Ah, venerable Church!
With none of the simple joys of those shepherds
who came first of all
to worship around your crib!
With nothing left of the peace of your stable.

fearing the coming of your kingdom,
tonight too Herod and his henchmen keep watch,
ready to lop off your young shoots,
keeping Christmas with glaring eyes.

And your disciples,
changing the colour of the Gospel
like a beaded dress displayed in a shop window,
the colour varying with the lighting,
with the enthusiastic mob,
and the Pharisees, today too,
all crowd around
you;

and like Zacchaeus perched in a tree,
one crow-like soul cries:
'On me and on all held in cursed bondage
turn, oh turn your eyes!'

# PART FIVE

# PARABLES

# The Treasure Hidden in a Field

*Matthew 13:44–45*

"The kingdom of heaven is like treasure hidden in a field, which someone found and hid; then in his joy he goes and sells all that he has and buys that field.

"Again, the kingdom of heaven is like a merchant in search of fine pearls; on finding one pearl of great value, he went and sold all that he had and bought it."

# The Bright Field

R. S. THOMAS

Wales, 1913–. See page 7 for biographical information on this poet.

I have seen the sun break through
to illuminate a small field
for a while, and gone my way
and forgotten it. But that was the pearl
of great price, the one field that had
the treasure in it. I realize now
that I must give all that I have
to possess it. Life is not hurrying

on to a receding future, nor hankering after
an imagined past. It is the turning
aside like Moses to the miracle
of the lit bush, to a brightness
that seemed as transitory as your youth
once, but is the eternity that awaits you.

# The Mustard Seed

*Mark 4:30–32*

He also said, "With what can we compare the kingdom of God, or what parable will we use for it? It is like a mustard seed, which, when sown upon the ground, is the smallest of all the seeds on earth; yet when it is sown it grows up and becomes the greatest of all shrubs, and puts forth large branches, so that the birds of the air can make nests in its shade."

# Song to the Virgin

## HILDEGARD OF BINGEN

Germany 1098–1179. See page 9 for biographical information on this poet.
"Song to the Virgin" is translated from the Latin by Barbara Newman.

Never was leaf so green,
for you branched from the spirited
blast of the quest
of the saints.

When it came time
for your boughs to blossom
(I salute you!)
your scent was like balsam
distilled in the sun.

And your flower made all spices
fragrant
dry though they were:
they burst into verdure.

So the skies rained dew on the grass
and the whole earth exulted,
for her womb brought forth wheat,
for the birds of heaven
made their nests in it.

Keepers of the feast, rejoice!
The banquet's ready. And you
sweet maid-child
are a fount of gladness.

But Eve?
She despised every joy.
Praise nonetheless,
praise to the highest.

# The Good Samaritan

*Luke 10:29−37*

[A lawyer] asked Jesus, "And who is my neighbor?" Jesus replied, "A man was going down from Jerusalem to Jericho, and fell into the hands of robbers, who stripped him, beat him, and went away, leaving him half dead. Now by chance a priest was going down that road; and when he saw him, he passed by on the other side. So likewise a Levite, when he came to the place and saw him, passed by on the other side. But a Samaritan while traveling came near him; and when he saw him, he was moved with pity. He went to him and bandaged his wounds, having poured oil and wine on them. Then he put him on his own animal, brought him to an inn, and took care of him. The next day he took out two denarii, gave them to the innkeeper, and said, 'Take care of him; and when I come back, I will repay you whatever more you spend.' Which of these three, do you think, was a neighbor to the man who fell into the hands of the robbers?" He said, "The one who showed him mercy." Jesus said to him, "Go and do likewise."

# The Neighbor

ANNETTE VON DROSTE-HÜLSHOFF

Germany, 1797–1848. Born of a noble Catholic family, Droste-Hülshoff, often referred to as Germany's greatest female poet, practiced her religion conscientiously throughout her life. Yet she was suspicious of external displays of piety, and in her cycle of poems based on the Sunday Gospel texts, *The Church Year*, from which "The Neighbor" is taken, she reveals her struggles with doubt. "This book," she writes, "is for those whose love is stronger than their faith, those unhappy but foolish people who ask more questions in one hour than seven sages can answer in seven years." "The Neighbor" is translated from the German by George Dardess.

> "Neighbor"? Who is he?
> Whom do I call my brother?
> My gifts—to him or another?
> My unasked hand—to whom reach it?
> O, let your rain wet my forehead,
> Drop on it your wisdom's dew!
> May I grip just the right stone
> To build the high temple for you!
>
> Is it he the same lap has held?
> Whom the same breast has nursed?
> The same cradle rocked—is it he?
> Blood-bonds cannot be torn.
> For those who have breathed the same air,
> Who have drunk from the same well,
> Nature has kindled a fire
> In every kindred heart,
>
> As also for those who kneel
> At the same altar rail.
> Tending the same way
> In mood and understanding,
> All are given to me
> In the embrace of kith and kin,
> Fibers of my own life,
> Drops of my own blood.

Yet if in some foreign air
Some sad soul anxiously seeks
To read the cryptic script
Where no one uses his name,
And if you approach and find that name,
And read every friendly word,
Then you will light a torch
Which nature has left cold!

And when at your temple's door
Stands someone lonely, shut out,
Whose tears yet flow before God,
Whose sighs still reach his ear,
To him stretch out your hand
And point up to the blue
Where the star-signs gleam in each eye,
And the mild dew sinks on us all.

And even if deep in you churns
Disgust for that homeless soul,
For manners that clash with those
Heaven has provided you;
If fault-finding, leagued with folly,
Is bent on stifling love's seed,
Reach him your hand! This is the hour
When the parable's test draws near.

Yes, even the hateful glare
Which scorns heaven and earth—
This must you gently accept.
You may tremble—but not yield.
O, in Christ embrace the hater,
Surveying his open wounds—
Then you have found the stone,
Then you know your "neighbor!"

# Thief and Samaritan

JAMES KEIR BAXTER

New Zealand, 1926–1972. See page 99 for biographical information on this poet.

You, my friend, fallen among thieves,
The parable is harder than we suppose.
Always we say another hand drives
Home the knife, God's malice or the gross
Night-hawking bandit, straddled Apollyon.
We are blinded by the fume of the thieves' kitchen.

To be deceived is human; but till deception end
What hope of a bright inn, Love's oil and wine?
One greasy cloth of comfort I bring, friend
Nailed at the crossroad—I, thief, have seen
The same dawn break in blood and negative fire;
Your night I too could not endure.

Friend, stripped of the double-breasted suit
That left no cold out—if by falling stars
Love come, with ointment for your deadly wound,
Carry you up the steep inn stairs—
What should a thief do, footloose and well,
But rape the landlord's daughter, rummage the till?

Search well the wound, friend: know to the quick
What pain is. Thieves are only taught by pain.
And when, no longer sick,
You sit at table in the bright inn,
Remembering that pain you may sing small, dine
On a little bread, less wine.

# One Lost Sheep

*Matthew 18:12−14*

"What do you think? If a shepherd has a hundred sheep, and one of them has gone astray, does he not leave the ninety-nine on the mountains and go in search of the one that went astray? And if he finds it, truly I tell you, he rejoices over it more than over the ninety-nine that never went astray. So it is not the will of your Father in heaven that one of these little ones should be lost."

# from *The Divine Narcissus*

JUANA INÉS DE LA CRUZ

Mexico, 1651–1695. See page 88 for biographical information on this poet. In this dramatic poem, Christ is represented by Narcissus, who appears in this scene in shepherd's dress. This selection from *The Divine Narcissus* is translated from the Spanish by Alan S. Trueblood.

Poor little lost sheep,
forgetful of your Master,
where can you be straying?
When you depart from me,
it's life you leave behind, will you not see?
    Drinking stagnant waters
out of ancient cisterns,
you slake your foolish thirst,
while, deaf to your mistake,
the spring of living waters you forsake.
    Call to mind my favors:
you'll see how lovingly
I watch over you
to free you of offense,
laying down my life in your defense.
    Covered with frost and snow,
I leave the flock behind,
to follow your foolish steps;
still you spurn this love of mind,
though for you I've left the other ninety-nine.
    Consider that my beauty,
beloved of every creature,
desired by them all—
by every single one—
has set its heart on winning you alone.
    Down paths through briary wastes,
I follow where you've trod,
I brave these rugged woods
until my feet are torn,
are stabbed and pierced by every passing thorn.
    Still, I shall seek you out
and, even if in the search
I risk my very life,
yours I shall not disown:
to find you I would sooner lose my own.

# The Place of Honor

## Luke 14:7–11

When he noticed how the guests chose the places of honor, he told them a parable. "When you are invited by someone to a wedding banquet, do not sit down at the place of honor, in case someone more distinguished than you has been invited by your host; and the host who invited both of you may come and say to you, 'Give this person your place,' and then in disgrace you would start to take the lowest place. But when you are invited, go and sit down at the lowest place, so that when your host comes, he may say to you, 'Friend, move up higher'; then you will be honored in the presence of all who sit at the table with you. For all who exalt themselves will be humbled, and those who humble themselves will be exalted."

# Luke 14: A Commentary

KATHLEEN NORRIS

U.S., 1947–. Author of the bestselling prose spiritual reflection, *Dakota*, Norris
has published many volumes of poetry. "Luke 14: A Commentary" shows Norris'
command of conversational diction and her sensitivity to wry connections.

<blockquote>

He is there, like Clouseau,
at the odd moment,
just right: when he climbs
out of the fish pond
into which he has spectacularly
fallen, and says condescendingly
to his hosts, the owners
of the estate: "I fail
where others succeed." You know
this is truth. You know
he'll solve the mystery,

unprepossessing
as he is, the last
of the great detectives.
He'll blend again into the scenery, and
more than once, be taken
for the gardener. "Come

now," he says, taking us
for all we're worth: "sit
in the low place."
Why not? we ask, so easy
to fall for a man
who makes us laugh. "Invite those
you do not know, people
you'd hardly notice." He puts
us on, we put him on; another
of his jokes. "There's
room," he says. The meal is
good, absurdly
salty, but delicious. Charlie

</blockquote>

PARABLES [ 239 ]

Chaplin put it this way: "I want to play
the role of Jesus. I look the part.
I'm a Jew.
And I'm a comedian."

# The Prodigal Son

*Luke 15:11—32*

Then Jesus said, "There was a man who had two sons. The younger of them said to his father, 'Father, give me the share of the property that will belong to me.' So he divided his property between them. A few days later the younger son gathered all he had and traveled to a distant country, and there he squandered his property in dissolute living. When he had spent everything, a severe famine took place throughout that country, and he began to be in need. So he went and hired himself out to one of the citizens of that country, who sent him to his fields to feed the pigs. He would gladly have filled himself with the pods that the pigs were eating; and no one gave him anything. But when he came to himself he said, 'How many of my father's hired hands have bread enough and to spare, but here I am dying of hunger! I will get up and go to my father, and I will say to him, "Father, I have sinned against heaven and before you; I am no longer worthy to be called your son; treat me like one of your hired hands."' So he set off and went to his father. But while he was still far off, his father saw him and was filled with compassion; he ran and put his arms around him and kissed him. Then the son said to him, 'Father, I have sinned against heaven and before you; I am no longer worthy to be called your son.' But the father said to his slaves, 'Quickly, bring out a robe—the best one—and put it on him; put a ring on his finger and sandals on his feet. And get the fatted calf and kill it, and let us eat and celebrate; for this son of mine was dead and is alive again; he was lost and is found!' And they began to celebrate.

"Now his elder son was in the field; and when he came and approached the house, he heard music and dancing. He called one of the slaves and asked what was going on. He replied, 'Your brother has come, and your father has killed the fatted calf, because he has got him back safe and sound.' Then he became angry and refused to go in. His father came out and began to plead with him. But he answered his father, 'Listen! For all these years I have been working like a slave for you, and I have never disobeyed your command; yet you have never given me even a young goat so that I might celebrate with my friends. But when this son of yours came back, who has devoured your property with prostitutes, you killed the fatted calf for him!' Then the father said to him, 'Son, you are always with me, and all that is mine is yours. But we had to celebrate and rejoice, because this brother of yours was dead and has come to life; he was lost and has been found.'"

# Mysterious Wealth

KU SANG

Korea, 1919–. See page 4 for biographical information on this poet. "Mysterious
Wealth" is translated from the Korean by Brother Anthony of Taizé.

Feeling today like the Prodigal Son
just arrived back in his father's arms,
I observe the world and all it contains.

June's milky sky glimpsed through a window,
the sunlight dancing over fresh green leaves,
clusters of sparrows that scatter, chirping,
full-blown petunias in pots on verandas,
all strike me as infinitely new,
astonishing and miraculous.

My grandson, too, rushing round the living-room
and chattering away for all he's worth,
my wife, with her glasses on,
embroidering a pillow-case,
and the neighbours, each with their particularities,
coming and going in the lane below,
all are extremely lovable,
most trustworthy, significant.

Oh, mysterious, immeasurable wealth!
Not to be compared with storeroom riches!
Truly, all that belongs to my Father in Heaven,
all, all is mine!

# Sunday in Saint Christina's in Budapest and Fruitstand Next Door

ANTONIO CISNEROS

Peru, 1942–. Cisneros teaches at the University of San Marcos in Lima. His poetry has been translated into many languages. He is the author of *Exile*, which received the National Poetry Prize, and *The Book of God and the Hungarians*. "Sunday in Saint Christina's. . . ." is translated from the Spanish by Wayne H. Finke.

It is raining on the peaches and pears,
their skins shiny under the deluge
like Roman helmets in their baskets.
It is raining midst the snoring of the surf
and the iron derricks. The priest
is wearing Advent green and a microphone.
I know neither his language
nor the century when this church was founded.
But I know the Lord is in his mouth:
for me guitars, the fattest calf,
the richest tunic, sandals,
for I was lost
more than a grain of sand in Black Point,
more than rainwater midst the waters
of the turbid Danube.
For I was dead and I am resurrected.

It is raining on the peaches and pears,
seasonal fruit whose name I know not, but I know
of their taste and smell, their color
that changes with the times.
I do not know the customs or face of the fruitseller
—his name is a sign—
but I know that this holiday season and the fattened cow
await him at the end of the labyrinth
like all good birds
tired of rowing against the wind.
For I was dead and I am resurrected,
praised be the name of the Lord,
Whatever his name under this vivifying rain.

# Return of the Prodigal Son

LÉOPOLD SÉDAR SENGHOR

Senegal, 1906–. See page 30 for biographical information on this poet. "Return of the Prodigal Son" is translated from the French by Melvin Dixon.

> to Jacques Maguilen Senghor,
> my nephew

### I

And my heart once again on the threshold of stone under the
      portal of honor.
And a tremor stirs the warm ashes of the lightning-eyed Man, my
      father.
On my hunger, the dust of sixteen years of wandering
And the uncertainty of Europe's many roads
And the noise of sprawling cities, and towns lashed by the waves
Of a thousand passions in my head.
My heart is still pure as the East Wind in March.

### II

I challenge my blood in this head empty of ideas, in this belly
Abandoned by courageous muscles.
Guide me by the golden note of the silent flute, guide me,
Herdsman, brother who shared my childhood dreams, naked under
      his milk belt
And with the flame tree's flower on his brow.
And pierce, herdsman, just pierce with a long surreal note
This tottering house where termites have eaten away windows and
      inhabitants.
And my heart once again under the great dwelling built by the Man's
      pride
And my heart once again on the tomb where he has piously laid his
      ancient lineage to rest.
He needs no paper, only the troubador's musical page
And the red-gold stylus of his tongue.

### III

How vast, how void is the courtyard smelling of nothingness,
Like the plain in the dry season trembling with emptiness,
But what woodcutting storm felled the secular tree?
An entire people had subsisted on its shade on the round terrace,
A whole household with stableboys and artisans and family herdsmen
On the red terrace that protected the surging sea of herds
On the great days of fire and blood.
Or is it now a district struck by four-engined eagles
And by lions of bombs with such powerful leaps?

### IV

And my heart once again on the steps of the high house.
I lay on the ground at your feet in the dust of my respect,
At your feet, Ancestors who are present, who proudly dominate
The great room of your masks defying Time.
Faithful servant of my childhood, here are my feet
Caked with the mud of Civilization.
Only pure water on my feet, servant, and only their white soles on the
        still mats.
Peace, peace, peace, my Fathers, on the Prodigal Son's head.

### V

You among them all, Elephant of Mbissel, shower your troubador
        poet with friendship
And he partakes with you of the dishes of honor, the oil highlighting
        the lips,
And the river horses, gifts from the Sine kings, masters of millet,
Masters of palms, the Sine kings who had planted in Diakhaw
The legitimate force of their lance. And among them all,
This Mbogou, of desert-colored skin; and the *Guelwârs*
Shed libations of tears at his departure
Pure rain of dew as when the Sun's death bleeds on the ocean plain
And on the waves of dead warriors.

VI

Elephant of Mbissel, through your ears invisible to our eyes,
Let my Ancestors hear my reverent prayer.
May you be blessed, my Fathers, may you be blessed!
Merchants and bankers, lords of gold and the outskirts of town
Where a chimney forest grows
—They have bought their nobility and blackened their mother's womb
The merchants and bankers have banished me from the Nation.
And they have carved "Mercenary" on my honorable weapons
And they knew I asked for no pay, only ten cents
To cradle the smoke of my dreams and milk to wash away my blue
        bitterness.
If I have planted my loyalty back in the fields of defeat,
It is because God has struck France with his leaden hand.
May you be blessed, my Fathers, may you be blessed.
You who have endured scorn and mockery, polite offenses,
Discreet slurs and taboos and segregation.
And you have torn from this too-loving heart
The ties that bind it to the world's pulse.
May you be blessed, you who refused to let hatred turn a man's heart
To stone. You know that I have made friends with the forbidden princes
Of intellect and the princes of form, that I have eaten the bread
That brings hunger to countless armies of workers
And those without work, that I dreamt of a world of sun
In fraternity with my blue-eyed brothers.


VII

Elephant of Mbissel, I applaud the emptiness of shops around the
noble house.
I applaud joyfully! Long live the merchant's bankruptcy!
I applaud this strip of sea abandoned by white wings—
The crocodiles now hunt deep in the woods
And the sea cows graze in peace!
I burn down the *seco!* The pyramid of peanuts towering above the land
And the hard wharf, an implacable will upon the sea.

But I bring back to life the sound of the herds, their neighing and
    bellowing,
The sound modulating the flutes and conch shells in the evening
    moonlight
I bring back the procession of servant girls on the dew
And the great calabashes of milk, steady, on their rhythmic, swaying
    hips.
I bring back to life the caravan of donkeys and camels
Smelling of millet and rice
In the glittering mirrors, in the tolling of faces and silver bells.
I bring back to life all my earthly virtues!


### VIII

Elephant of Mbissel, hear my reverent prayer.
Give me the skilled knowledge of the great Timbuktu doctors,
Give me Soni Ali's strong will, born of the Lion's slobber—
A tidal wave to the conquest of a continent.
Blow upon me the Keïtas' wisdom.
Give me the Guelwâr's courage, gird my loins with the strength of a
    tyedo.
Give me the chance to die for the struggles of my people,
And if necessary in the odor of gunpowder and cannon.
Preserve and root in my freed heart the foremost love of my people.
Make me your Master Linguist; No, no,
Appoint me his ambassador.


### IX

May you be blessed, my Fathers, who bless the Prodigal Son!
I want to see again the room on the right where the women worked,
Where I played with the doves and my brothers, sons of the Lion.
Ah! to sleep once again in the cool bed of my childhood
Ah! to have loving black hands once again tuck me in at night,
And see once again my mother's white smile.
Tomorrow I will continue on my way to Europe, to the embassy,
Already homesick for my black Land.

# Wheat and Tares

*Matthew 13:24–30, 36–43*

He put before them another parable: "The kingdom of heaven may be compared to someone who sowed good seed in his field; but while everybody was asleep, an enemy came and sowed weeds among the wheat, and then went away. So when the plants came up and bore grain, then the weeds appeared as well. And the slaves of the householder came and said to him, 'Master, did you not sow good seed in your field? Where, then, did these weeds come from?' He answered, 'An enemy has done this.' The slaves said to him, 'Then do you want us to go and gather them?' But he replied, 'No; for in gathering the weeds you would uproot the wheat along with them. Let both of them grow together until the harvest; and at harvest time I will tell the reapers, Collect the weeds first and bind them in bundles to be burned, but gather the wheat into my barn.'"

. . . Then he left the crowds and went into the house. And his disciples approached him, saying, "Explain to us the parable of the weeds of the field." He answered, "The one who sows the good seed is the Son of Man; the field is the world, and the good seed are the children of the kingdom; the weeds are the children of the evil one, and the enemy who sowed them is the devil; the harvest is the end of the age, and the reapers are angels. Just as the weeds are collected and burned up with fire, so will it be at the end of the age. The Son of Man will send his angels, and they will collect out of his kingdom all causes of sin and all evildoers, and they will throw them into the furnace of fire, where there will be weeping and gnashing of teeth. Then the righteous will shine like the sun in the kingdom of their Father. Let anyone with ears listen!"

# Self-Ordained

VASSAR MILLER

U.S., 1924–. See page 146 for biographical information on this poet.

> Lithe shadows flickering across a rock
> Flashed the expressions of his face, the heir
> Of heretic and rebel, forged from shock
> Of lust dark in some granite-tufted lair.
> I watched him kneel down like a buckled rod
> Over his darkness gathered in a gulf,
> An upstart Jacob wrestling with his God
> Or some inflated image of himself,
> Or both, who knows? His words dropped blazing brands
> Upon injustice, which, smoked out, still lingers.
> But as he lifted proud and angry hands
> I saw the victims dangling from his fingers.
> Then I remembered what his Master said
> Of wheat and tares, and mildly bowed my head.

# The Grain of Wheat

## *John 12:24*

"Very truly, I tell you, unless a grain of wheat falls into the earth and dies, it remains just a single grain; but if it dies, it bears much fruit."

# The Day of My Death

PIER PAOLO PASOLINI

Italy, 1922–1975. Novelist, poet, and internationally renowned neo-realist filmmaker, Pasolini strove to achieve a truly popular art that would reach every level of society. A Catholic and a Communist, he was a dedicated adherent of the Marxist critic, Antonio Gramsci. His 1964 film, *The Gospel According to St. Matthew*, remains one of the finest and most original cinematic versions of scripture. "The Day of My Death" is translated from the Italian by Lawrence R. Smith.

> In a city, Trieste or Udine,
>     down in a valley of lime trees,
> when the leaves
>     change color . . .
>     a person lived,
> with the strength of a young man
>             in the heart of the world,
> and he gave, to those few men
> he knew, everything.
>
> Then, for love of those
>     who were boys
> like him—until shortly before
>     the stars changed
>     their light on his head—
> he would have wanted to give his life
>             for the whole unknown world,
> he, unknown, little saint,
> seed fallen in the field.
>
> And instead he wrote
>     poems of holiness
> believing that in this way
>     his heart would become larger.

# The Eternal Dialogue

YŪSUF AL-KHĀL

Lebanon, 1917–1987. Son of a Lebanese Protestant minister, al-Khāl is best known as a creative journalist, publisher, and founder of the magazine *Shi'r*, which fostered the free verse movement in Arabic poetry, He published many volumes of avante-garde poetry and extensively translated Frost, Eliot, Whitman, and others. al-Khāl saw the poet as a Christ-like figure who brings life through sacrifice; in "The Poet" he wrote: "Crucified, I bleed while my hands touch the heavens / But tomorrow I arise from my grave . . . " "The Eternal Dialogue," a meditation on human sinfulness, ponders whether our sins are so great as to be beyond redemption. "The Eternal Dialogue" is translated from the Arabic by Issa J. Boullata.

I

When will our sins be blotted out? When will
The pains of the humble leaf? When will
The fingers of doubt touch us? Are we dead
On the road and don't know it, I wonder?
We are hidden from sight by shrouds
Of sand, of dust diffused by hoofs
In the arena of the sun.
                                              You tell me
I am still a child. Look well at me
For the flood has stains
On my damp shirt, and in my eyes
Are virgin secrets not yet awake, passions
That shed the first tear, wounds
That fill my tender body.
Are you thirsty? Take the rock and strike it,
Are you in the dark? Roll it away from the tomb.
If hunger bites you take manna
And quails. If you become naked
Take a garment of fig leaves
To cover your pudenda from people.
In great tribulation bear out
With the fortitude of Job and don't despair
If evil is rampant: God's cross
Is raised on the hill of time. On the shore
Are lighthouses and when they shine we shall strike

The brow of dawn with our hands, and bring forth
From the rock gushing water that carries the sand
To the sea. In the horizon are a bird's wings
Settled on the skull of night,
And a dark star relating the story
Of the manger to passers-by. And in secret,
When stark, is a God who fills the sight,
A God who is not dead yet, a God who pours
Love on the wound.


II

                              On my way
Are crocodiles and pseudo-crocodiles,
Owls filling the house and ravens,
And black clouds threatening with a violent storm
With flood, with death
On the roadside: bones grown stiff
In humiliation, in solitude, in the Now.
This naked creeping being—is he a man,
Is he a man in the image of God?
I see he is sliced from the devil's flesh,
I see he has killed the dragon in the wood
And let its blood run in the earth to quench
The thirst for conquest, for meeting a world
Which beginning has not yet begun with;
I see he has carried the universe in his palms,
Thrown it in corridors, built a hut
Of steel unattainable by death
Or the secret. I see he has emptied the sea
Into his eyes, and hidden his head in the sand
In fear of his enemies: I wonder, does the blind man
See his enemies?
                              His enemies are:
Veins that throb no more with love
Or hate, a tongue that says anything but
What speaking is for, and a mind astray
On the way, exhausted by the way.

III

We are slaves of the past, slaves
Of the future, slaves nursing on humiliation
From birth to death. Our sins?
The hand of days did not make our sins.
We made our sins with our own hands:
Perhaps the sun did not shine to revive us:
Here is the cemetery of light, here the sand,
Here harmless little birds become eagles, here the first wheat grain
Dies. Here doubt does not exist,
Speech dies on truthful tongues,
God's cross has not blotted out our sins,
Will they be blotted out if our wings
Compete with the wind, if the seal
Of the secret is broken, or the world obeys us?
My morrow is the making of appointments with phantasy
This has been the case of my forefathers since the beginning:
The raven of separation has no mercy on our victims
Only God arose from the dead
Only something which was God. We ate His flesh
As bread, drank His blood as wine,
Neither the bread satiated us, nor the wine
Intoxicated us. Yet is light of any use
If it is hidden under a bushel?


IV

I wonder, will death attain us perplexed
As we are? We have neither understood, accepted,
What has become nor what was.
We disbelieved, neither the hand of faith will redeem us
Like Isaac nor will the atonement of love:
God's cross is still raised
On the hill of time. By it our sins will be blotted out,
By it the pains of the humble will leaf,
By it doubt will touch us
And the story of the dead on earth will end.

# The Rich Man and Lazarus

## Luke 16:19—31

There was a rich man who was dressed in purple and fine linen and who feasted sumptuously every day. And at his gate lay a poor man named Lazarus, covered with sores, who longed to satisfy his hunger with what fell from the rich man's table; even the dogs would come and lick his sores. The poor man died and was carried away by the angels to be with Abraham. The rich man also died and was buried. In Hades, where he was being tormented, he looked up and saw Abraham far away with Lazarus by his side. He called out, "Father Abraham, have mercy on me, and send Lazarus to dip the tip of his finger in water and cool my tongue; for I am in agony in these flames." But Abraham said, "Child, remember that during your lifetime you received your good things, and Lazarus in like manner evil things; but now he is comforted here, and you are in agony. Besides all this, between you and us a great chasm has been fixed, so that those who might want to pass from here to you cannot do so, and no one can cross from there to us." He said, "Then, father, I beg you to send him to my father's house—for I have five brothers—that he may warn them, so that they will not also come into this place of torment." Abraham replied, "They have Moses and the prophets; they should listen to them." He said, "No, father Abraham; but if someone goes to them from the dead, they will repent." He said to him, "If they do not listen to Moses and the prophets, neither will they be convinced even if someone rises from the dead."

# *from* Homily on Dives and Lazarus

ROMANOS

Constantinople, 6th c. See page 139 for biographical information on this poet.
"Homily on Dives and Lazarus" is translated from the Greek by Marjorie Car-
penter.

The rich man, who was being condemned for the enormity of his
      sins,
  Probably thought: "I have sinned greatly,
But what is the reason
  For my being roasted here in the fire without any pity?"
When the Lord, who knows all, heard these words,
  He revealed to the sinner the cause of his punishment.
For while he was in Hades he looked on high,
  And he saw Lazarus in the bosom of Abraham.
Then he recognized the man who formerly was poor, and was
      amazed as he saw
  The one whom he scorned on earth, while he enjoyed himself and
      did not cry:
  "Have pity, Lord."

Astonished, then, the greedy fellow said to himself:
DIVES: "Is this the fellow who was formerly lying at my gate,
Whom I did not consider worthy of scraps?
  What splendor and glory he has—such as I have not seen on earth!
What cry for help am I going to utter now? What am I to imagine?
    Shall I ask Lazarus
  To moisten my tongue with a drop of water?
I am ashamed to ask the poor fellow now,
  When I formerly saw him in need of my scraps;
So I shall beg Abraham, saying, 'Father, pity your son,
  And quickly send Lazarus who cried out:
  "Have pity, Lord".'

DIVES: "Unjustly I formerly set snares for Lazarus because he was
      poor;
  I was filled with iniquities; I proceeded unrighteously,
Priding myself on my riches;

As a braggart, I wandered from the path of truth,
And the light did not shine on me, for I did not recognize
   The paths of holiness, as I missed my life.
Wealth passed as a spider's web and a shadow
   And as grass that flourishes near the house,
And like a ship it has run in the depths of the sea, and one cannot
      find a trace of it.
   It is, then, useless for me to cry out:
   'Have pity, Lord.'


"Wealth and life have passed; just as the chaff blown by the storm,
   Or the smoke driven by the wind are not visible,
Just so my breath, suddenly
   Snuffed out, is now dispersed like empty air.
Life is only a shadow for every mortal; there is no release
   In my end, for I have sinned grievously.
But the souls of the just are in the hands of God,
   And the lash does not draw near their habitation.
Therefore, now I shall cry out to Abraham to propitiate God,
   So that Lazarus may be sent to me—Lazarus whom I know who
      cries:
   'Have pity, Lord.'"

# To Saint Lazarus

## (Babalú Ayé)

JOSÉ SÁNCHEZ-BOUDY

Cuba, 1928–. A prolific writer in many genres, Sánchez-Boudy preserves Cuba's popular language and customs in his work. He is a leading representative of Afro-Cuban poetry, which celibrates the heritage of Cubans of African descent. In Afro-Cuban culture, Yoruba gods are identified with particular Catholic saints: for instance, Babalú Ayé, the old man who can cure all diseases, merges with St. Lazarus, who has a shrine in a hospital for lepers near Havana. "To Saint Lazarus" is translated from the Spanish by Claudio Freixas.

I

From Havana, from all the roads,
Cripples arrived in Rincón with their laments,
showing their bruised stumps in the open air
Or moving their legless bodies on rolling boards.

Dreaming of their cure while suffering torments,
Their knees bleeding from walking on cobblestones,
Kissing the pedestal of Saint Lazarus' image,
Their prayers going up, ripping firmaments.

There, away from home, the saint in his chapel
With his dog licking his wounds
Showed them his generous and touching charity.

The seed of faith, singing prayers,
Was slowly rising toward the heights,
And, in heaven, hope was chanting arias.

# Ballad of Dives and Lazarus

JAMES KEIR BAXTER

New Zealand, 1926–1972. See page 99 for biographical information on this poet.

Two men lived in the same street
But they were poles apart
For Lazarus had crippled bones
But Dives a crippled heart
That made him stare both night and day
At a production chart.

The springtime came, the springtime went,
The tide flowed up the sand;
Lazarus murmured to himself,
'It is a pleasant land;
The sun that shines upon my coat
Is the comfort of God's Hand.'

But Dives in anger cried aloud,
'I spend too much on you!
A blind man cannot watch the dials
That help my engines go;
A deaf man cannot hear the whistle
To tell the end of smoko;

'A lame man cannot fetch and carry
The cheques that I must write—
The graph of my production chart
Is lovely in my sight
As Jacob's ladder was to him
Upon a starry night.

'And you will live, since live you must,
But at a cheaper rate;
A cripple cannot ask the World
To carry his dead weight—
My engines run too slowly
Because of the Welfare State.'

God spoke to Dives upon the hour
(Since God and God alone
Knows what can turn a human heart
Into a heart of stone)—
'My poor blind crippled son,' He said,
'Sit here beneath My Throne,

'Why force My Hand? I did not make
Man for the gap of Hell;
I gave the wild sea and the wind
And limbs that serve him well,
And a heart that is My dwelling place
Where none may buy or sell.

'Go back and learn from Lazarus
To walk on My highway
Until your crippled soul can stand
And bear the light of day,
And you and Lazarus are one
In holy poverty.'

# The Laborers in the Vineyard

## Matthew 20:1–16

For the kingdom of heaven is like a landowner who went out early in the morning to hire laborers for his vineyard. After agreeing with the laborers for the usual daily wage, he sent them into his vineyard. When he went out about nine o'clock, he saw others standing idle in the marketplace; and he said to them, "You also go into the vineyard, and I will pay you whatever is right." So they went. When he went out again about noon and about three o'clock, he did the same. And about five o'clock he went out and found others standing around; and he said to them, "Why are you standing here idle all day?" They said to him, "Because no one has hired us." He said to them, "You also go into the vineyard." When evening came, the owner of the vineyard said to his manager, "Call the laborers and give them their pay, beginning with the last and then going to the first." When those hired about five o'clock came, each of them received the usual daily wage. Now when the first came, they thought they would receive more; but each of them also received the usual daily wage. And when they received it, they grumbled against the landowner, saying, "These last worked only one hour, and you have made them equal to us who have borne the burden of the day and the scorching heat." But he replied to one of them, "Friend, I am doing you no wrong; did you not agree with me for the usual daily wage? Take what belongs to you and go; I choose to give to this last the same as I give to you. Am I not allowed to do what I choose with what belongs to me? Or are you envious because I am generous?" So the last will be first, and the first will be last.

# Do You Honor God?

## HIPPOLYTUS OF ROME

Italy, c.165–235. A vehement controversialist, Hippolytus withdrew from communion with Pope Calixtus over disputes about the relationship between God and Jesus. He was later consecrated antipope by his followers. In less contentious moments he was also a poet. The hymn included here, from a treatise on Easter, was written in Greek, which was still the language of the Roman Empire. "Do You Honor God?" is translated from the Greek by Walter Mitchell.

Do you honour God? Do you love him
–here's the very feast for your pleasure.
Are you his servant, knowing his wishes?
—be glad with your Master, share his rejoicing.
Are you worn down with the labour of fasting?
—now is the time of your payment.

Have you been working since early morning?
—now you will be paid what is fair.
Have you been here since the third hour?
—you can be thankful, you will be pleased.

If you came at the sixth hour,
you may approach without fearing:
you will suffer no loss.
Did you linger till the ninth hour?
—come forward without hesitation.
What though you came at the eleventh hour?
—have no fear; it was not too late.

God is a generous Sovereign,
treating the last to come as he treats the first arrival.
He allows all his workmen to rest—
those who began at the eleventh hour,
those who have worked from the first.
He is kind to the late-comer
and sees to the needs of the early,
gives to the one and gives to the other:
honours the deed and praises the motive.

Join, then, all of you, join in our Master's rejoicing.
You who were the first to come, you who came after,
come and collect now your wages.
Rich men and poor men, sing and dance together.
You that are hard on yourselves, you that are easy,
honour this day.
You that have fasted and you that have not,
make merry today.

The meal is ready: come and enjoy it.
The calf is a fat one: you will not go hungry away.
There's kindness for all to partake of and kindness to spare.

Away with pleading of poverty:
the kingdom belongs to us all.
Away with bewailing of failings:
forgiveness has come from the grave.
Away with your fears of dying:
the death of our Saviour has freed us from fear.
Death played the master: he has mastered death . . .
The world below had scarcely known him in the flesh
when he rose and left it plunged in bitter mourning.

Isaias knew it would be so.
The world of shadows mourned, he cried, when it met you,
mourned at its bringing low, wept at its deluding.

The shadows seized a body and found it was God;
they reached for earth and what they held was heaven;
they took what they could see: it was what no one sees.
Where is death's goad? Where is the shadows' victory?

Christ is risen: the world below is in ruins.
Christ is risen: the spirits of evil are fallen.
Christ is risen: the angels of God are rejoicing.
Christ is risen: the tombs are void of their dead.
Christ has indeed arisen from the dead,
the first of the sleepers.

Glory and power are his for ever and ever. Amen.

# The Wicked Tenants

*Mark 12:1b—*

"A man planted a vineyard, put a fence around it, dug a pit for the wine press, and built a watchtower; then he leased it to tenants and went to another country.

When the season came, he sent a slave to the tenants to collect from them his share of the produce of the vineyard.

But they seized him, and beat him, and sent him away empty-handed.

And again he sent another slave to them; this one they beat over the head and insulted.

Then he sent another, and that one they killed. And so it was with many others; some they beat, and others they killed.

He had still one other, a beloved son. Finally he sent him to them, saying, "They will respect my son."

But those tenants said to one another, "This is the heir; come, let us kill him, and the inheritance will be ours."

So they seized him, killed him, and threw him out of the vineyard.

What then will the owner of the vineyard do? He will come and destroy the tenants and give the vineyard to others.

# To Christ

FADWĀ TŪQUĀN

Palestine, 1917–. Considered one of the most distinguished female poets of the Arab world, Fadwā Tūquān, like all Palestinian poets, was painfully affected by the establishment of Israel, especially after her home town of Nablus fell to the Israelis in the June 1967 war. Poetry became her—and her fellow poets'—only means of protest, as "To Christ" makes clear. "To Christ" is translated from the Arabic by Abdullah al-Udhari.

> *But those husbandmen said among themselves, this is*
> *the heir; come let us kill him, and the inheritance shall*
> *be ours.*
> *And they took him, killed him, and cast him out of the*
> *vineyard.*
>
> Mark 12:7–8

Lord, Glory of the Universe,
On Christmas Day 1967
Jerusalem's feasts were nailed upon the Cross.
Lord, on the day of your feast
The bells were silent.

For two thousand years
The bells always rang
On the day of your birth
But not this year.

Under the weight of the Cross
On the road of agony
Jerusalem is whipped:
The soldier's lashes draw blood.
But the world's heart is closed to the tragedy.
This stone-cold world, Lord, is
                              Blind
For the eye of the sun has turned to glass.

Not a candle was lit,
Not a tear was shed
To wash away Jerusalem's grief.

Lord, the vineworkers killed the heir
And took the vines;
The bird of sin
Feathered the sinners of the world
And swooped down to stain Jerusalem's chastity.

Lord, Glory of Jerusalem,
From the well of grief
From the abyss
        From the depth of the night
From the heart of pain
To you Jerusalem's groans rise.
Mercy, O Lord,
Let this cup pass from her.

# The Vigilant Servant

## Luke 12:35–40

Be dressed for action and have your lamps lit; be like those who are waiting for their master to return from the wedding banquet, so that they may open the door for him as soon as he comes and knocks. Blessed are those slaves whom the master finds alert when he comes; truly I tell you, he will fasten his belt and have them sit down to eat, and he will come and serve them. If he comes during the middle of the night, or near dawn, and finds them so, blessed are those slaves.

But know this: if the owner of the house had known at what hour the thief was coming, he would not have let his house be broken into. You also must be ready, for the Son of Man is coming at an unexpected hour.

# For the Veiling of Sister Isabel
# De Los Angeles

TERESA OF AVILA

Spain, 1515–1582. See page 36 for biographical information on this poet. "For
the Veiling of Sister Isabel De Los Angeles" is translated from the Spanish by
Adrian J. Cooney.

*So that you will be watchful, Sister,*
*Today they have veiled you;*
*On that your Heaven depends;*
*Do not be careless.*

This veil so graceful
Proclaims you keep vigil,
The watchful sentinel
Awaiting her Bridegroom,
Who as the famed thief
Will come with surprise;
*Do not be careless.*

That hour is unknown,
What watch it will be,
First, second, or third;
All Christians know not,
So watch, watch, sister,
Lest your treasure be stolen.
*Do not be careless.*

Hold always in your hand
A candle bright;
Veiled, keep the watch
With loins girded well.
Be free of deep sleep,
Mindful of the danger near.
*Do not be careless.*

Keep ready your oil jar
Of merit and deeds,

Ample to keep
Your lamp aflame
Lest outside you be kept
When He comes.
*Do not be careless.*

No one will lend you oil
If you hasten to buy it;
Late you could be,
Once the Bridegroom is within,
The door then is closed;
Your cries will avail you not.
*Do not be careless.*

Be constant in care,
Fulfilling all bravely,
What you vowed today
Until death comes.
In keeping well your watch,
With the Bridegroom you will enter.
*Do not be careless.*

# The Wise and Foolish Virgins

*Matthew 25:1—13*

Then the kingdom of heaven will be like this. Ten bridesmaids took their lamps and went to meet the bridegroom. Five of them were foolish, and five were wise. When the foolish took their lamps, they took no oil with them; but the wise took flasks of oil with their lamps. As the bridegroom was delayed, all of them became drowsy and slept. But at midnight there was a shout, "Look! Here is the bridegroom! Come out to meet him." Then all those bridesmaids got up and trimmed their lamps. The foolish said to the wise, "Give us some of your oil, for our lamps are going out." But the wise replied, "No! there will not be enough for you and for us; you had better go to the dealers and buy some for yourselves." And while they went to buy it, the bridegroom came, and those who were ready went with him into the wedding banquet; and the door was shut. Later the other bridesmaids came also, saying, "Lord, lord, open to us." But he replied, "Truly I tell you, I do not know you." Keep awake therefore, for you know neither the day nor the hour.

# The Virgins' Hymn to Christ

## METHODIUS OF OLYMPUS

Greece, d.c.312. Little is known of Methodius, except that he was an opponent of Origen and that he died a martyr. His only writing to survive intact is *The Symposium of the Ten Virgins*, a series of Platonically-inspired discourses in praise of chastity. Attached to the end is "The Virgins' Hymn to Christ," an acrostic poem modeled on Psalm 119; each stanza (or "Psalm") begins with a different letter of the Greek alphabet, in sequence. "The Virgins' Hymn to Christ" is translated from the Greek by Walter Mitchell.

### ANTIPHON

My purity intact for you, my lamp alight in my hand,
Bridegroom, I come out to meet you.

### PSALM 1

That cry from the heights, virgins,
could have wakened the dead.
'Out to the Bridegroom together,' it said;
'take your lamps and white dresses;
make for the east.
Wake up, or else the King
will be indoors before you.'

### ANTIPHON

My purity intact for you, my lamp alight in my hand,
Bridegroom, I come out to meet you.

### PSALM 2

Not for me the pale joys,
the pleasures, loves, of an existence
fed with mortal pleasure.
I long for you to take me in your arms
and give me life;
I want to look at you for ever,
my Blessed One, my Beauty.

My purity intact for you, my lamp alight in my hand,
Bridegroom, I come out to meet you.

PSALM 3

Men offered me their beds: I scorned them;
scorned their houses too.
For you, my golden King,
I come in this fresh white dress.
I cannot wait to go inside that blissful place
and be with you.

ANTIPHON

My purity intact for you, my lamp alight in my hand,
Bridegroom, I come out to meet you.

PSALM 5

I have forgotten the land I was born in,
so deep your grace absorbs me, Word.
I have no heart for friendly girls and dances,
I no more care who my forebears were.
You, Christ, you, are all in all to me.

ANTIPHON

My purity intact for you, my lamp alight in my hand,
Bridegroom, I come out to meet you.

PSALM 6

Joy to you, Christ, Master of life's ballet,
Light of our days, undimmed at evening.
The virgins acclaim you; take what they bring you:
Flower of all flowers, our Love, our Joy,
Understanding, Wisdom, Word.

My purity intact for you, my lamp alight in my hand,
Bridegroom, I come out to meet you.

## PSALM 7

Stand by the open doors,
queen in the glittering gown;
bid us too welcome to the marriage-room.
Virgin your body, bride,
splendid your victory,
sweet the scent of your breath.
See us now beside Christ,
dressed like you, ready to celebrate
your marriage, blest branch of God's olive.

### ANTIPHON

My purity intact for you, my lamp alight in my hand,
Bridegroom, I come out to meet you.

## PSALM 11

Clear the colours Abel used
to paint your death before you died,
my Blessed.
Down streamed his blood,
his eyes sought heaven, as he said:
'My brother's hand has made this cruel wound.
Take me, Word, I beseech you.'

### ANTIPHON

My purity intact for you, my lamp alight in my hand,
Bridegroom, I come out to meet you.

## PSALM 17

John washed the crowds in the cleansing waters:
you were to wash them too.
A bad man sent him undeserved to death,
for purity.
Blood drenched the dust, but still he cried to you:

### ANTIPHON

My purity intact for you, my lamp alight in my hand,
Bridegroom, I come out to meet you.

## PSALM 18

The mother, my Life, that bore you
stood firm and fast in your grace.
The womb that held you, spotless Germ,
no man has sown with his seed.
Virgin she was, though seeming to betray
the marriage-bed. Big with her blissful fruit she said:

### ANTIPHON

My purity intact for you, my lamp alight in my hand,
Bridegroom, I come out to meet you.

# The Wise Virgins

CARLOS MARTÍNEZ RIVAS

Nicaragua, 1924–. Called Nicaragua's best living poet by Ernesto Cardinal, Martínez Rivas writes a dense poetry of layered meanings. His poems' protagonists are often social outcasts. "The Wise Virgins" is translated from the Spanish by Steven F. White.

*. . . he will come like a thief in the night*

Who is that woman who sings
in the night? Who is calling her sister?
From country to country, that rhapsodist flying on the wind
over the murky sea where the sky slithers?

Go out to meet him!
She, the woman in love,
only she, and her sister.
That wind singing?

It is the voice of love. The voice of love's desire rising
in the high night.
Over the potency of the city, that voice spinning.
That exquisite aria!

Only that note vibrates in the frozen night.
That lonely harp in the vast night.
That single penetrating whistle of purity.
Only that bewitched serenade.

And the sisters' love!
The stars' love protecting their flames
for the Desired who is late in coming.
Nothing but that: the betrothed sisters' fields of cane
and the lengthening shadow of the climbing Thief.

The night sings and the lonely plains
beneath the spell of the moon. Suddenly
clear, empty, as the sisters pass.
As the white flock of virgin sisters passes.

Those who surrendered themselves to love.
To whom nothing was granted but love.

The Wise Virgins whispering in the starry bedroom.
Lowering their voices and raising the flame.
Closing themselves in the middle of their shadow.
        Disappearing behind their lamp.

Here you have only abyss. Here there is only one fixed point:
the quiet wick burning and the cold halo.

Here you will rip the veil.
Here you will invent the center.
Here you will touch the body
as a blind man touches the dream.

Here you may blow and put out your secret.

Here you may stay and die.

# The Talents

## Matthew 25:14–30

For it is as if a man, going on a journey, summoned his slaves and entrusted his property to them; to one he gave five talents, to another two, to another one, to each according to his ability. Then he went away. The one who had received the five talents went off at once and traded with them, and made five more talents. In the same way, the one who had the two talents made two more talents. But the one who had received the one talent went off and dug a hole in the ground and hid his master's money. After a long time the master of those slaves came and settled accounts with them. Then the one who had received the five talents came forward, bringing five more talents, saying, "Master, you handed over to me five talents; see, I have made five more talents." His master said to him, "Well done, good and trustworthy slave; you have been trustworthy in a few things, I will put you in charge of many things; enter into the joy of your master." And the one with the two talents also came forward, saying, "Master, you handed over to me two talents; see, I have made two more talents." His master said to him, "Well done, good and trustworthy slave; you have been trustworthy in a few things, I will put you in charge of many things; enter into the joy of your master." Then the one who had received the one talent also came forward, saying, "Master, I knew that you were a harsh man, reaping where you did not sow, and gathering where you did not scatter seed; so I was afraid, and I went and hid your talent in the ground. Here you have what is yours." But his master replied, "You wicked and lazy slave! You knew, did you, that I reap where I did not sow, and gather where I did not scatter? Then you ought to have invested my money with the bankers, and on my return I would have received what was my own with interest. So take the talent from him, and give it to the one with the ten talents. For to all those who have, more will be given, and they will have an abundance; but from those who have nothing, even what they have will be taken away. As for this worthless slave, throw him into the outer darkness, where there will be weeping and gnashing of teeth."

# Brief Is Our Life

## To Adelhard, Archbishop of Canterbury

ALCUIN

England, c.735–804. A distinguished English clerical schoolmaster, Alcuin was summoned to France in 785 by Charlesmagne to reform the King's Palace school. Retiring from the court in 796 to become Abbot of St. Martin's at Tours, Alcuin wrote poetry and hymns, revised the liturgy, and produced an improved edition of the Latin Vulgate bible. "Brief Is Our Life" is translated from the Latin by Helen Waddell.

Brief is our life, now in the midst of the years,
And death with silent footfall draweth near.
　　His dreaded fingers are upon the gates,
　　And entering in, takes all thou hast.
Look forward to that day, and to that unloved hour
　　That when Christ come from heaven
He find the father of the house still watching,
　　And then thou shalt be blessed.
Happy the day when thou shalt hear the voice
Of thy gentle Judge, and for thy toil rejoicing:
　　'Come, my most faithful servant, enter in
　　The kingdom of the Father everlasting.'
That day, remember me, and say:
　　'O Christ most gentle,
　　Have mercy on a poor man, Alcuin.'
And now,
Beside the shore of the sail-winged sea
I wait the coming of God's silent dawn.
Do thou help this my journey with thy prayer.
　　I ask this, with a devoted heart.

# Meditation Forty-Nine

EDWARD TAYLOR

U.S. 1642?–1729. Born in England during Cromwell's Protectorate, Taylor em-
igrated to Massachusetts in 1668 to avoid having to sign an oath of loyalty to the
Church of England. Educated at Harvard College, he accepted in 1671 a post
as minister in the frontier town of Westfield, Massachusetts, where he re-
mained for the rest of his life. Taylor's poetry, unpublished during his lifetime
and discovered only in the 1930s, bristles with paradoxes and conceits, probably
due to the unfluence of JOHN DONNE, GEORGE HERBERT, and other English
metaphysical poets whom Taylor had read in his youth.

MATTHEW XXV: 21: *Enter thou into the joy of thy lord.*

Lord, do away my Motes and Mountains great.
  My nut is vitiate. Its kirnell rots:
Come, kill the Worm that doth its kirnell eate,
  And strike thy sparkes within my tinderbox.
    Drill through my metall heart an hole, wherein
    With graces Cotters to thyselfe it pin.

A Lock of Steel upon my Soule, whose key
  The serpent keeps, I feare, doth lock my doore:
O pick 't: and through the key-hole make thy way,
  And enter in, and let thy joyes run o're.
    My Wards are rusty. Oyle them till they trig
    Before thy golden key: thy Olye makes glib.

Take out the Splinters of the World that stick
  Do in my heart. Friends, Honours, Riches, and
The Shivers in't of Hell whose venoms quick
  And firy, make it swoln and ranckling stand.
    These wound and kill: those shackle strongly to
    Poore knobs of Clay, my heart: hence sorrows grow.

Cleanse and enlarge my kask: it is too small:
  And tartariz'd with worldly dregs dri'de in 't.
It's bad mouth'd too: and though thy joyes do Call
  That boundless are, it ever doth them stint.

Make me thy Chrystall Caske: those wines in't tun
That in the Rivers of thy joyes do run.
Lord, make me, though suck't through a straw or Quill,
Tast of the Rivers of thy joyes, some drop.
'Twill sweeten me: and all my Love distill
Into thy glass; and me for joy make hop.
'Twill turn my water into wine, and fill
My Harp with Songs my Masters joyes distill.

# Matthew XXV: 30

JORGE LUIS BORGES

Argentina, 1899–1986. One of the giants of twentieth-century world literature, Borges was born in Buenos Aires and educated in Europe, where he received a multilingual education. Influenced by the Spanish *ultraismo* movement, Borges went on to create borderless literary forms that ingeniously challenge traditional genres. One of his most bizarre stories is "The Gospel According to Mark." "Matthew XXV: 30" is translated from the Spanish by Alastair Reid.

The first bridge, Constitution Station. At my feet
The shunting trains trace iron labyrinths.
Steam hisses up and up into the night,
Which becomes at a stroke the night of the Last Judgment.

From the unseen horizon
And from the very center of my being,
An infinite voice pronounced these things—
Things, not words. This is my feeble translation,
Time-bound, of what was a single limitless Word:

"Stars, bread, libraries of East and West,
Playing cards, chessboards, galleries, skylights, cellars,
A human body to walk with on the earth,
Fingernails, growing at nighttime and in death,
Shadows for forgetting, mirrors busily multiplying,
Cascades in music, gentlest of all time's shapes,
Borders of Brazil, Uruguay, horses and mornings,
A bronze weight, a copy of the Grettir Saga,
Algebra and fire, the charge at Junín in your blood,
Days more crowded than Balzac, scent of the honeysuckle,
Love and the imminence of love and intolerable remembering,
Dreams like buried treasure, generous luck,
And memory itself, where a glance can make men dizzy—
All this was given to you and with it
The ancient nourishment of heroes—
Treachery, defeat, humiliation.
In vain have oceans been squandered on you, in vain
The sun, wonderfully seen through Whitman's eyes.
You have used up the years and they have used up you,
And still, and still, you have not written the poem."

PART SIX

# SAYINGS AND
# DISCOURSES

# The Beatitudes

*Matthew 5:1—12*

When Jesus saw the crowds, he went up the mountain; and after he sat down, his disciples came to him. Then he began to speak, and taught them, saying:

"Blessed are the poor in spirit, for theirs is the kingdom of heaven.

"Blessed are those who mourn, for they will be comforted.

"Blessed are the meek, for they will inherit the earth.

"Blessed are those who hunger and thirst for righteousness, for they will be filled.

"Blessed are the merciful, for they will receive mercy.

"Blessed are the pure in heart, for they will see God.

"Blessed are the peacemakers, for they will be called children of God.

"Blessed are those who are persecuted for righteousness' sake, for theirs is the kingdom of heaven.

"Blessed are you when people revile you and persecute you and utter all kinds of evil against you falsely on my account. Rejoice and be glad, for your reward is great in heaven, for in the same way they persecuted the prophets who were before you."

# The Sermon on the Mount

TAUFĪQ SĀYIGH

Syria, 1923–1971. Son of a Presbyterian minister, Sāyigh moved with his family from Syria to Palestine when he was two. Educated in Lebanon, he spent most of the rest of his life abroad, teaching in Cambridge, London, and Berkeley, and becoming one of the pioneers of Arabic free verse. Kenneth Cragg says that Sāyigh "writes out of a Christian nurture that strives within him to interpret how it faces the contradictions of the world. There is no more wistful voice of Christian Arabism."

I too followed him,
married my frailty to his virtue, and
helped him reveal himself.

On the lisping hill, long waited for
by the dull arms of drowsy Kinnereth
(like a couple of tears the cheeks expect,
that cling to feeble eyes), I shared the meal
of the thick-necked multitude. Well-fed,
they hailed him Lord and rolled down after him.
Alone I lay upon the hill, watched him
accept the silent homage of water
amid the crow-like shrieks of his elect.
Alone I lay, waiting for his return.

I knew he would return.
Cold crumbs and fish (though by a mother's hands
wrapped and with a mother's blessings salted)
left me starved. Water-turned-to-wine
tasted water to my lips. The mud
that cleared Bartimeus' eyes of mud, made mine
unsatisfied with what they feasted on.
The call that once restored to life the lad
of Nain, left my mother in black. Upon
the fertile hill, and the candle-like
corn, by the lake, wherein the sleepless fish
make weary passes at the blushing corn,
I starved.
I too was tempted, in no wilderness.

And he came.
Divinities of love spring out of sea.
He came and talked (some say he prayed, and some
he sang). Did others hear? I thought he talked
only to me. He called me not, and I
came forth. He broke no loaves, and touched no jars,
baskets were full again; the wedding-guests,
unconscious, conscious sipped the better wine.

He spat not on the brown converted ground,
I saw the tempters join the seven from
adjacent Magdala. He only talked.

On the hill I lie. And when the sun
steps in, increases then the heat but not
the light, I go to meet the oarless wave.
I am a pilgrim in my native land.

I know he will return, and wait for him
(the cemetery now stands upon the hill).
Thither, leaving all, he would repair,
as he was wont, to seek the fox's lair
and pray. Haply he may repeat:

"Blessed are . . ."

# Stumble Between Two Stars

CÉSAR VALLEJO

Peru, 1892–1938. Influential in the development of Latin American poetry, Vallejo crafted a surrealism of stream-of-consciousness imagery to express his personal, dark vision. He suffered great poverty as an adult, and the compassion in his poetry focuses on the pain of physical and spiritual hunger. About his own life, he is grim: "I was born on a day when God was sick." "Stumble Between Two Stars" is translated from the Spanish by Rachel Benson.

There are people so unfortunate that they don't even
have bodies; hair they have in quantity—
it lowers by inches the weight of genius;
their position, upright;
do not seek me, grindstone of oblivion,
they seem to come out of the air, to add up sighs mentally,
to hear sharp blows in their words.

They shed their skins, scratching at the tomb in which they were born,
and climb up their deaths hour by hour
and fall the length of their icy alphabet to the ground.
Alas for so much! Alas for so little! Alas for them!
Alas in my room, hearing them with eyeglasses!
Alas in my throat when they buy suits!
Alas for my white filth joined with their excrement!

Beloved be the ears of the Joneses,
beloved be those who sit down,
beloved be the stranger and his wife,
our neighbor with sleeves, collars and eyes!

Beloved be he who has bedbugs,
he who wears a torn shoe in the rain,
he who holds a wake with two matches for the corpse of a loaf of bread,
he who catches his finger in the door,
he who has no birthdays,
he who lost his shadow in the fire,
he who looks like an animal, he who looks like a parrot,
he who looks like a man, the poor rich,
the simply miserable, the poor poor!

Beloved be
he who hungers
or thirsts, but has no hunger with which to slake his thirst,
and no thirst that can satisfy all his hungers.
Beloved be he who works by the day, by the month, by the hour,
he who sweats from pain or shame,
he who goes to the movies by the work of his hands,
he who pays with what he lacks,
he who sleeps on his back;
he who no longer remembers his childhood; beloved be
the bald man without a hat,
the just man without thorns,
the thief without roses,
the man who wears a watch and has seen God,
the man who bears an honor and does not weaken!

Beloved be the child who still cries when he falls
and the man who has fallen and cries no longer.

Alas for so much! Alas for so little! Alas for them!

# An Old Man in Church

OSWALD MBUYOSENI MTSHALI

South Africa, 1940–. See page 24 for biographical information on this poet.

I know an old man
who during the week is a machine working at full throttle:
productivity would stall,
spoil the master's high profit estimate,
if on Sunday he did not go to church
to recharge his spiritual batteries.

He never says his prayer in a velvet-cushioned pew—
it would only be a whisper on God's ear.
He falls on raw knees
that smudge the bare floor with his piety.
He hits God's heart with screams as hard as stones
flung from the slingshot of his soul.
He takes the gilded communion plate with gnarled hands,
he lowers his eyes into the deep pond of serenity,
his brow rippling with devotion,
his ears enraptured by rustling silk vestments of the priest.
He drinks the Lord's blood from a golden chalice
with cracked lips thirsty for peace.

The acolyte comes around with a brass-coated
                                        collection plate
the old man sneaks in a cent piece
that raises a scowl on the collector's face
whose puckered nose sneezes at such poor generosity
instead of inhaling the aromatic incense smoke.
Then the preacher stands up in the pulpit
his voice fiery with holy fervour:
"Blessed are the meek for they shall inherit the earth."

# If You Are Angry

*Matthew 5:21−22*

You have heard that it was said to those of ancient times, "You shall not murder"; and "whoever murders shall be liable to judgment." But I say to you that if you are angry with a brother or sister, you will be liable to judgment; and if you insult a brother or sister, you will be liable to the council; and if you say, "You fool," you will be liable to the hell of fire.

# The Impatience Which Makes Us Lose All We Have Won

JACOPONE DA TODI

Italy, c.1230–1306. Italy's major vernacular poet before Dante, Jacopone wrote nearly a hundred *Lauds* (Praises): poems on spiritual themes. His poetry draws less on the Gospel itself than on the medieval allegory of virtues and vices, as well as Franciscan motifs like love of poverty and condemnation of church corruption; he joined a Franciscan Order after his wife died. "The Impatience Which Makes Us Lose All We Have Won" is translated from the Italian by Serge and Elizabeth Hughes.

I work hard to lay away treasure—
If only I could hold on to what I've gained!

I am a friar. I've studied Scripture, I've prayed,
Endured illness with patience, and helped the poor.

I've patiently kept my vows of obedience and poverty,
Gladly practiced chastity as well as I could;

Meekly accepted hunger, heat, and cold,
And made long, hard pilgrimages.

I've risen early for divine office—from beginning to end—
Terce, none, and vespers, and vigils after compline.

But let someone say something harsh to me,
And I am quick to take offense, and spit out fire.

Now see the good the habit has done me,
The riches and ease it has won for me!

Let someone make just one comment that upsets me,
And I can barely find it in me to forgive and forget!

# The Lord's Prayer

*Matthew 6:9–13*

Pray then in this way:

> Our Father in heaven,
>> hallowed be your name.
>>
>> Your kingdom come.
>>
>> Your will be done,
>>> on earth as it is in heaven.
>>
>> Give us this day our daily bread.
>>
>> And forgive us our debts,
>>> as we also have forgiven our debtors.
>>
>> And do not bring us to the time of trial,
>>> but rescue us from the evil one.

# Paternoster to Pan

RUBÉN DARÍO

Nicaragua, 1867–1916. See page 49 for biographical information on this poet.
"Paternoster to Pan" is translated from the Spanish by Lysander Kemp.

Our father, ambiguous father
of the eternal miracles
that we moderns admire because
of your great and ancient fame.

The nymph passes by the fountain,
and her whiteness includes
what inspires, what perdures,
what perfumes, and what provokes.

For on seeing the living flower
or the statue that moves,
made all of roses and snow,
our souls are captured by love.

Our Pan, which art on earth
because the universe might take fright,
hallowed be thy name
for all that it signifies.

Bring us back your joyous kingdom
in which you come singing
with the throngs of bacchantes
crashing through the thickets.

You are always violently alive;
with your wild impulsiveness,
shake your celestial horns in the sky,
sink your goat's feet in the earth.

Give us rhythm and measure
through the love of your song;
and through the love of your flute, give us
this day our daily love.

The debts the loving soul incurs
are in your hands,
and do not grant forgiveness
to him who has never loved.

# Lord's Prayer

D. H. LAWRENCE

England, 1885–1930. A poet, prophet, and polemicist in the great Noncon-
formist Protestant tradition, Lawrence was the son of a coal miner. Though
twentieth century literary criticism doesn't recognize the fact, St. Paul probably
brings us closer to Lawrence's genius than does Sigmund Freud. Much of
Lawrence's writing—from the magnificent *The Rainbow* to his novella of Jesus,
"The Man Who Died"—is immersed in Scripture. Lawrence's quarrels with
Christianity, especially with what he regarded as its Sunday School sentimen-
tality, are endless; yet he wrote of his religious education that he was "eternally
grateful for the wonder with which it filled my childhood."

> For thine is the kingdom
> the power, and the glory—
>
> Hallowed be thy name, then
> Thou who art nameless—
>
> Give me, Oh give me
> besides my daily bread
> my kingdom, my power, and my glory.
>
> All things that turn to thee
> have their kingdom, their power, and their glory.
>
> Like the kingdom of the nightingale at twilight
> whose power and glory I have often heard and felt.
>
> Like the kingdom of the fox in the dark
> yapping in his power and his glory
> which is death to the goose.
>
> Like the power and the glory of the goose in the mist
> honking over the lake.
>
> And I, a naked man, calling
> calling to thee for my mana,
> my kingdom, my power, and my glory.

# Agoué-Taroyo
## from *Epiphanies of the Voodoo Gods*

RENÉ DEPESTRE

Haiti, 1926–. See page 27 for biographical information on this poet. Depestre calls his *Epiphanies of the Voodoo Gods*, in which he blends political passion with images from Haitian folk religion, a "Voodoo mystery poem." "Agoué-Taroyo" is translated from the French by Ellen Conroy Kennedy.

I am Agoué-Taroyo
I press my symbols
On the naked belly of your wife:
A ship a fish and the vast ocean
Here I am her master and her pilot
Here I am her sails and her woman isles
She raises her Alabama head to me
To tell me with tears shining in her eyes
"Forgive us Papa-Agoué we are all your children
We are the scabbard of your saber of sweet water
We are the radar of your sweet fruits of the sea
Have pity on us, have pity on us
Oh! Papa-Taroyo! Oh! Good Papa-Woyo!
Forgive us our errors, pardon our sins"
No I tell her I am a Negro without forgiveness
My last pardon no longer has Negro eyes
To see you nor ears for your prayers
You lynched him you martyred him
You have dried up the last drop of dew
That glistened at the end of my forgiveness
I am the proud Agoué a *marine creature*
*Who lives upon the earth and also knows how to fly*
At my neck I wear a collar of green pearls
I am come to squeeze your spongy souls
Thirsty sponges in which the blood of my trees is weeping
I am come to scatter reefs of coral in your path
I am come to break your masts and oars
I am Agoué-Taroyo the great sea monster
Who drags you down beneath his undertow!

# Our Father

HJALMAR FLAX

Puerto Rico, 1942–. Flax is one of Puerto Rico's leading contemporary poets. The political protest frequent in recent Latin American verse turns, in Flax's "Our Father," to parodic fun. "Our Father" is translated from the Spanish by Wayne H. Finke.

Our Father who art in the office,
hallowed be thy name.
Thy will be done at home
as at thy desk.
Favor us in thy will.
Give us this day our steak, French fries,
and chocolate ice cream.
Force not upon us the Brussels sprouts
and we shall forgive the cook
if our steak is too well done
and our fries uncrisp.
Endow us with sports cars;
keep away the police.
Exempt us from serving in the army.
For thine is the country,
the power and the dollars,
for ever and ever,
amen.

# In My Father's House

DEWITT CLINTON

U.S., 1946–. Professor of English Clinton uses poetry to (in his own words) "retell, reconstruct, and reimagine our past histories." "In My Father's House" exemplifies this effort at what Clinton calls "historical improvisation" by blending the remembered boyhoods of a Christian and a Jew.

*for Rev. John J. Clinton (1906–1979)*
*and Rabbi David A. Lipper (1961– )*

Friday mornings, while challah rises,
I walk to shul to practice desert prayers.
Inside the domed sanctuary
I took up into the cupola,
count the many stars of David,
and wonder who keeps calling me,
calling me back to this lovely house.

Sometimes it's father,
robed, standing behind the pulpit,
sending shivers down our backs
or lulling some to gentle sleep.
Sunday mornings, Mother and I
would perch almost out of sight.
Up there, I knew, someday, I could
work this flock just like poppa
leading wayward Methodists
back into the fold.

In the quiet, shadow filled sanctuary,
the flicker of the eternal light
brings me back to *Veahavta eit Adonai*,
loving God with all mind,
all strength, all being.
Someday I'll know it, with feeling,
the rabbi says, with feeling.
How old was I when I learned,
by heart, Our Father, who Art in Heaven,
Hallow wood be thy name?

Waking, this morning, I heard
parts of Thy kingdom come
in between *Shema Yisraeil:*
Hear O Israel:
*Adonai Eloheinu, Adonai Echad!*
the Lord is our God, the Lord is One!
I can feel the quick breath
of Hebrew, feel the Crescent wind
swirl around Sarah, Isaac, Isaac's father.
Now I'm almost inside that love,
only a few days away from a moyel
taking a nick, a drop of blood,
choosing, like Ruth,
your people shall be my people.

On cue, when Father finishes
a drosh somewhere in the Galilee,
we all rise with Faith of our Fa ha thers
li hi ving still,
in spite of dun geon fi ire and sword.
Trying to hear, in memory, the next word,
the rabbi calls me in, and together,
almost like blood brothers,
we practice a slow and solemn chant
for reading prophets in a minor key.
Wrapped in prayer shawls,
wrapped in this ancient tongue,
both of us feel a desert breeze
as we practice, once more,
what will soon come from the heart.

# I Am Their Father, Says God

CHARLES PÉGUY

France, 1873–1914. Although Péguy is now considered France's major 20th century religious poet, his mammoth *Mysteries* —three volumns of continuous verse, unbroken into separate poems—were virtually ignored while he was alive. Most striking in his poetry is the narrative voice of God, who ponders Christian faith sounding like a blend of rigorous Church logician and wry French peasant. Like his compatriot, composer Olivier Messiaen, Péguy crafted the repeated phrase to evoke a sense of eternity's timelessness. "I Am Their Father, Says God" is translated from the French by Julian Green.

I am their father, says God. *Our Father who art in Heaven.* My son
told them often enough that I was their father.
I am their judge. My son told them so. I am also their father.
I am especially their father.
Well, I am their father. He who is a father is above all a father. *Our
        Father who art in Heaven.* He who has once been a father
        can be nothing else but a father.
They are my son's brothers; they are my children; I am their father.
*Our Father who art in Heaven,* my son taught them that prayer.
        *Sic ergo vos orabitis.* After this manner therefore pray ye.
*Our Father who art in Heaven,* he knew very well what he was doing
        that day, my son who loved them so.
Who lived among them, who was like one of them.
Who went as they did, who spoke as they did, who lived as they did.
Who suffered.
Who suffered as they did, who died as they did.
And who loved them so, having known them.
Who brought back to heaven a certain taste for man, a certain taste
        for the earth.
My son who loved them so, who loves them eternally in heaven.
He knew very well what he was doing that day, my son who loved
        them so.

When he put that barrier between them and me, *Our Father who art
        in Heaven,* those three or four words.
That barrier which my anger and perhaps my justice will never pass.
Blessed is the man who goes to sleep under the protection of that
        outpost, the outpost of those three or four words.

Those words that move ahead of every prayer like the hands of the
     suppliant in front of his face.
Like the two joined hands of the suppliant advancing before his face
     and the tears of his face.
Those three or four words that conquer me, the unconquerable.
And which they cause to go before their distress like two joined and
     invincible hands.
Those three or four words which move forward like a beautiful
     cutwater fronting a lowly ship.
Cutting the flood of my anger.
And when the cutwater has passed, the ship passes, and back of them
     the whole fleet.
That, actually, is the way I see them, says God;
During my eternity, eternally, says God.
Because of that invention of my Son's, thus must I eternally see them.
(And judge them. How do you expect me to judge them now.
After that.)
*Our Father who art in Heaven,* my son knew exactly what to do
In order to tie the arms of my justice and untie the arms of my mercy.
(I do not mention my anger, which has never been anything but my
     justice.
And sometimes my charity.)
And now I must judge them like a father. As if a father were any good
     as a judge. A *certain man had two sons.*
As if he were capable of judging. A *certain man had two sons.*
     We know well enough how a father judges. There is a famous
     example of that.


We know well enough how the father judged the son who had gone
     away and come back.
The father wept even more than the son.
That is the story my son has been telling them. My son gave them
The secret of judgement itself.
And now this is how they seem to me; this is how I see them;
This is how I am obliged to see them.
Just as the wake of a beautiful ship grows wider and wider until it
     disappears and loses itself,
But begins with a point, which is the point of the ship itself.
So the huge wake of sinners grows wider and wider until it disappears

and loses itself.

But it begins with a point, which is the point of the ship itself, and
     it is that point which comes towards me,

Which is turned towards me.

It begins with a point, which is the point of the ship itself.

And the ship is my own son, laden with all the sins of the world.

And the point of the ship is the two joined hands of my son.

And before the look of my anger and the look of my justice

They have all hidden behind him.

And all of that huge cortège of prayers, all of that huge wake grows
     wider and wider until it disappears and loses itself.

But it begins with a point and it is that point which is turned towards
     me.

Which advances towards me.

And that point is those three or four words: *Our Father who art in
     Heaven*; verily my son knew what he was doing.

And every prayer comes up to me hidden behind those three or four
     words. —

*Our Father who art in Heaven.* — And behind (these words) widens
     until it disappears and loses itself.

The wake of innumerable prayers

As they are spoken in their text for innumerable days

By innumerable men,

(By simple men, his brothers).

Morning prayers, evening prayers;

(Prayers said on all other occasions);

On so many other occasions during innumerable days;

Prayers for noon and for the whole day;

Prayers of monks for all hours of the day,

And for the hours of the night;

Laymen's prayers and clerics' prayers

As they were said innumerable times

For innumerable days.

(He spoke like them, he spoke with them, he spoke as one of them.)

All of that huge fleet of prayers laden with the sins of the world.

All of that huge fleet of prayers and penances attacks me

Having the spear you wot of,

Advances towards me having the spear you wot of.

It is a fleet of freighters, *classis oneraria*.

And a fleet of the line,
A combat fleet.
Like a beautiful fleet of yore, like a fleet of triremes
Advancing to attack the king.
And what do you expect me to do: I am attacked
And in that fleet, in that innumerable fleet
Each *Our Father* is like a high riding ship
Having itself its own spear, *Our Father who art in Heaven*
Turned towards me, and coming behind this selfsame spear.
*Our Father who art in Heaven,* not so smart after all. Of course,
      when a man says that, he can get behind what he has said.

# When You Fast

## *Matthew 6:16—18*

And whenever you fast, do not look dismal, like the hypocrites, for they disfigure their faces so as to show others that they are fasting. Truly I tell you, they have received their reward. But when you fast, put oil on your head and wash your face, so that your fasting may be seen not by others but by your Father who is in secret; and your Father in secret will reward you.

# A Hymn After Fasting

## PRUDENTIUS

[Aurelius Clemens Prudentius] Spain, c.348–410. Prudentius had two distinguished careers, first as a civil servant under emperor Theodosius and second, after his retirement from court at age 57, as a poet. Often judged "the first great Christian poet," he is also called "the Christian Virgil" because of his incorporation of Virgilian pastoral into his Christian lyrics. "A Hymn After Fasting" is translated from the Latin by Sister M. Clement Eagan.

Christ, the sovereign master of all Thy faithful,
Thou dost rule and guide us with reins that lightly
Curb our wayward tendencies, round us hedging
      Mild regulations.

Though Thou Thyself, laden with mortal body,
Didst endure hard labors and racking anguish,
Stern example setting, Thy hand is gentle
      On Thy dear servants.

Now the ninth hour turns the sun to his setting,
Which through scarce three parts of his course has glided,
Leaving yet one fourth of his shining journey
      Through the heavens.

Brief the fast we break at this hour appointed,
And our vigil ended, we now enjoy
Bounty spread on tables high to replenish
      Languishing nature.

Such the gracious love of the eternal Master,
So benign the counsel our kind Teacher gives us,
That observance of His law does not burden
      Man's feeble body.

Further, He ordains that none with sordid vesture
Clothe himself, nor his comely brow disfigure,
But fair make his face and his head ennoble
      With the hair's glory.

'When you fast,' He said, 'Keep the body stainless;
Let no sallow hue on your cheeks appearing
Drive away the roses, and let no pallor
      Whiten your visage.'

It is more just for us to hide with joy
All the good works done for the Father's glory,
For God who in secret sees all things hidden
      Will recompense us.

When one ailing sheep lags behind the others
And loses itself in the sylvan mazes,
Tearing its white fleece on the thorns and briers,
      Sharp in the brambles,

Unwearied the Shepherd, that lost one seeking,
Drives away the wolves and on His strong shoulders
Brings it home again to the fold's safekeeping,
      Healed and unsullied.

He brings it back to the green fields and meadows,
Where no thorn-bush waves with its cruel prickles,
Where no shaggy thistle arms trembling branches
      With its rough briers,

But where palm trees grow in the open woodland,
Where the lush grass bends its green leaves, and laurels
Shade the glassy streamlet of living water
      Ceaselessly flowing.

For all Thy gifts, O Shepherd true and faithful,
What service is meet ever to requite Thee?
For salvation's cost no devoted worship
      Makes due repayment.

Although by refraining from daily nurture
We should gladly weaken the laggard body,
Night and day spend singing Thy holy praises,
      Scorning all comfort,

This atoning service would not be equal
To the gift bestowed by the Heavenly Father,
And severe austerities would but shatter
        Frail earthen vessels.

Therefore, lest this fragile clay lose its vigor
And grow faint from watery fluids flowing
In the pallid veins, and the sickly body
        Perish with weakness,

Light and easy is the precept of fasting
Laid on all the faithful, and no stern rigor
Impels us; his own capacity urges
        Each to observe it.

Enough, if we sanctify all our actions
By invoking first the divine approval,
Whether we accept the food that is given
        Or shun the table.

God of His great bounty bestows these blessings
And with His favoring smile looks upon us,
As we take the bread we have dedicated,
        Trusting His goodness.

Grant, I humbly pray, that this food be healthful,
And as it spreads throughout all our members,
May we who adore Thee, O Christ, now nourish
        Body and spirit.

# Knock and the Door Will Be Opened

## Matthew 7:7–11

Ask, and it will be given you; search, and you will find; knock, and the door will be opened for you. For everyone who asks receives, and everyone who searches finds, and for everyone who knocks, the door will be opened. Is there anyone among you who, if your child asks for bread, will give a stone? Or if the child asks for a fish, will give a snake? If you then, who are evil, know how to give good gifts to your children, how much more will your Father in heaven give good things to those who ask him!

# Knock With Your Little Fist

## ANNA AKHMATOVA

Russia, 1889–1966. Revered in Russia for her resistance to government repression, Akhmatova expressed in her poetry the sufferings and longings that she shared with her compatriots during this turbulent century. Her first husband, NIKOLAI GUMILYOV, was executed by the Bolsheviks; her third husband died as a political prisoner. Though her poems were officially banned in her country for many years, they were memorized by millions of Russians. "Knock With Your Little Fist" is translated from the Russian by Judith Hemschemeyer.

Knock with your little fist—I will open.
I always opened the door to you.
I am beyond the high mountain now,
Beyond the desert, beyond the wind and the heat,
But I will never abandon you . . .
I didn't hear your groans,
You never asked me for bread.
Bring me a twig from the maple tree
Or simply a little green grass,
As you did last spring.
Bring me in your cupped palms
Some of our cool, pure, Neva water,
And I will wash the bloody traces
From your golden hair.

# Wolves in Sheep's Clothing

## Matthew 7:15

Beware of false prophets, who come to you in sheep's clothing but inwardly are ravenous wolves.

# The Need to Guard Oneself Against Wolves in Sheep's Clothing

## JACOPONE DA TODI

Italy, c.1230–1306. See page 291 for biographical information on this poet. "The Need to Guard Oneself Against Wolves in Sheep's Clothing" is translated from the Italian by Serge and Elizabeth Hughes.

O faithful soul, intent on salvation,
Beware the fangs of the wolf.

Beware the wolf who comes by stealth;
In the guise of a friend
He gains entry to your house,
Sure of deceiving you with his pious talk.

The Lord bless you for the counsel you give me!
You help to disentangle me from this web;
Their assaults have cut me off from help,
And I know not where to find refuge.

Be on guard; remember the Lord's warning
About the wolf disguised as a lamb.
By stealth he comes among the flock,
Then suddenly attacks and scatters them.

I will tell you a story that's hard to believe:
One came among us pretending to be a learned healer,
And once unmasked, set himself to poisoning those
Who had discovered and exposed his fraud.

Speak up; do not be afraid;
Now that you know, defend yourself.
Remember, once the wolf has you in his grip
He sinks his fangs into your throat.

But how can I defend myself when I am besieged
By those from whom I should expect counsel?

They act like lambs until I drop my guard,
And then quick as lightning they pounce.

Wisdom lies in trusting no one;
He who is bitten by a snake comes to fear the lizard.
Keep a wary eye on all sheep you do not know,
And your conscience will not reproach you.

# Here Are My Mother and My Brothers

*Mark 3:31–35*

Then his mother and his brothers came; and standing outside, they sent to him and called him. A crowd was sitting around him; and they said to him, "Your mother and your brothers and sisters are outside, asking for you." And he replied, "Who are my mother and my brothers?" And looking at those who sat around him, he said, "Here are my mother and my brothers! Whoever does the will of God is my brother and sister and mother."

# Jesus and His Relatives

PAUL WEGNER

Germany, 1887–?. Born in Flatow, Wegner was awarded the Doctor of Philosophy and lived after World War I in Berlin. "Jesus and His Relatives" is translated from the German by George Dardess.

His Word delivered, he stood apart
in a glow among them. His heart
still rang, overcome by its own beat,
like the swinging clapper of a mighty bell.

And his glance, rapt in the spell
of God's face, shuddered like the sea
in the sun's kiss, glittering cool, empty,
amid the swarm of men, the swooning girls.

He still stood, arm outfurled
in blessing posture, yet
just as if there were no columns, roof, or wall
but only himself towering over them all,
over a distant Here, a There right under his feet.

A disciple touched his cloak.
"Mary, your mother, spoke
to me, told me to call you.
She's just outside. Your brothers too."

Hesitating, he turned
like one facing the plunge
from the clear burn
of the evening sky
into a dingy night.
His family stood before him.
His voice was black.
"Who gave you all the right
to say 'my son,' 'my brother,' to me?
My God made me a light
to this whole blundering crew,

not just to you, or you.
You have no claim on me.
To possess and be possessed is your obsession.
My will is my own—
I am my own possession
by being God's.
For who takes God into himself
must be alone.

# from *A Woman Wrapped in Silence*

JOHN W. LYNCH

U.S., 1904–1990. See page 60 for biographical information on this poet.

The inference is left us that He turned
Away then, and continued on with speech
That had endured this small parenthesis,
But was resumed again, oblivious
Of all save that He had a more considered
And a longer word to tell to them.
He had been interrupted, but His voice
Broke strong again, and they were listening.

She felt attention tighten, and around
Her shoulders strained and pushed ahead, and little
Shuffles moved them closer in. He'd had
Enough of pause. They had distracted Him
A moment with the word of her. He'd learned
That she was near, that she was near and stood
So, just beyond the crowd's edge and had come
To Him, and like a man who hewed to larger
Business, He'd dismissed her and gone on,
Forgetting her.

                    She'd heard Him. She had heard
These sentences and knew them. They were hers.
She'd known they were to be, and that they'd fall
For her and were to be her own against
A world of men that might be free in them,
But could not own them, nor the pain in them
As she would own. This is her day's completion.
This is night, fulfillment. This is thrusted
Sword that had been entered to the wound,
The hurt, the pain of now, the bared pain, stark
And stripped of more delay and faced to her.
She'd held this hour and tried in prophecy
The sharpened edge of it. Had she not heard
That one day He'd be gone and would be gone

Without her? That she'd keep no part, and He
No plan, nor place, nor reference for her?
He'd asked her once did she not know of this!

She'd grown since then, in strength, for that was long
Ago when she was young, and she'd not had
The years to ponder then, nor words of His
To turn in hid foreboding of a way
That would be hers. She was not now untutored,
Unprepared, with inner strength unlearned
And tentative, and standing here, she should
Not now be quivering by any anguish
Keener than the years had taught to her.
She should have known of this, and in her heart
She had perceived His words were only meanings
Risen up to hard and present outlines
Out of dreams. But she'd not grown so far,
Nor come to such acceptance, she was lost
To all except a bloodless revery
That said, "How true," and gave a little sigh
And turned away.

                    She was a woman here,
A woman who had seen a long love close
To her; who heard a sound that was an end
Awaited, and who knew that no appeal
Or cry or staggering of hers could stay
This certainty, or turn again the sound
Until it still was only time expected
And not time begun. She was a life
That came to withering within a word,
That felt a sudden silence fall and widen
Till the brief endurance through the length
Of only one quick breathing, seemed a space
That had no edge, beginning, nor progression,
And would have no end. She was a woman
Who was made bereft, who felt a pall
Close suddenly upon a warmth that had
Been hers against a hundred lesser pains,

And now was gone. And she'd not grown beyond
The reach of *that* denial, nor advanced
By any prayer or virtue to a sphere
Where loss of Him could be another loss
Than what was hers to bear and what was real.
She knew no time that was pretended time.
We must not mistranslate the dark scars healed
Above the wounds. She'd heard the word He spoke.
She stood here lonely at Capharnaum,
And when her hand had fallen from her brow,
And strove no more to give a shade against
The sun that she might see, and find Him there,
And when she moved away and left Him speaking
On, and did not pause, nor turn, nor waver,
She had gone one distance more, and found
Almost her last maturity.

# The Scorner (2)

## GÉRALD FÉLIX TCHICAYA U TAM'SI

Congo, 1931–1988. From age 15 until his death, U Tam'si lived in voluntary
exile in France. Like most African poets educated under European colo-
nialism, he agonized over tensions between his African heritage and adopted
European culture. But wry self-mockery joins political critique in U Tam'si's
poetic voice. "The Scorner," a sequence of six poems addressed to Christ, was
written during the 1960 Congolese Civil War, when U Tam'si returned briefly
to Leopoldville to edit its daily newspaper. In his anguish at his country's self-
destruction, the poet both identifies with and scorns Christ. "The Scorner (2)"
is translated from the French by Gerald Moore.

Am I only your brother
They have already killed me in your name
Was I guilty of my death
I held all the shadow of love's flowers at my eyes
my hands played like latania palms at evening
In kissing your cross my mouth was stained with blood

Was I not your brother
I dance at your sadness
I take neither father nor mother to witness
for me but my sadness equals yours
The water of my river is sweet fly swallows
The rock loves the sea which beats it wildly and lazily

You tempt me
and I rejoice
I am lost in the music of your soul
though it is only the false singing of hogs
And I dance in death for the slow sadness
The vices in my flesh are the three iron nails
in your hands and your feet
But you soil yourself by mixing with the bourgeois
Their luxury is a golden calf on the necks of their wives

# Take Up the Cross

*Matthew 10:38*

Whoever does not take up the cross and follow me is not worthy of me.

# The Progeny of Cain

NIKOLAI GUMILYOV

Russia, 1886–1921. See page 3 for biographical information on this poet. "The Progeny of Cain" is translated from the Russian by Simon Franklin.

He did not lie to us, that spirit, mournfully severe,
Whose name was borrowed from the morning star,
When he said: "Don't fear requital from above;
Taste the fruit, and you will be as gods."

For youths all roads were opened,
For elders—all forbidden works,
For girls—amber fruits,
And unicorns white as snow.

But why, then, do we stoop in impotence,
Feeling, perhaps, that Some One has forgotten us,
Seeing, perhaps, the horror of that first temptation,
Whenever any hand unites
Two sticks, two blades of grass, two poles,
Into a casual, momentary cross?

# Come to Me All Who Are Weary

## *Matthew 11:28—30*

Come to me, all you that are weary and are carrying heavy burdens, and I will give you rest. Take my yoke upon you, and learn from me; for I am gentle and humble in heart, and you will find rest for your souls. For my yoke is easy, and my burden is light.

# I Tire So Beneath This Ancient Load
## Sonnet 81 from *Rime Sparse*

PETRARCH

[Francesco Petrarca] Italy, 1303–1374. In Petrarch's *Rime Sparse*, the most influential sequence of love lyrics ever written in the vernacular, Sonnet 81 is one of the few poems that touch on Gospel themes. The poem's simple and direct appeal for Christian salvation contrasts strongly with the intricate linguistic play of the rest of the sequence. Throughout his career, Petrarch's attitude toward the Church was highly ambivalent; he was the first to describe its thousand year supremacy after the Fall of Rome as "the Dark Ages." "I Tire So Beneath This Ancient Load" is translated from the Italian by Jack Roberts.

I tire so beneath this ancient load
of sin and bitter use: I pray
I will not falter on the way
and fall into the hands of my foe.

True, once a great friend eased it so
in his ineffable courtesy;
but then he hastened off so quickly
that soon I had no friend to behold.

Even so, his voice rings from above:
"O you who labor, here is the way;
Come to me, if the way stands clear."

What grace, what love, O what fate
will grant me wings as of a dove,
that I might rest and fly from here?

# Paradox

VASSAR MILLER

U.S., 1924–. See page 146 for biographical information on this poet.

Mild yoke of Christ, most harsh to me not bearing,
You bruise the neck that balks, the hands that break you;
Sweet bread and wine, bitter to me not sharing,
You scar and scorch the throat that will not take you;
Mount where He taught, you cripple feet not bloody
From your sharp flints of eight-fold benediction;
Bright cross, most shameful stripped of the stripped body,
You crucify me safe from crucifixion:
Yet I, who am my own dilemma, jolting
My mind with thought lest it unthink its stiffness,
Rise to revolt against my own revolting.
Blind me to blindness, deafen me to deafness.
So will Your gifts of sight and hearing plunder
My eyes with lightning and my ears with thunder.

# I Have Come to Cast Fire

*Luke 12:49*

I came to bring fire to the earth, and how I wish it were already kindled!

# Fire

## from *The Christ of Velasquez*

MIGUEL DE UNAMUNO

Spain, 1864–1936. See page 77 for biographical information on this poet. "Fire" is translated from the Spanish by Y. R. Pérez.

Fire you came to cast upon the earth
fire, You Yourself, a raining white light.
Fire tongues upon your apostles
descended—You in glory—tongues
of the Word made Man in the dome
of the heavens;
of the luminous body
that sustains itself on fish—offspring of water—
silent and cold fish of the abyss
that makes its nest far beneath raging gales.

You are fire, which ever rises toward heaven
seeking the sun, its father, its home forever,
fire which sets ablaze our blood and burns
the flesh of sin, the pulp of the fruit
of the tree of knowledge, for your blood
is fire on the cross, Seraph of Sorrow;
yes truly you are the Seraph, glowing ember
of love, rose of the tree of the cross.

Two black wings envelop your head,
a pair hovered about your feet
on the heights of Tabor and of Calvary,
and You fly to your Father, with your arms,
wings of fire, splitting the darkness.
And the joints of your cross shudder
at the mystical rumbling of your flight.

# The Needle's Eye

*Mark 10:23–25*

Then Jesus looked around and said to his disciples, "How hard it will be for those who have wealth to enter the kingdom of God!" And the disciples were perplexed at these words. But Jesus said to them again, "Children, how hard it is to enter the kingdom of God! It is easier for a camel to go through the eye of a needle than for someone who is rich to enter the kingdom of God."

# Humility Is the Eye of the Needle

YELENA RUBISOVA

Russia, 1910?–. Humility is an appropriate theme for Yelena Rubisova, who lived in relative obscurity as an emigré in France. Very little is known of her life. "Humility Is the Eye of the Needle" is translated from the Russian by Thomas E. Bird.

> Humility is the eye of the needle
> And I am a camel, hulking, clumsy.
> Go through! Go through! And suddenly everything
> Is easy and simple and paradise for us, mortals, ordained.
>
> In the sandy sea the waves are yellow,
> Among them I am lost, a desert ship.
> O God, let me go through! Let the Will of the Pilot
> Henceforth change the set of sail.
>
> Let me become like thread, and put anxiety aside,
> So the doorkeeper's hand will lead
> Me through the triumphal gates
> Of the eye of the needle.

# The Greatest Commandment

*Mark 12:28—31*

One of the scribes came near and heard them disputing with one another, and seeing that he answered them well, he asked him, "Which commandment is the first of all?" Jesus answered, "The first is, 'Hear, O Israel: the Lord our God, the Lord is one; you shall love the Lord your God with all your heart, and with all your soul, and with all your mind, and with all your strength.' The second is this, 'You shall love your neighbor as yourself.' There is no other commandment greater than these."

# As Thyself!

D. H. LAWRENCE

England, 1885–1930. See page 295 for biographical information on this poet.

Supposing I say: dogs are my neighbours
I will love dogs as myself!

Then gradually I approximate to the dog,
wriggle and wag and slaver, and get the mentality of a dog!
This I call a shocking humiliation.

The same with my robot neighbours.
If I try loving them, I fall into their robot jig-jig-jig,
their robot cachinnation comes rattling out of my throat—
and I had better even have approximated to the dog.

Who then, O Jesus, is my neighbour?
If you point me to that fat money-smelling man in a motor-car,
or that hard-boiled young woman beside him
I shall have to refuse entirely to accept either of them.

My neighbour is not the man in the street, and never was:
he jigs along in the imbecile cruelty of the machine
and is implacable.

My neighbour, O my neighbour!
Occasionally I see him, silent, a little wondering
with his ears pricked and his body wincing
threading his way among the robot machine-people.

O my neighbour
sometimes I see her, like a flower, nodding her way and shrinking
from the robot contact on every hand!

How can that be my neighbour
which I shrink from!

# Love of One's Neighbor

MAX JACOB

France, 1876–1944. A poet and painter who combined the roles of humorist and mystic, Jacob was, during the early years of the century, a close friend of Picasso and Apollinaire. He became a mentor to younger poets after the Armistice. A Jew, he converted to Catholicism in 1915 after having seen a vision of Christ on one of his watercolors hanging on the wall. His poetry then became a kind of clowning before the Lord. Forced to wear the yellow star during World War II, he died at the Nazi concentration camp in Drancy. "Love of One's Neighbor" is translated from the French by Wallace Fowlie.

Who saw the toad cross the street? He's a very small man. A doll isn't smaller. He drags himself on his knees. Might you say he's ashamed? No, he has rheumatism. One leg drags behind and he brings it forward! Where is he going? The poor clown comes out of the sewer. No one noticed this toad in the street. At one time no one paid any attention to me in the street, and now the children make fun of my yellow star. Happy toad! you have no yellow star.

# Proverbs and Songs (XLII)

ANTONIO MACHADO Y RUIZO

Spain, 1875–1939. One of Spain's leading modernist poets, Machado wrote a pristine, denuded verse. "Christ teaches . . . " is from a series of ninety-nine "Proverbs and Songs." "Proverbs and Songs (XLII)" is translated from the Spanish by Alan S. Trueblood.

> Christ teaches love your neighbor
> as yourself. But never forget
> he is someone else.

# The Stones Would Shout

## Luke 19:37–40

As [Jesus] was now approaching the path down from the Mount of Olives, the whole multitude of the disciples began to praise God joyfully with a loud voice for all the deeds of power that they had seen, saying,

"Blessed is the king
> who comes in the name of the Lord!
Peace in heaven,
> and glory in the highest heaven!"

Some of the Pharisees in the crowd said to him, "Teacher, order your disciples to stop." He answered, "I tell you, if these were silent, the stones would shout out."

# The Amen of the Stones

LUDWIG THEOBUL KOSEGARTEN

Germany, 1758–1818. A pastor's son, Kosegarten took orders after studying theology at Greifswald University. After some time as pastor in Rügen, he returned to Greifswald as professor of theology. His *Gedichte* was published in 1776; later he wrote two sentimental hexameter epics, for which he is best known. "The Amen of the Stones" is translated from the German by Charles T. Brooks, D.D.

Blind with old age, the Venerable Bede
Ceased not, for that, to preach and publish forth
The news from heaven,—the tidings of great joy.
From town to town—through all the villages—
With trusty guidance, roamed the aged saint,
And preached the word with all the fire of youth.

One day his boy had led him to a vale
That lay all thickly sowed with mighty rocks.
In mischief more than malice spake the boy:
"Most reverend father! there are many men
Assembled here, who wait to hear thy voice."

The blind old man, so bowed, straightway rose up,
Chose him his text, expounded, then applied,
Exhorted, warned, rebuked, and comforted,
So fervently, that soon the gushing tears
Streamed thick and fast down to his hoary beard.
When, at the close, as seemeth always meet,
He prayed, "Our Father," and pronounced aloud,
"Thine is the kingdom and the power,—thine
The glory now and through eternity,"—
At once there rang through all that echoing vale
A sound of many thousand voices crying,
"Amen! most reverend sire, amen! amen!"

Trembling with terror and remorse, the boy
Knelt down before the saint, and owned his sin.
"Son," said the old man, "hast thou then never read,
'When men are dumb, the stones shall cry aloud'?—

Henceforward mock not, son, the word of God!
Living it is, and mighty, cutting sharp,
Like a two-edged sword. And when the heart
Of flesh grows hard and stubborn as the stone,
A heart of flesh shall stir in stones themselves!"

# I Am Not of This World

## John 8:21–23

Again he said to them, "I am going away, and you will search for me, but you will die in your sin. Where I am going, you cannot come." Then the Jews said, "Is he going to kill himself? Is that what he means by saying, 'Where I am going, you cannot come'?" He said to them, "You are from below, I am from above; you are of this world, I am not of this world."

# Explanation Without Words

SIMON ZHAO

China, 1925?–. Zhao and his wife were imprisoned in 1951 for working to spread Christianity in a remote Chinese province. Though his wife died in prison in 1960, Zhao did not know until 1973. "Explanation without Words" is his response to the news. Released in the 1980s, he remains an active pastor, writing poems and hymns to encourage Chinese Christians. "Explanation Without Words" is translated from the Chinese by Kim-Kwong Chan and Alan Hunter.


Some people
To evaluate the life                         of a dead person
As a yard-stick                              use social effect
(i.e. what and                               how much that person
contributed to society)

Some people
To evaluate the life                         of a dead person
As a yard-stick                              use the beauty of a garland
(i.e. the magnificent                        but spurious things
associated with the dead person)

Other people
To evaluate the life                         of a dead person
As a yard-stick                              use sunglasses
(i.e. everything                             is black
associated with the dead person)

She alone used her own blood
Explained without words that
To evaluate the life of a dead person
As a yard-stick                              use the dead person's blood

(but as for her blood, nobody cared to look)
Although she was part of the world
She did not belong to the world
Her body was abandoned at an unmarked burial ground
Her corpse bore witness to the Lord

The theoretical logic of this world
Also left her far away          far away

Ah   eyes attached to this world—
How can they recognize footprints of heaven
When the love of God    sacrificed on the cross
Consumed her like fire
In the midst of fire          from the altar of sacrifice

# I Am the Good Shepherd

## *John 10:14–15, 27–28a*

I am the good shepherd. I know my own and my own know me, just as the Father knows me and I know the Father. And I lay down my life for the sheep. . . . My sheep hear my voice. I know them, and they follow me. I give them eternal life, and they will never perish.

# Shepherd Who With Your Tender Calls

## FELIX LOPE DE VEGA Y CARPIO

Spain, 1562–1613. Famous for writing 1500 plays, of which 500 survive, Lope de Vega also wrote some of Spanish literature's fondest religious sonnets. "Shepherd Who With Your Tender Calls" *(Pastor que con tus silbos amorosos)* is one of his most widely anthologized poems in Spain. "Shepherd Who With. . ." is translated from the Spanish by Kate Flores.

Shepherd who with your tender calls
From deep slumber has wakened me,
You who made of this log the staff
On which your powerful arms are held,

Upon my faith turn your pitying eyes,
For I confess you my love and lord,
And to follow you pledge my word,
Your beauteous feet and calls so mild.

Hear me, Shepherd who dies for love,
Flinch not at my frightful sins,
You to the humbled so much a friend,

Stay, and let my cares be heard . . .
Though why do I ask that you stay for me,
When to make you stay your feet are nailed?

# The Last Judgment

*Mark 13:5a, 7–8, 19*

Then Jesus began to say to them, ". . . When you hear of wars and rumors of wars, do not be alarmed; this must take place, but the end is still to come. For nation will rise against nation, and kingdom against kingdom; there will be earthquakes in various places; there will be famines. This is but the beginning of the birth pangs. . . . For in those days there will be suffering, such as has not been from the beginning of the creation that God created until now, no, and never will be."

# Judgement Day

ODIA OFEIMUN

Nigeria, 1950–. Called the Jeremiah of modern Nigeria, Ofeimun writes angry
poetry attacking the pomposity of those in power in his country. "Judgement
Day" is typical of the energetic satire with which he decries "public sins."

They will tumble down from rooftops
treetops and hilltops
where they once glowed with the bravura of gods
Their bloated robes smudged by public sins
will billow in the winds as they squirm and gutter
rocking to unbelief the sheep, the touts and clowns
who bleated 'Amen' to their every whip and lash.
They will tumble down
From their towers of illusions,
they will tumble down as they awaken
to the speed of thunderbolts, nemetic music
Their ears, deal to hometruths
will flap in their bullfrog run
amidst the leer and contempt
aimed by the menials
yesterday's carriers of gongs and talking drums
who spread hossana-green palmfronds
halleluyah palmfronds
for their motorcades

They will fall from the dais
dazed by hammerblows
shunned by the neon-lights that once called them,
the feverish handclaps which saw them through,
from whoredoms to whirldoms of insentiate grogginess
They will fall from the dais
bald lives, vultures with clipped wings
They will fall to be received by the sizzling spittle
the aimed rejection, our collective spite
And if they still outwit
the contrition that is theirs
through overdrafts from their long-filliped sin

And if they still outwit the shame that is theirs
in the pride-tall sins that have swamped us all
they cannot escape the healing floods
the legations of looming storms that will break
storms that will stick their hearts to the roofs of their mouths
making of them cheap rodents in the blitz
that must weed and sweep the streets
sweeping away the banana skins
that have slimed and could slime
the path of those who would rather throw
than be thrown by the ghomids of public sins.

## Luke 21:25–27

There will be signs in the sun, the moon, and the stars, and on the earth distress among nations confused by the roaring of the sea and the waves. People will faint from fear and foreboding of what is coming upon the world, for the powers of the heavens will be shaken. Then they will see 'the Son of Man coming in a cloud' with power and great glory.

# In Emanuel's Nightmare:
# Another Coming of Christ

GWENDOLYN BROOKS

U.S., 1917–. Through a long, distinguished poetic career, Brooks has crafted a range of voices to express African American experience. Her ballad of Black life in Chicago, *Annie Allen*, won her the Pulitzer Prize for Poetry in 1950.

*(Speaks, among spirit questioners, of marvelous spirit affairs.)*

There had been quiet all that afternoon.
Just such a quiet afternoon as any,
Though with a brighter and a freer air.
The sleepy sun sat on us, and those clouds
Dragged dreamily. Well, it was interesting—
How silence could give place to such a noise.
But now—is noise the word? Is that exact?
I think not.

I'll try to name it. Naming is my line.
I won the Great War-Naming Contest. Ah,
I put it over on them all. I beat
Them all. I wear an honor on my name—
Sound wasn't in it. Though it was loud enough.
I'd say it was a heat.

But it took us. Did with us as it would.
Wound us in balls, unraveled, wound again.
And women screamed, "The Judgment Day has come."
And little children gathered up the cry.
It was then that they knocked each other down
To get to—Where? But they were used to Doors.
Thought they had but to beat their Fellow Man
To get to and get out of one again.

It wasn't Judgment Day. (For we are here.)
And presently the people knew, and sighed.
Out of that heaven a most beautiful Man
Came down. But now is coming quite the word?

It wasn't coming. I'd say it was—a Birth.
The man was born out of the heaven, in truth.
Yet no parturient creature ever knew
That naturalness, that hurtlessness, that ease.

How He was tall and strong!
How He was cold-browed! How He mildly smiled!
How the voice played on the heavy hope of the air
And loved our hearts out!
Why, it was such a voice as gave me eyes
To see my Fellow Man of all the world,
There with me, listening.

He had come down, He said, to clean the earth
Of the dirtiness of war.

Now tell of why His power failed Him there?
His power did not fail. It was that, simply,
He found how much the people wanted war.
How much it was their creed, and their good joy.
And what they lived for. He had not the heart
To take away their chief sweet delectation.

We tear—as a decent gesture, a tact—we tear
Laxly again at our lax, our tired hair.

The people wanted war. War's in their hearts.
    (In me, in your snag-toothed fool
Who won the Great War-Naming Contest and
All the years since has bragged how he did Beat
His Fellow Man.) It is the human aim.
Without, there would be no hate. No Diplomats.
And households would be fresh and frictionless.

God's Son went home. Among us it is whispered
He cried the tears of men.

Feeling, in fact,
We have no need of peace.

# Separating the Sheep from the Goats

## Matthew 25:31−33

When the Son of Man comes in his glory, and all the angels with him, then he will sit on the throne of his glory. All the nations will be gathered before him, and he will separate people one from another as a shepherd separates the sheep from the goats, and he will put the sheep at his right hand and the goats at the left.

# A Bidding Grace

A. D. HOPE

Australia, 1907–. One of the twentieth century's rare poets of wit and classicism, Hope was born in Coomo in New South Wales and educated both at Sydney University and Oxford. Hope, who converted to Catholicism (one of his most esteemed poems is the "Ode on the Death of Pius the Twelfth"), was nearly fifty when he published his first volume of poetry. For many years he was Professor of English at the Australian National University at Canberra.

For what we are about to hear, Lord, Lord,
The dreadful judgement, the unguessed reprieve,
The brief, the battering, the jubilant chord
Of trumpets quickening this guilty dust,
Which still would hide from what it shall receive,
Lord, make us thankful to be what we must.

For what we are now about to lose, reprove,
Assuage or comfort, Lord, this greedy flesh,
Still grieving, still rebellious, still in love,
Still prodigal of treasure still unspent.
Teach the blood weaving through its intricate mesh
The sigh, the solace, the silence of consent.

For what we are about to learn too late, too late
To save, though we repent with tears of blood:
The innocent ruined, the gentle taught to hate,
The love we made a means to its despair —
For all we have done or did not when we could,
Redouble on us the evil these must bear.

For what we are about to say, urge, plead,
The specious argument, the lame excuse,
Prompt our contempt. When these archangels read
Our trivial balance, lest the shabby bill
Tempt to that abjectness which begs or sues,
Leaves us one noble impulse: to be still.

For what we are about to act, the lust, the lie
That works unbidden, even now restrain
This reckless heart. Though doomed indeed to die,
Grant that we may, still trembling at the bar
Of Justice in the thud of fiery rain,
Acknowledge at last the truth of what we are.

In all we are about to receive, last, last,
Lord, help us bear our part with all men born
And, after judgement given and sentence passed,
Even at this uttermost, measured in thy gaze,
Though in thy mercy, for the rest to mourn,
Though in thy wrath we stand, to stand and praise.

# Whatever You Do
# for the Least of These

*Matthew 25:34–40*

"Then the king will say to those at his right hand, 'Come, you that are blessed by my Father, inherit the kingdom prepared for you from the foundation of the world; for I was hungry and you gave me food, I was thirsty and you gave me something to drink, I was a stranger and you welcomed me, I was naked and you gave me clothing, I was sick and you took care of me, I was in prison and you visited me.' Then the righteous will answer him, 'Lord, when was it that we saw you hungry and gave you food, or thirsty and gave you something to drink? And when was it that we saw you a stranger and welcomed you, or naked and gave you clothing? And when was it that we saw you sick or in prison and visited you?' And the king will answer them, 'Truly I tell you, just as you did it to one of the least of these who are members of my family, you did it to me.'"

# On the Swag

R. A. K. MASON

New Zealand, 1905–1971. See page 109 for biographical information on this poet.

His body doubled
under the pack
that sprawls untidily
on his old back
the cold wet dead-beat
plods up the track.

The cook peers out:
'oh curse that old lag—
here again
with his clumsy swag
made of a dirty old
turnip bag.'

'Bring him in cook
from the grey level sleet
put silk on his body
slippers on his feet,
give him fire
and bread and meat.

Let the fruit be plucked
and the cake be iced,
the bed be snug
and the wine be spiced
in the old cove's night-cap:
for this is Christ.'

# PART SEVEN

# FINAL JERUSALEM MINISTRY

# The Triumphal Entry into Jerusalem

*Matthew 21:1—9*

When they had come near Jerusalem and had reached Bethphage, at the Mount of Olives, Jesus sent two disciples, saying to them, "Go into the village ahead of you, and immediately you will find a donkey tied, and a colt with her; untie them and bring them to me. If anyone says anything to you, just say this, 'The Lord needs them.' And he will send them immediately." This took place to fulfill what had been spoken through the prophet, saying,

"Tell the daughter of Zion,

Look, your king is coming to you,

humble, and mounted on a donkey,

and on a colt, the foal of a donkey."

The disciples went and did as Jesus had directed them; they brought the donkey and the colt, and put their cloaks on them, and he sat on them. A very large crowd spread their cloaks on the road, and others cut branches from the trees and spread them on the road. The crowds that went ahead of him and that followed were shouting,

"Hosanna to the Son of David!

Blessed is the one who comes in the name of the Lord!

Hosanna in the highest heaven!"

# Hymn to Christ the Saviour

## CLEMENT OF ALEXANDRIA

Egypt, c.150–215. An independent Christian teacher who did much to recon-
cile Christianity with Greek philosophy and to defend it from the esoteric doc-
trines of Gnosticism, Clement prepared for baptism the younger members of
cultivated Christian families in the Greek community of Alexandria. His
"Hymn to Christ the Saviour" may have served as the school song. "Hymn to
Christ the Saviour" is translated from the Greek by Walter Mitchell.

You who bridle colts untamed,
who wing unerring birds in flight,
who steer ships along their course
and shepherd the royal lambs,
gather together
your artless children
for honest praising,
guileless hymning
of Christ, the guide of his children.

King of the saints,
invincible Word
of the Father most High,
wisdom's Prince,
Ground of exertion,
eternal Joy;
Jesus, Saviour
of this mortal race,
you the Shepherd,
Cultivator,
you the Helmsman
and the Rider,
you the Wing that lifts to heaven
all the company of the saints;
Fisher of men:
them you came to deliver
from the waters of sin;
to fish untainted
by the envious sea
you cast the bait

of sweet fresh life.
Guide your flock
of spiritual sheep;
guide, holy King,
guide your unsullied children.
The prints of Christ's feet
show the way to heaven.

Word everlasting,
Age without end,
undying Light,
Fountain of mercy,
Doer of virtuous deeds,
exalted Life
of them that sing God's praises.

Jesus Christ,
celestial Milk out-pressed
from a young bride's fragrant breasts
(your Wisdom's graces),
your little children
with their tender mouths
slake their thirst there,
drink their fill
of the Spirit flowing
from those incorporeal nipples.

Let us together
sing simple praises,
true hymns
to Christ the King,
our blessed reward
(such is his life-giving teaching).

With hearts undivided
let us sing to the Son in his might.
Votaries of peace,
we the Christ-born,
people of wisdom,
hymn we together
the God of tranquillity.

# Gloria, Laus et Honor

## THEODULF OF ORLEANS

Spain, c.750–821. Theodulf rose high in Charlesmagne's court, the emperor making him bishop of Orleans and abbot of Fleury, then later his chief theological adviser. Imprisoned on suspicion of treason by Charlesmagne's son and successor, Louis the Pious, Theodulf is said to have composed "Gloria, Laus et Honor" in his cell and to have sung it from behind bars as the king passed in procession on Palm Sunday, 821. The king, according to legend, was so moved that he ordered Theodulf's immediate release. "Gloria, Laus et Honor" is translated from the Latin by John Mason Neale.

*All glory, laud, and honour*
*To thee, Redeemer, King,*
*To whom the lips of children*
*Made sweet hosannas ring.*

Thou art the King of Israel,
Thou David's royal Son,
Who in the Lord's name comest,
The King and Blessed One.

The company of angels
Are praising thee on high,
And mortal men and all things
Created make reply.

The people of the Hebrews
With palms before thee went;
Our praise and prayer and anthems
Before thee we present.

In hastening to thy Passion,
They raised their hymns of praise;
In reigning 'midst thy glory,
Our melody we raise.

Thou didst accept their praises:
Accept the prayers we bring,
Who in all good delightest,
Thou good and gracious King.

# Palm Sunday

## GIAMBATTISTA MARINO

Italy, 1569–1625. Known for his ornate poetry, Marino was one of the most influential poets of his time. His rhetorical exaggerations and emphasis on novelty were widely imitated, and the term "Marinism" was coined to designate his version of the baroque style. Though often protected by powerful patrons, Marino courted trouble through his unruly conduct and satirical verse and in 1615 was forced to leave Italy for Paris, where he found refuge and recognition at the court of Louis XIII. "Palm Sunday" is translated from the Italian by Thomas Stanley.

> Where thy victorious feet, Great God, should tread,
>   In honor this green tapestry is spread;
> And as all future things are past to thee,
>   The triumph here precedes the victory.

# Easter

WOLE SOYINKA

Nigeria, 1934–. Educated in England, Soyinka was director of the Drama School of Ibadan University in Nigeria until 1967, when he was arrested for his support of secessionist Biafra. He spent nearly two years in prison. Soyinka's writings include both poetry and plays, and often combine a radical political vision with intense sympathy for ancient folk wisdom. In 1986 he became the first African to win the Nobel Prize for Literature.

> This slow day dies, a wordless wilt
> Shades of silence reaping
> Soft frangipanes
>
> Pollen's wings are thorned; bosoms
> Too welcoming fold later chills
> Take death to innocents
>
> Kinder these hard mangoes, greendrops
> At the ear of god-apparent, coquettes
> To the future decadence.
>
> Do we not truly fear to bleed? We hunt
> Pale tissues of the palm, fingers groping
> Ever cautious on the crown.
>
> These pink frangipanes of Easter crop
> Eager to the wind; by repetition weak
> And rain's in-breeding,
>
> One bough to slake the millions? Decay
> Caulks earth's centre; spurned we pluck
> Bleached petals for the dreamer's lair.
>
> Borne passive on this gift, wound-splashes
> From wind scavenger, sap fragrance for
> A heady brew, I rode my winged ass and raged—
>
> As children wove frond yellow from the palm
> Plucked at the core, within the spadix heart.

# Palm Sunday

ADAM ZAGAJEWSKI

Poland, 1945 –. Born in Lvov, Zagajewski grew up in Krakow and studied phi-
losophy at the Jagiellonian University. The author of several highly acclaimed
volumes of poetry and essays, he lives in Paris and teaches periodically in
the United States. "Palm Sunday" is translated from the Polish by Renata
Gorczynski.

> Christ crucified at daybreak,
> a week too early, unshaven,
> in soiled clothes, with a grimace
> of bewilderment on his skinny face,
> surrounded by soldiers
> in half-buttoned uniforms,
> nailed to the wood in haste.
> The exaltations of the Week called off,
> murky Wednesday and the hatred of Friday.
> They discontinued the retreat
> and the mystical ascent
> of adolescent boys, we've lost our chance for
> the seven ascetic days, there's no time
> for penance, new feasts are forthcoming,
> full of the unknown triumphs of fire.

# Jesus's Lament Over Jerusalem

*Luke 19:41–44*

As he came near [Jerusalem] and saw the city, he wept over it, saying, "If you, even you, had only recognized on this day the things that make for peace! But now they are hidden from your eyes. Indeed, the days will come upon you, when your enemies will set up ramparts around you and surround you, and hem you in on every side. They will crush you to the ground, you and your children within you, and they will not leave within you one stone upon another; because you did not recognize the time of your visitation from God."

# The Destruction of Jerusalem

GYÖRGY RÓNAY

Hungary, 1913–1978. See page 91 for biographical information on this poet. "The Destruction of Jerusalem" is set during the siege of Budapest at the start of 1945, when for two months the Russian army fought to capture the city from the Germans, with the Hungarians caught in the middle of the horror. "The Destruction of Jerusalem" is translated from the Hungarian by Dalma Hunyadi Brunauer.

Here before your door I stand and knock—said the Lord
and stood before the door and knocked     Jerusalem's
every door was locked     in vain the Lord rapped
and pleaded   doors hearts houses windows
everything was locked.

                   He knocked and already there banged
the hail   He knocked and His fists
were bleeding     every door was locked
and He wept: City the hour
of your visitation has come     I'm here, I'm knocking
and it is not opened to me!     I see already the destruction
no stone remains upon stone, hear ye?     Here come the
eagles claws infant cries pestilence
and begs for food

             and He saw already the Beast
and the Hell of explosives.

                 The city was throbbing
it had no time to open for Him it was bargaining
the Ancient of the City just sold his temple
no one had time     nasty punks with machine-guns were
herding trembling women     on the Danube
corpses were floating     blood-oozing, blind-eyed
corpses like bloated boats.

                 I'm knocking
said He for the last time.

                 Armed men ransacked
houses     War arrived.

                 He knocked
and covered His face.

                 Night wild night blind night

blindly surging blood-soaked night!

                                War

knocked and locks fell and walls
collapsed homes toppled gods
whined and crumbled among the carrion
with turned-out-eyes and straw-filled innards.        Night wild night
blind night deadly night!
Under the scarlet ruins the
suffocating people imprisoned
in bunkers were knocking but every door was locked
every exit was cocked      in the streets
bullets were hissing        in the sky with flaming
swords angry angels were chasing
the souls of the damned—

                                Judas strewing his silver
money thirty pieces of silver among
exploding rockets' cutting glare runs
his neck in a rope

                and the winter wind blew the snow whistled
they ate every rat every newborn
they chewed off their own arms and thighs
and they froze to death and burned and died and
no stone remained on stone.
As it was foretold.

# Cleansing the Temple

## Luke 19:45–46

Then he entered the temple and began to drive out those who were selling things there; and he said, "It is written,

'My house shall be a house of prayer';

but you have made it a den of robbers."

# The Scorner (6)

## GÉRALD FÉLIX TCHICAYA U TAM'SI

Congo, 1931–1988. See page 319 for biographical information on this poet.
"The Scorner (6) " is translated from the French by Gerald Moore.

The wine weighs on my heart I suffer with joy
Christ I hate your Christians

I am emptied of joy by loving all your cowards
I spit at your joy
having to right and left of me
these bourgeois women
drinking it has made me ill
Your temple is full of merchants who sell your cross Christ

four for a hundred sous
And take a chance
on the bartered Indies

Ah what continent lacks its false negroes
I have them to spare
Even Africa has some
The Congo has its false negroes
So Christian, were they a little less cautious
Oh I die for your glory
for you have tempted me
by making me so sad

# The Withered Fig

*Mark 11:12—14, 20—21*

On the following day, when they came from Bethany, he was hungry. Seeing in the distance a fig tree in leaf, he went to see whether perhaps he would find anything on it. When he came to it, he found nothing but leaves, for it was not the season for figs. He said to it, "May no one ever eat fruit from you again." And his disciples heard it. . . . In the morning as they passed by, they saw the fig tree withered away to its roots. Then Peter remembered and said to him, "Rabbi, look! The fig tree that you cursed has withered."

# The Miracle

## BORIS PASTERNAK

Russia, 1890–1960. Born to artistically gifted, partly-Jewish parents in Moscow, Pasternak may have been secretly baptized into the Greek Orthodox Church by a governess. Influenced by RILKE and Mayakovsky, Pasternak studied music and philosophy before linking up with the Futurists, who helped sponsor his earliest poetry. Though the author of several remarkable volumes of poetry, Pasternak is best known internationally for his novel *Doctor Zhivago*, which stirred up so much political controversy that he was forced to decline the Nobel Prize in 1958. "The Miracle" is translated from the Russian by Nina Kossman.

He was walking from Bethany to Jerusalem,
Brooding over sad premonitions.

The sun scorched the slope's prickly shrubs.
No smoke was rising over a nearby hut,
The air was hot and the reeds motionless,
And the calm of the Dead Sea lay still.

And with a bitterness rivalling the sea's,
He walked with a small throng of clouds
Along a dusty road, to somebody's backyard,
On His way to a gathering of disciples.

And so immersed was He in His thoughts,
That the field, dejected, sent off a wormwood smell.
All was still. He stood alone in the midst of it,
While the land lay prostrate in swoon.
All became muddled, the heat, the desert,
The lizards, the springs, the streams.

A fig tree rose not too far off,
Fruitless, nothing but branches and leaves.
And He said to it: "Of what use are you?
What joy does your stupor bring me?

"I thirst and hunger, yet you stand barren,
My meeting you is joyless as granite.

O, how offensive and ungifted you are!
Remain as you are, then, till the end of time."

A tremor of condemnation ran through the tree,
Like a spark of lightning down a rod.
The fig tree was reduced to ashes.

If only a moment of freedom had been given
To the leaves, the branches, roots, trunk,
The laws of nature could have intervened.
But a miracle is a miracle, and a miracle is God.
When we're in confusion, in the midst of disorder,
It overtakes us instantly, by surprise.

# A Pun for Al Gelpi

JACK KEROUAC

U.S., 1922–1969. A victim of his notoriety as the author of *On the Road*, Kerouac, the so-called "King of the Beats," was long regarded as simply an amoral seeker of "kicks" and pleasure. Yet a close, unbiased study of his more than seventeen published volumes reveals a powerful Catholic consciousness.

Jesus got mad one day
    at an apricot tree.
He said, "Peter, you
    of the Holy See,
Go see if the tree is ripe."
        "The tree is not yet ripe,"
        reported back Peter the Rock.
"Then let it wither!"
Jesus wanted an apricot.
In the morning, the tree
    had withered,
Like the ear in the agony
    of the garden,
Struck down by the sword.
    Unready.
    What means this parable?
Everybody
    better see.
You're really sipping
When your glass
    is always empty.

# Judas's Betrayal

*Matthew 26:14–16*

Then one of the twelve, who was called Judas Iscariot, went to the chief priests and said, "What will you give me if I betray him to you?" They paid him thirty pieces of silver. And from that moment he began to look for an opportunity to betray him.

# And So It Came to Pass . . .

FUNSO AVEJINA

Nigeria, 1950–. One of the best known of Nigeria's new generation of poets, Avejina studied in Canada and the West Indies, returning to Nigeria to teach English Literature. "And So It Came to Pass . . ." is from a sequence of poems castigating the native leaders who continue to betray African societies.

And so it came to pass
many seasons after the death of one Saviour
that a new crop of saviours, armed with party programmes
came cascading down our rivers of hope;
poised for the poisoning of our atlantic reservoir
they sought out the foxes in the family
to whom they gave their thirty pieces of silver
in local and foreign exchange
for the secrets of the passage—
way into the castle of our skins . . .

men we had taken for fearless warriors
as protectors of our secret recipes
suddenly turned crabs, carapace and all
shedding shame like water from duck-backs,
seeing sideways beyond the good of all
to the comfort of the selves;
and with their divination bags of tricks
slung over arrogant shoulders
they crawl over our dreams
under the cover of moonless nights
sidestepping traps, destroying hope
they turn our green august of rains,
of showers with which to persuade crops
towards harvest-circles
around whose fire we would have exchanged
happy tales of toil
into an orgy of furious flames . . .
And so it came to pass
that our saviours gave us a gift of tragedy
for which we are too dumb-struck to find a melody.

# When a Cloud Shades the Sun

EMMANUEL LACABA

Phillipines, 1948–1976. In Manila, the young poet Lacaba developed a Byronic reputation. But responding to the martial law regime of Ferdinand Marcos, he joined the left-wing guerrilla underground, the New People's Army, in the 1970s. Captured in 1976, he was shot by a military patrol at the age of 27. Though written in English, "When a Cloud Shades the Sun" uses Tagalog (native Filipino) verse forms. Its identification of the poet with both Judas and Jesus is found in other contemporary Filipino poets as well.

When a cloud shades the sun all penumbras are one
and my eyes' blue pouches to Magdalene are moles
like my secreted bag's two most delicate coins,
like Shadow my true friend whom water cannot drown.

Styx and salt, salt and Styx. They'll look back, fugitives
who bother if there should be dots untouched by feet;
passing through rain prisons, the strings of puppet trees,
prepare with three roosters notes for the Pharmacist.

Antiseptically masked and aproned, the skies
knife with fire and brimstone abdomens of cities.
In the oboe distance: the first successful lies
predict a savage death dance of adulteries.

Let gazes be brassieres. Processions of black robes.
Holy Friday faces. The whitening of crows.
A fist of cowards I: who sing from a tau cross,
my sons by my daughters calling their mothers whores.

Named Judas, born Jesus, named Jesus, born Judas,
I am not what I am, I am what I am not:
a shower of insects under an outside bulb,
the Genuine Guitarist's indiscriminate scars.

# The Last Supper

## *Luke 22:7, 14–16*

Then came the day of Unleavened Bread, on which the Passover lamb had to be sacrificed. . . . When the hour came, [Jesus] took his place at the table, and the apostles with him. He said to them, "I have eagerly desired to eat this Passover with you before I suffer; for I tell you, I will not eat it until it is fulfilled in the kingdom of God."

# The Last Supper

RAINER MARIA RILKE

Germany, 1875–1926. See page 107 for biographical information on this poet. "The Last Supper" is translated from the German by David Curzon and Will Alexander Washburn.

They are assembled, astounded, bewildered,
round him who, like a sage centered at last,
withdraws from those to whom he once belonged
and flows beyond them as some foreigner.
The former solitude comes over him
which raised him to perform his profound acts;
again he'll wander in the olive grove,
and those who love him will now run from him.

He summons them to the final meal
and (as a shot shoos birds from sheaves)
he shoos their hands from bread
with his word: they flutter up to him;
they flap about the table anxiously
searching for some way out. But *he*,
like an evening hour, is everywhere.

# The Last Supper

JACQUES PRÉVERT

France, 1900–1977. One of France's most popular twentieth-century poets, the Parisian Prévert began his career in a surrealist and anarchist mode. An established scriptwriter and social satirist who often attacked religion and bourgeois life, he achieved his major success with the publication of *Paroles* in 1946, one of the few volumes of modern poetry to become a bestseller. "The Last Supper" is translated from the French by Lawrence Ferlinghetti.

They are at table
They eat not
Nor touch their plates
And their plates stand straight up
Behind their heads.

## Luke 22:19–20

Then he took a loaf of bread, and when he had given thanks, he broke it and gave it to them, saying, "This is my body, which is given for you. Do this in remembrance of me." And he did the same with the cup after supper, saying, "This cup that is poured out for you is the new covenant in my blood."

# For Holy Saturday

ANONYMOUS

4th–5th century. "For Holy Saturday" is translated from the Greek by Walter
Mitchell.

Today we have seen
our Lord Jesus Christ on the altar.
Today we have gained possession
of the burning coal in whose shadow
the cherubim sing.
Today we have heard
a voice say, sweet and strong:

This body burns the thorns
of sin.
This body gives light to the souls
of all believers.
This body the woman touched
that had the flux of blood,
and gone was her bitter anguish.

This body the Canaanite's daughter
saw and was healed.
This body the harlot approached
with eager heart,
and all her filthy sins
were washed away.
This body Thomas touched and cried:
'My Lord, my God.'
Great is this body and more than great
the salvation it brings us.

The Word who is life
said also: 'This is my blood,
shed for you, poured for you,
bringing you pardon for sin.'

We have drunk, beloved, this blood;
it is holy and deathless.
We have drunk, beloved, the blood
that flowed from his side,

that heals all disease and gives freedom
to every soul.

We have drunk the blood
that ransomed us, redeemed us,
gave us light and knowledge.

See, children, what a body
we have eaten, see what blood
we have drunk, what a covenant
we have made with our God.
O to be proof against shame
on the day of requital.

Who can sufficiently praise
the mystery of your grace?
We have been enabled
to take our share of the gift;
may we keep it safe to the end,
that so we may come to hear
the blessed voice,
the sweet, the holy, saying:
Come, you that have received
a blessing from my Father;
take possession of the kingdom
that awaits you.

Then they that crucified the Lord
will be afraid,
and they that have not believed
in Father, Son and Holy Spirit
will be ashamed,
that they have denied and not acknowledged
the holy Trinity in the one godhead.

But we, beloved, will celebrate, as we ought,
Christ's baptism and his holy resurrection,
that gave us life and gave the world salvation:
which may we all achieve through Jesus Christ,
our Lord, and through his grace and kindness.
Glory, worship, honour are his due.

# Communion

GÉRALD FÉLIX TCHICAYA U TAM'SI

Congo, 1931–1988. See page 319 for biographical information on this poet.
"Communion" is translated from the French by John Reed and Clive Wake.

When man is more loyal to man
woman more heedful of the moon
the child gentle under his father's touch
my hands tracing a dawn
life will reinvent my body
my memory suddenly made flint
no longer mould the clay of crime
on the back of any brother of mine

O light of the Last Supper's bread!
O warmth of wine in that cup!
all in the image of a blessed womb!
already my life has stopped devouring me . . .

Once it was sad to be a man
each colour of the body was a ghetto
no way out through the pores but sweat
wherever I was shadow the whip cracked
but now it is my tongue I crack
at the sweet taste that now the nettle has
since I learnt to make my voice a balm

# African Easter: Easter Eve

ABIOSEH NICOL

Sierra Leone, 1924–. Nicol studied at Cambridge, England. His stories and poems have been published in Europe and the United States. He is Principal of Fourah Bay College, Freetown, Sierra Leone. "African Easter" is a three-part poem exploring what Good Friday, Easter Eve, and the Resurrection mean to an African intellectual surrounded by tribal religions and by Islam. See p. 421 and pp. 516–18 for the other parts.

THE AFRICAN PRIEST:

I have sat me down by the waterside
Watching the grey river pulling away.
I have listened me with willing ears
To your vesper bells across the fields.

Come close to me, God, do not keep away,
I walk towards you but you are too far,
Please try and meet me here halfway,
Because you are my all, my all.

What are you, Negro, Lebanese or Jew,
Flemish, Italian, Indian, Greek?
I know within my heart exactly what you are—
What we would like to be, but never are.

The warm blood sticks to your whipped shoulders
(Drink this in remembrance of me).
Only when the whirling thongs have raised the red weals
On our complacent bodies, then we remember you.
Change our salty tears of brown remorse

Into your flowing blood, it tastes the same.
(Oh, River Niger, you too have come from far away),
Fill my uplifted silver calabash
With your new sacrificial wine.

And I, your least novitiate, will sip,
With my thick lips, your ancient memory
So God the Father who art above,
Christ His Son, our only love,
Holy Ghost, eternal Dove,
Make of me a goodly man.

# The Foot-Washing

## John 13:4—8

[Jesus] got up from the table, took off his outer robe, and tied a towel around himself. Then he poured water into a basin and began to wash the disciples' feet and to wipe them with the towel that was tied around him. He came to Simon Peter, who said to him, "Lord, are you going to wash my feet?" Jesus answered, "You do not know now what I am doing, but later you will understand." Peter said to him, "You will never wash my feet." Jesus answered, "Unless I wash you, you have no share with me."

# Foot-Washing

JACOBUS REVIUS

Netherlands, 1586–1658. A minister of the Dutch Reformed Church, Revius preached a militant Calvinism. Some of his poetry displays this zealous passion, but other poems, like "Foot-Washing," are more quiet and reflective. "Foot-Washing" is translated from the Dutch by Henrietta Ten Harmsel.

> Why wonder that he doffed his garments willingly,
> Who had unclothed himself of heavenly majesty?
> Why wonder that he tied a towel round his waist,
> Who, for our sakes, as Master, assumed a servant's place?
> Why wonder that he washed the feet of humble men,
> Who later with his blood would wash away their sin?

# The Foot-Washing

## GEORGE ELLA LYON

U.S., 1949–. Teacher, poet, and author of many books for children, Lyon expresses deftly and humorously in "The Foot Washing" her belief that "all of us are given different gifts which require that we give up our ego selves in order to receive and pass the gift on. We do this imperfectly, of course, but in the labor we feel God's presence, and in the synthesis of song or poem, dance or painting, we share in the joy of the Maker."

> *"I wouldn't take the bread and wine if I didn't wash feet."*
> OLD REGULAR BAPTIST

They kneel on the slanting floor
before feet white as roots.
humble as tree stumps.
Men before men
women before women
to soothe the sourness
bound in each other's journeys.
Corns, calluses, bone knobs
all received and rinsed
given back clean
to Sunday shoes and hightops.

This is how they prepare
for the Lord's Supper,
singing and carrying a towel
and a basin of water,
praying while kids put soot
in their socks—almost as good
as nailing someone in the outhouse.

Jesus started it: He washed feet
after Magdalen dried His ankles
with her hair. "If I wash thee not,
thou has no part with me."

All servants, they bathe
flesh warped to its balance.
God of the rootwad,
Lord of the bucket in the well.

# The Beloved Disciple

## *John 13:21–25*

[Then] Jesus was troubled in spirit, and declared, "Very truly, I tell you, one of you will betray me." The disciples looked at one another, uncertain of whom he was speaking. One of his disciples—the one whom Jesus loved—was reclining next to him; Simon Peter therefore motioned to him to ask Jesus of whom he was speaking. So while reclining next to Jesus, he asked him, "Lord, who is it?"

# Verbi Vere Substantivi

## Sequence for the Feast Day of John the Evangelist

ADAM OF ST. VICTOR

France, d.1192. Adam's contribution to liturgical poetry was enriching the genre of the *sequence*, the verses expanding the *Alleluia* at Mass. His over fifty sequences are dense with the medieval symbolism which saw all of nature and human life as Christian allegory. Especially informing Adam's poetry, which — like much medieval liturgical verse — was meant to teach as well as to praise, is typology: the view of Old Testament figures and events as "types" of the life of Christ. In "Verbi Vere Substantivi" ("Of the Truly Self-Existent World"), Adam makes the traditional identification of the evangelists with living creatures: John with the eagle, Mark with the lion, Luke with the ox, Matthew with a winged man. "Verbi Vere Substantivi" is translated from the Latin by George Dardess.

How God's Word
Will last forever down the ages
Though mated with the flesh's rages
And sunk in the anxiety of time —
So John teaches.

Reclining at Jesus' side,
John drinks deep from wisdom's streams,
And as he forward leans,
His faith joins Jesus' Word,
His ear, his voice,
His mind, his God.

From there he mounts in visionary flight
Above the path of flesh,
Above all clouds of error —
His guide the true Sun's light —
And fixes eagle-like
Upon the vision and the summit of the heart.

If the sense is dull, the style is empty.
Not so with John. His style so high,
His faith so wide,
No heretical depravity

Can keep stride
With the saving Word—

That inexpressible Word
Whose creative power
Made all things good:
That same Word, says John,
Inseparable from God,
Except in the mystery
Of the Trinity.

He whom Matthew feeds
On virgin's milk,
Then bends to labor and to loss;
He whom Luke, the Ox,
Lifts high with quill-pen on the cross,
As Moses lifted the serpent on his staff;

He whom Lion Mark leads back
To life from death's dark,
Shaking the earth, splitting rock—
This same Christ, writes untutored John,
Is God from true God,
Beginning and the end,
Source and goal to which we tend.

John's visionary light
Ezekiel foresaw in his own heavenly flight—
The four living creatures,
Each with four wings, four features,
And wheels whirling within wheels—
Before John saw them here,
Or Christ drove them,
Their charioteer.

Those three describe the pain
Christ suffered, Pilate's power,
The crown of thorn,
While John, drawn up by his light quill,

Traces Christ's everlasting reign,
And avenging sword.

But all four,
Ordinary, mortal men,
Lift the king's wheels on their songs,
While angelic throngs
Throw themselves before the throne
Singing alleluia and amen.

# The Dream of John

## TADEUSZ RÓZEWICZ

Poland, 1921–. See page 206 for biographical information on this poet. "The Dream of John" is translated from the Polish by Victor Contoski.

John fell asleep
on the breast of the Master

he saw himself
with the face of Judas
felt the heft of
the moneybag in his hand
kissed the godly face

he did it all
because he was chosen

the tree was covered
with leaves and flowers
the fruit in secret
ripened
and fell

Awake
he saw that love and hate
are like the left hand
resting
motionless
on the lap

# Lord, I'm Afraid

PAUL VERLAINE

France, 1844–1896. Exerting, with Mallarmé, an important influence on the Symbolist movement in French poetry, Verlaine led a notoriously dissolute life, and his poems express his wild mood swings. During a remorseful spell in prison for having aimed a shot at his companion and fellow poet Rimbaud, Verlaine converted to Catholicism and wrote the spiritually ardent poems of *Sagesse* (1881), including "Lord, I'm Afraid." At the same time as he wrote these poems, however, he continued to write wild, even blasphemous verse. "Lord, I'm Afraid" is translated from the French by C. F. MacIntyre.

Lord, I'm afraid. My soul is all aquiver
I know I ought to love you, but how could
a poor thing, like myself, God, be your lover,
O Justice feared by the virtuous and good?

Yes, how? Beneath this troubled canopy
where my heart's been digging out its tomb
and where I feel the heavens flow toward me,
I ask you, by what road you'd have me come.

Stretch forth your hand to me, so I can raise
this sickened spirit and this flesh that cowers.
But shall I have the blessèd accolade?

Is it possible to find, one of these days,
in your breast, on your heart, what once was ours,
the place where the apostle's head was laid?

# Judas Leaves

## *John 13:26–30*

Jesus answered, "It is the one to whom I give this piece of bread when I have dipped it in the dish." So when he had dipped the piece of bread, he gave it to Judas son of Simon Iscariot. After he received the piece of bread, Satan entered into him. Jesus said to him, "Do quickly what you are going to do." Now no one at the table knew why he said this to him. Some thought that, because Judas had the common purse, Jesus was telling him, "Buy what we need for the festival"; or, that he should give something to the poor. So, after receiving the piece of bread, he immediately went out. And it was night.

# Seguidilla

JOSÉ DE VALDIVIELSO

Spain, 1560–1638. A priest, Valdivielso adapted popular songs to religious sub-
jects. A *seguidilla* is a complexly rhymed verse form developed in sixteenth
century Spanish poetry from traditional folk lyrics. "Seguidilla" is translated
from the Spanish by Thomas Walsh.

I who once was free,
Sold unto death you see;
*Trust not, Mother dear,*
*Hearts ungrateful here!*
With a honeyed smile,
Mother, a false friend
At the banquet's end,
His hand within my dish the while,
Like a lamb betrayed me vile.
*Trust not, Mother dear,*
*Hearts ungrateful here!*
I placed him at my side
And passed the dish to him;
I shared and did provide
The best unto the brim.
His bargain rare and grim,—
He sold Thy Son away,
*Trust not, Mother dear,*
*Hearts ungrateful here!*
The garden flowers were wet
With the tears I shed thereon;
'Twas Holy Thursday, yet
With me had Judas gone;
He gave unto Thy Son
The kiss I'll not forget—
*Trust not, Mother dear,*
*Hearts ungrateful here!*

# The Last Supper

OSCAR HAHN

Chile, 1938–. A leading figure of Chilean poetry, Hahn now lives in the United States, teaching at the University of Iowa. His books of poetry include *This Black Rose* and *Art of Dying*. "The Last Supper" is translated from the Spanish by Wayne H. Finke.

> Corruption sits
> on clean bodies
> with napkin, knife and fork.

# Judas Iscariot

R. A. K. MASON

New Zealand, 1905–1971. See page 109 for biographical information on this poet.

Judas Iscariot
　　sat in the upper
　　room with the others
　　at the last supper

And sitting there smiled
　　up at his master
　　whom he knew the morrow
　　would roll in disaster.

At Christ's look he guffawed—
　　for then as thereafter
　　Judas was greatly
　　given to laughter,

Indeed they always said
　　that he was the veriest
　　prince of good fellows
　　and the whitest and merriest.

All the days of his life
　　he lived gay as a cricket
　　and would sing like the thrush
　　that sings in the thicket

He would sing like the thrush
　　that sings on the thorn
　　oh he was the most sporting bird
　　that ever was born.

# As the Father Has Loved Me

## John 14:23; 15:9, 12−13

Jesus answered him, "Those who love me will keep my word, and my Father will love them, and we will come to them and make our home with them. . . . As the Father has loved me, so I have loved you; abide in my love. . . . No one has greater love than this, to lay down one's life for one's friends."

# Wilt Thou Love God?

## JOHN DONNE

England, 1572–1631. One of English literature's most gifted and influential poets, Donne was so revered by his immediate followers that they thought him "a king that ruled as he thought fit/The universal monarchy of wit." Raised a Roman Catholic, Donne later converted to Anglicanism, though his sensibility—as shown in his late religious poetry—seems always to have remained with the Roman Church. Unable to find civil employment, Donne was eventually persuaded of his calling and took Anglican orders in 1615. Acclaimed for his brilliant sermons, he was soon appointed Dean of St. Paul's Cathedral.

Wilt thou love God, as he thee? then digest,
My Soule, this wholsome meditation,
How God the Spirit, by Angels waited on
In heaven, doth make his Temple in thy brest.
The Father having begot a Sonne most blest,
And still begetting, (for he ne'r begonne)
Hath deign'd to chuse thee by adoption,
Coheire to his glory, and Sabbaths endless rest;
And as a robb'd man, which by search doth finde
His stolne stuffe sold, must lose or buy it againe:
The Sonne of glory came downe, and was slaine,
Us whom he had made, and Satan stolne, to unbinde.
'Twas much, that man was made like God before,
But, that God should be made like man, much more.

# Peace I Leave With You

## *John 14:27a*

Peace I leave with you; my peace I give to you.

# In the Refectory

ALCUIN

England, c.735–804. See page 279 for biographical information on this poet. "In the Refectory" is translated from the Latin by Helen Waddell.

Lord Christ, we pray thy mercy on our table spread,
And what thy gentle hands have given thy men
Let it by thee be blessed: whate'er we have
Came from thy lavish heart and gentle hand,
And all that's good is thine, for thou art good.
And ye that eat, give thanks for it to Christ,
And let the words ye utter be only peace,
For Christ loved peace: it was himself that said,
Peace I give unto you, my peace I leave with you.
Grant that our own may be a generous hand
Breaking the bread for all poor men, sharing the food.
Christ shall receive the bread thou gavest his poor,
And shall not tarry to give thee reward.

# Jesus's Promise of the Holy Spirit

## John 16:7, 13

I tell you the truth: it is to your advantage that I go away, for if I do not go away, the Advocate will not come to you; but if I go, I will send him to you. . . . When the Spirit of truth comes, he will guide you into all the truth; for he will not speak on his own, but will speak whatever he hears, and he will declare to you the things that are to come.

# Veni Creator Spiritus

(attrib.) RABANUS MAURUS

Germany, 780–856. Born at Mainz, Rabanus studied under ALCUIN at Tours. He served as abbot of the monastery at Fulda and later as archbishop of Mainz, writing numerous homilies and commentaries. "Veni Creator Spiritus" ("Come, Creator Spirit"), attributed to him, remains a popular Pentecost hymn, still found in both Protestant and Catholic hymnals. "Veni Creator Spiritus" is translated from the Latin by John Dryden.

Creator Spirit, by whose aid
The world's foundations first were laid,
Come visit every pious mind,
Come pour Thy joys on human kind;
From sin and sorrow set us free
And make Thy temples worthy Thee.
O Source of uncreated light,
The Father's promised Paraclete!
Thrice holy fount, thrice holy fire,
Our hearts with heavenly love inspire;
Come and Thy sacred unction bring
To sanctify us while we sing.
Plenteous of grace, descend from high,
Rich in Thy sevenfold energy!
Thou strength of His almighty hand,
Whose power does heaven and earth command.
Proceeding Spirit, our defense,
Who dost the gifts of tongues dispense,
And crown'st Thy gift with eloquence!
Refine and purge our earthly parts;
But, oh, inflame and fire our hearts!
Our frailties help, our vice control,
Submit the senses to the soul;
And when rebellious they are grown
Then lay Thy hand and hold them down.
Chase from our minds the infernal foe,
And peace, the fruit of love bestow;
And lest our feet should step astray,
Protect and guide us on the way.

Make us eternal truths receive,
And practice all that we believe;
Give us Thyself that we may see
The Father and the Son by Thee.
Immortal honor, endless fame
Attend the Almighty Father's name;
The Saviour Son be glorified,
Who for lost man's redemption died;
And equal adoration be,
Eternal Paraclete, to Thee!

# PART EIGHT

# THE PASSION

# The Agony in the Garden

*Luke 22:39–46*

[Jesus] came out and went, as was his custom, to the Mount of Olives; and the disciples followed him. When he reached the place, he said to them, "Pray that you may not come into the time of trial." Then he withdrew from them about a stone's throw, knelt down, and prayed, "Father, if you are willing, remove this cup from me; yet, not my will but yours be done." [Then an angel from heaven appeared to him and gave him strength. In his anguish he prayed more earnestly, and his sweat became like great drops of blood falling down on the ground.] When he got up from prayer, he came to the disciples and found them sleeping because of grief, and he said to them, "Why are you sleeping? Get up and pray that you may not come into the time of trial."

# Gethsemane

ANNETTE VON DROSTE-HÜLSHOFF

Germany, 1797–1848. See page 233 for biographical information on this poet.
"Gethsemane" is translated from the German by George Dardess.

As Christ lay in Gethsemane,
Face down, with closed eyes,—
The breezes seeming nothing but sighs,
And a spring,
Reflecting the moon's pale face,
Murmuring its sorrow apace,—
That was the hour for the angel to bring,
In tears, from God, the bitter cup.

Then before Christ the cross rose up.
He saw his own body hanging there
Torn and wrenched, joints jutting where
The ropes stretched each limb back.
He saw the nails, the crown.
At each thorn a drop of blood hung down.
The thunder growled under its breath.
He heard a drip. Down the cross
Softly slid a whimper, then blurred out.
Christ sighed. In every pore
Sweat found a door.

The air went dark. In the grey ocean
A dead sun swam.
Through the murk he made out
The thorn-crowned head thrashing about.
Three forms lay at the cross's foot.
He saw them lying, grey as soot.
He heard the catching of their breath,
Saw how their trembling set their clothes in motion.
Was ever love as hot as his?
He knew them, knew them well.
His heart glowed.
Still harder his sweat flowed.

The sun's corpse vanished—just smoke, black day.
Cross and sighs both sank away.
A silence grimmer than a storm's roar
Swam through starless paths of air.
No breath of life anywhere.
And, all around, a crater, burnt, empty,
And a hollow voice crying for pity,
"My God, my God, why have you forsaken me?"
Death's grip seized him.
He wept. His spirit broke.
Sweat turned blood. He shook.
His mouth formed words of pain and spoke.
"Father, if it's possible, let this hour
Pass me by."

A bolt of lightning cut the night!
In that light
Swam the cross, its martyr-symbols bright.
Hands by millions he saw reaching,
Hands large and small from near and far beseeching,
And hovering spark-like over the crown of thorn
The souls of millions yet unborn.
The murk slunk back into the ground,
While the dead in their graves their voices found.
In love's fulness Christ raised himself on high.
"Father," he cried, "not my
Will but yours be done."

The moon swam out in quiet blue.
Before him, on the dewy green,
A stem of lily stretched up its length.
Then out of the calyx-cup
An angel stepped
And gave him strength.

# And Once More

ANNA AKHMATOVA

Russia, 1889–1966. See page 309 for biographical information on this poet.
"And Once More" is translated from the Russian by Judith Hemschemeyer.

> And once more the autumn blasts like Tamerlane,
> There is silence in the streets of Arbat.
> Beyond the little station or beyond the haze
> The impassable road is dark.
>
> So here it is, the latest one! And the rage
> Subsides. It's as if the world had gone deaf . . .
> A mighty, evangelical old age
> And that most bitter Gethsemane sigh.

# Lord, You Have Ripped Away

ANTONIO MACHADO Y RUIZO

Spain, 1875–1939. See page 332 for biographical information on this poet.
"Lord, You Have Ripped Away" is translated from the Spanish by Robert Bly.

Lord, you have ripped away from me what I loved most.
One more time, O God, hear me cry out inside.
"Your will be done," it was done, and mine not.
My heart and the sea are together, Lord, and alone.

# Gethsemane

NILS FERLIN

Sweden, 1898–1961. A seaman, laborer, actor, and song-writer, the legendary
Ferlin was one of Sweden's most popular lyric poets. Many of his poems have
been set to music. His work, shaped by melancholy and compassion for life's
outcasts, often concentrates on biblical subjects, though without a doctrinal
perspective. Gethsemane was a favorite theme of Scandinavian poetry. "Geth-
semane" is translated from the Swedish by Martin S. Allwood and Thorild
Fredenholm.

> He was such a feeble, confused artiste
> That he felt quite hopelessly sad and triste.
>
> He took up his No. 2 Faber and wrote
> On one fine evening the following, quote:
>
> In God's photographic salon there will be
> A dark-room that's called Gethsemane.
>
> And there clear pictures soon appear
> To him who is quiet and sincere.
>
> But he who is frightened of rod and ice
> Shall never have flowers in paradise.
>
> His life will be like a barren hell
> Where never a silvern tear fell.
>
> Maybe the purple path he took,
> But his look was always a beggar's look.
>
> He ashes became, but could never burn.
> The smiling moon from his hand will turn.
>
> For he who's afraid of Gethsemane
> Shall never nor giving nor getting see.

# The Arrest

## Mark 14:43-45

Immediately, while he was still speaking, Judas, one of the twelve, arrived; and with him there was a crowd with swords and clubs, from the chief priests, the scribes, and the elders. Now the betrayer had given them a sign, saying, "The one I will kiss is the man; arrest him and lead him away under guard." So when he came, he went up to him at once and said, "Rabbi!" and kissed him.

# In All Ages

YULIYA DRUNINA

Russia, 1924–1991. A national deputy during Perestroika, Yuliya Drunina had experienced the horrors of World War II as a young girl while serving in the front lines as a nurse. Her first volume of poetry, published in 1948, reveals the powerful effects of her war experience. Her poem on Judas' betrayal is especially significant since she herself spoke out against her former mentor, the gifted poet Pavel Antokolsky, during the ideological campaign against the "cosmopolitans." "In All Ages" is translated from the Russian by Albert C. Todd.

In all ages, always, everywhere, and everywhere
It repeats itself, that cruel dream—
The inexplicable kiss of Judas
And the ring of the accursed silver.

To understand such things is a task in vain.
Humanity conjectures once again:
Let him betray (when he cannot do else),
But why a kiss on the lips? . . .

# The Scare-Crow Christ

RICAREDO DEMETILLO

Phillipines, 1911–. Like most twentieth century Filipino poets, Demetillo chose to write in English. Simultaneous identification with Jesus and Judas, as in "The Scare-Crow Christ," is a recurrent theme in modern Filipino poetry on Christ.

I mourn man, man diminished, unfulfilled,
Whose shadow drags the darkness of his night
Across the endless dreariness of days,
Where no oasis greens the sand-choked waste.
I mourn for man, my brother crucified.

Though doom ticks through the clammy cells of blood,
Hope pendulums the marrow of each nerve.
I know his hungers scoop the lake for snails,
His guts Gehenna with their appetite
Prowling to thieve the larders for his lack.

In rooms where locusts crunch the dog-eared crop,
Despair bisecting thought in fields of blight;
In farms where claw-like fingers wear to shreds
And huts precarious sag down to the grave,
This man still sidles in a search for light.

Is he not neighbor to my creaking bed
When sleep weighs at the eyelids like a rock?
His cries croak down the echoes of my heart
Though often I would spurn his rattled knock.
Is he not neighbor to my creaking bed?

And you, my reader in this cramp of words,
Are you not party to his hang-dog gait?
You tear his blankets to a chill of shreds,
Snatching your fat feasts from his patient plate?
Are you not Judas to this scare-crow Christ?

# John 18:12

So the soldiers, their officer, and the Jewish police arrested Jesus and bound him.

# The Prisoner

RAÏSSA MARITAIN

France, 1883–1960. Born Raïssa Oumansov of Jewish parents in Rostov-on-
Don, Raïssa Maritain, wife of French philosopher Jacques Maritain and his
collaborator on many projects, was a poet and Christian contemplative. For
her, poetry was an aspect of the contemplative life: "Poetry appears to me as the
fruit of a contact of the spirit with reality in itself ineffable, and with its source
which is in truth God himself in the impulse of love which leads him to create
images of his beauty." "The Prisoner" is translated from the French by Shelley
Salamensky.


Thy servant in irons
In the shadow of death
Lord deliver him
I see his face through the grille
Like saints' faces in icons
His face wide his prominent eyes
And the fringe of black hair on his brow
White wool streaked
He looks like the Christ
Of Quentin Matsys
He stares straight ahead
Stunned by misfortune
He views God's sky and
Sees all will be well
But no he has not yet been painted in icons
He sits on his cot
Head bent over his arms and
He cries
All alone amidst enemies
Who hate all he reveres
To whom his kindness his spirit
Are naught but objects of mockery
He is the prisoner of his own innocence and
He is patient
Like his Master Jesus Christ
Like Him sorrowful unto death
He has so loved justice
He is like to the Christ of Quentin Matsys
He is learning the language of Heaven

## Mark 14:51–52

A certain young man was following him, wearing nothing but a linen cloth. They caught hold of him, but he left the linen cloth and ran off naked.

# Often Have I Tried to Follow You

JEAN DE LA CEPPÈDE

France, 1548–1623. Caught up in the political-religious wars of post-Reformation France, La Ceppède saw his fortunes rise or fall depending on whether Catholics or Protestants were in power. He wrote his *Theorems*, 520 sonnets on Christian themes, to prove his Catholic faith, but "proof" for a Baroque poet often took the form of unexpected metaphorical conceit. Though honored at his death, La Ceppède fell into oblivion and has been rediscovered only this century; his poems are just beginning to be anthologized. "Often Have I Tried To Follow You" is translated from the French by Keith Bosley.

Often have I tried to follow you, my life
Along familiar paths your mercy shows
But always, but always your several foes
Have seized me by the sheet, my strength borne off.

Now that I hear your Spirit's holy call
To mark your footsteps with these measured feet
This world, this charmer, this foe is a cheat
Clutching me by the cloak, thwarting my will.

By a thousand vanities I am possessed,
So much, so long besotted, I am pressed
For time to follow you to Calvary:

Henceforth, Lord, grant that learning by your favour
From the young man who slipped his captors, I
May leave these habits to the world for ever.

# Peter's Denial

## *Luke 22:54–62*

Then they seized [Jesus] and led him away, bringing him into the high priest's house. But Peter was following at a distance. When they had kindled a fire in the middle of the courtyard and sat down together, Peter sat among them. Then a servant-girl, seeing him in the firelight, stared at him and said, "This man also was with him." But he denied it, saying, "Woman, I do not know him." A little later someone else, on seeing him, said, "You also are one of them." But Peter said, "Man, I am not!" Then about an hour later still another kept insisting, "Surely this man also was with him; for he is a Galilean." But Peter said, "Man, I do not know what you are talking about!" At that moment, while he was still speaking, the cock crowed. The Lord turned and looked at Peter. Then Peter remembered the word of the Lord, how he had said to him, "Before the cock crows today, you will deny me three times." And he went out and wept bitterly.

# In the Servants' Quarters

THOMAS HARDY

England, 1840–1928. Hardy's career bridged not only two centuries but also two genres: the nineteenth century saw him as a novelist, the twentieth as a poet. The son of a stonemason, Hardy, who was largely self-educated, learned architecture and church restoration before writing the novels that made him famous. After his last novels, *Tess of the D'Urbervilles* (1891) and *Jude the Obscure* (1895), were attacked on moral grounds, Hardy quit writing fiction and devoted the rest of his life to poetry. His poems often view a scriptural passage from a folklorist's perspective.

'Man, you too, aren't you, one of these rough followers of the criminal?
All hanging hereabout to gather how he's going to bear
Examination in the hall.' She flung disdainful glances on
The shabby figure standing at the fire with others there,
      Who warmed them by its flare.

'No indeed, my skipping maiden: I know nothing of the trial here,
Or criminal, if so he be.—I chanced to come this way,
And the fire shone out into the dawn, and morning airs are cold now;
I, too, was drawn in part by charms I see before me play,
      That I see not every day.'

'Ha, ha!' then laughed the constables who also stood to warm
      themselves,
The while another maiden scrutinized his features hard,
As the blaze threw into contrast every line and knot that wrinkled them,
Exclaiming, 'Why, last night when he was brought in by the guard,
      You were with him in the yard!'

'Nay, nay, you teasing wench, I say! You know you speak mistakenly.
Cannot a tired pedestrian who has legged it long and far
Here on his way from northern parts, engrossed in humble marketings,
Come in and rest awhile, although judicial doings are
      Afoot by morning star?'

'O, come, come!' laughed the constables. 'Why, man, you speak the
      dialect
He uses in his answers; you can hear him up the stairs.

So own it. We sha'n't hurt ye. There he's speaking now! His syllables
Are those you sound yourself when you are talking unawares,
    As this pretty girl declares.'

'And you shudder when his chain clinks!' she rejoined. 'O yes, I
        noticed it.
And you winced, too, when those cuffs they gave him echoed to us
        here.
They'll soon be coming down, and you may then have to defend
        yourself
Unless you hold your tongue, or go away and keep you clear
    When he's led to judgment near!'

'No! I'll be damned in hell if I know anything about the man!
No single thing about him more than everybody knows!
Must not I even warm my hands but I am charged with blasphemies?' . . .
—His face convulses as the morning cock that moment crows,
    And he droops, and turns, and goes.

# Aeterne Rerum Conditor

AMBROSE

Germany, 340–397. Bishop of Milan and tower of the Church's defense against Arianism (the belief that Jesus is not one with God but a created being), Ambrose composed hymns like "Aeterne Rerum Conditor" ("Eternal Creator of the World") during the siege of his cathedral by Arian forces. He wanted his flock to sing "lest"—in his admirer Augustine's words—"they faint through fatigue and sorrow." Ambrose is often called the "father of Church song in the West." "Aeterne Rerum Conditor" is translated from the Latin by Walter Mitchell.

Creator of the world, O God
eternal, Lord of night and day,
at whose command the seasons come
and, lest they weary us, depart:

the bird that watches all night long
and cries aloud to pierce the dark
and guide the lightless traveller
now sounds the approach of day;

the morning star, aroused from sleep,
draws back the veils that shroud the sky,
while errant sinners at the sound
take fright and leave the hellward road;

the sailor sloughs his weariness,
the angry sea grows mild again,
the rock on which the Church is built
at cock-crow weeps his sin away.

Up, then, and out: the cock has crowed
to prod the sluggard from his sleep;
he puts the stay-abed to shame
and proves him late who says, 'Too soon'.

At cock-crow hope returns and health
flows back to wilting minds and limbs,
the murderer's knife is stowed away,
the weak find trust again and faith.

Jesus, we fall; a look from you
will pull us firmly to our feet:
sin quails and falters at your glance,
and guilt dissolves in timely tears.

Shine on our torpid minds, O Light,
and set the dormant thoughts astir;
and may our earliest action be
to speak the name of God in prayer.

# Rooster

ROBERT OBERG

U.S., 1957 –. Born in Providence, Rhode Island, Oberg is director of The Olney Street Group, an independent poetry association which he founded in 1982. Winner of the 1991 Galway Kinnell Poetry Prize, he has published poetry in a variety of periodicals. His recent poems reflect the Christian contemplative tradition in which he is immersed.


And when we return
from the garden's anguish or vision
doesn't the rooster's crown
look different against the scratched ground
and chicken fence of the pit,
razors of our weakness wedged in its talons,
glutinous talons that will be handed over with the neck,
severed beneath the axe of the man who fed it.

Will we remember the fight
when the neck, feet and entrails simmer on the stove,
and the breast, halved, with garlic and crushed pepper, roasts.
Will we eat only what the spirit demands
not for the sensuous melding of flesh,
to eat the hacked limbs unhastily,
taste our own limbs that too will be hacked,
that too will cry out *I do not know the man,*
do not know love, do not know how to overcome
desire's longing for more flesh pricked from the carving block,
the body sated, knives and forks washed,
eaten as if saying *if only it would bleed,*
as we will bleed, feed on our death.

Will we ever say *yes,*
the blood dripping from our mouths,
the bones broken.
Will we stay awake when the hour is come,
our feet clutching the perch,
sing our natures beneath death's folding wing,
accepting the rooster's red comb,
the runes and excrement scratched into earth
along the paths of laying hens.

# African Easter: Good Friday

ABIOSEH NICOL

Sierra Leone, 1924–. See page 380 for biographical information on this poet.


THE WOUNDED CHRIST:

I am not your God
If you have not denied me once, twice,
If I have not heard you complaining,
Or doubting my existence.

I am not your Love,
If you have not rejected me often.
For what then am I worth to you
If you are always sinless.

Pace these sandy corridors of time,
Turn again and live for me your youth, listening
To the gently falling rain, the distant cock crow
Then proceed once more to deny

That I had a part in your being. Say
That I am an invention to keep you held
Always in thralldom. That I was
The avant-garde of your disintegration.

After me, the stone jars of cheap gin, the ornamental
Glass beads, the punitive expeditions, your colonial status,
I have heard it all before; hide your face,
Bury it, for fear that finding me, you may find peace.

For in this hour when the dying night lingers
Unwilling to surrender its waking darkness
Over your face and fevered brow, my torn fingers
Will stray bringing such comfort
As may claim your doubting heart.

# The Meaning of the Look

## ELIZABETH BARRETT BROWNING

England, 1806–1861. A precocious child, Browning could read Greek at the age of 8 and at 13 had written a four-book epic. An invalid who also suffered from tuberculosis, she eloped in 1846 with Robert Browning, who at the time was a far less prominent poet than his wife. The Brownings lived in Italy, where Elizabeth became a devotee of spiritualism and a supporter of socialist and humanitarian causes. Essentially Evangelical in her faith, she disliked ritual and religious institutionalization.

> I think that look of Christ might seem to say,
> "Thou Peter! art thou, then, a common stone
> Which I at last must break my heart upon,
> For all God's charge to His high angels may
> Guard my foot better? Did I yesterday
> Wash *thy* feet, my beloved, that they should run
> Quick to deny me 'neath the morning sun?
> And do thy kisses, like the rest, betray?
> The cock crows coldly.—Go, and manifest
> A late contrition, but no bootless fear!
> For when thy final need is dreariest,
> Thou shalt not be denied, as I am here:
> My voice to God and angels shall attest,
> '*Because I* KNOW *this man, let him be clear.*'"

# Saint Peter's Denial

CHARLES BAUDELAIRE

France, 1821–1867. First achieving literary recognition in France for his trans-
lations of Edgar Allan Poe, Baudelaire became notorious for his profligate life.
When his single book of poems, *Fleurs du Mal*, was published in 1857, the poet
and his publisher were tried in court for obscenity. Though during Baudelaire's
lifetime, *Fleurs du Mal* remained scorned for its depravity, it soon became the
inspiration for the Symbolist movement and changed the course of world
poetry. The book has been translated into every major language. Its spiritual
vision is deliberately, provocatively satanic. "Saint Peter's Denial" is translated
from the French by Richard Howard.

The tide of curses day by day ascends
unto His hosts—and God, what does He do?
Like a tyrant gorged on meat and wine, He sleeps—
the sound of our blasphemies sweet in His Ears.

The martyrs' sobs, the screaming at the stake
compose, no doubt, a heady symphony;
indeed, for all the blood their pleasure costs,
the Heavens have not yet had half enough!

Remember the Mount of Olives, Jesus? When
you fell on your knees and humbly prayed to Him
Who laughed on high at the sound of hammering
as the butchers drove the nails into your flesh?

And when they spat on your divinity,
the jeering scullions and the conscript scum—
that moment when you felt the thorns impale
the skull which housed Humanity itself;

when the intolerable weight of your tormented flesh
hung from your distended arms; when blood
and sweat cascaded from your whitening brow;
when you were made a target for all eyes—

did you dream then of the wonder-working days
when you came to keep eternal promises,

riding an ass, and everywhere the ways
strewn with palms and flowers—those were the days!

when, your heart on fire with valor and with hope,
you whipped the moneylenders out of that place—
you were master then! But now, has not remorse
pierced your side even deeper than the spear?

Myself, I shall be satisfied to quit
a world where action is no kin to dreams;
would I had used—and perished by—the sword!
Peter denied his Master . . . He did well!

# The Trial

## Matthew 26:57, 59—66

Those who had arrested Jesus took him to Caiaphas the high priest, in whose house the scribes and the elders had gathered. . . . Now the chief priests and the whole council were looking for false testimony against Jesus so that they might put him to death, but they found none, though many false witnesses came forward. At last two came forward and said, "This fellow said, 'I am able to destroy the temple of God and to build it in three days.' " The high priest stood up and said, "Have you no answer? What is it that they testify against you?" But Jesus was silent. Then the high priest said to him, "I put you under oath before the living God, tell us if you are the Messiah, the Son of God." Jesus said to him, "You have said so. But I tell you,

From now on you will see the Son of Man

seated at the right hand of Power

and coming on the clouds of heaven."

Then the high priest tore his clothes and said, "He has blasphemed! Why do we still need witnesses? You have now heard his blasphemy. What is your verdict?" They answered, "He deserves death."

# Comrade Jesus

SARAH N. CLEGHORN

U.S., 1876–1959. A political activist, the Virgina-born Cleghorn was known for what she termed her "burning poems" on such social topics as poverty and child labor. The author of two novels, she published her collected poems, *Portraits and Protests*, in 1917; her autobiography, *Threescore*, appeared in 1936.

Thanks to St. Matthew, who had been
At mass-meetings in Palestine,
We knew whose side was spoken for
When Comrade Jesus took the floor.

"Where sore they toil and hard they lie,
Among the great unwashed, dwell I: —
The tramp, the convict, I am he;
Cold-shoulder him, cold-shoulder me."

By Dives' door, with thoughtful eye,
He did to-morrow prophesy: —
"The kingdom's gate is low and small;
The rich can scarce wedge through at all."

"A dangerous man," said Caiaphas,
"An ignorant demagogue, alas!
Friend of low women, it is he
Slanders the upright Pharisee."

For law and order, it was plain,
For Holy Church, he must be slain.
The troops are there to awe the crowd:
And violence was not allowed.

Their clumsy force with force to foil
His strong, clean hands he would not soil.
He saw their childishness quite plain
Between the lightnings of his pain.

Between the twilights of his end,
He made his fellow-felon friend:
With swollen tongue and blinded eyes,
Invited him to paradise.

Ah, let no Local him refuse!
Comrade Jesus hath paid his dues.
Whatever other be debarred,
Comrade Jesus hath his red card.

# The Tale of a Dzeleka Prison Hard-Core Hero

JACK MAPANJE

Malawi, 1944–. With a doctorate in linguistics from the University of London, Mapanje teaches oral literature at the University of Malawi. He edits a journal of oral literature and has compiled several anthologies of African poetry, oral and written.

*For Madhala*

"The landrover stops one hundred yards from
Dzeleka Prison gate; the two rows of those

Notorious guards you have heard about blur,
Their clubs or truncheons raised high to kill.

They unlock your leg-irons whose clump now
Numbs; they take off your handcuffs in blood.

Your garments are like Jesus's, except that
Like the other thief you have indeed robbed,

Many times, and several even armed. It was
The Congress Party wallet you threw in Shire

River that has brought you to Dzeleka Prison;
You could not stop pinching just to please

The name they gave this prison; how could
You stop picking the Congress Party mango?

It's the only fruit you pick without guilt:
They forced it off the poor, you off them,

Wash out! But you must run very fast between
Those rows to get to the end of that human

Tunnel alive. I remember only the sudden
Naked shiver; the rest you can guess. Yet

Imagine the whole Presidential tour to Taiwan
To import for us the one and only hard-core!

(Indeed, fancy all those Western freedoms he
Watched, wasted on such dull despot desires—

*The streets of Taiwan are so tidy; no thieves,*
*No beggars; that's a nation for you!* he boasts.)

God, I miss those juicy avocado pears behind
The Congress Party fence in Kabula Old Museum!

And awaiting to hang must be dead end here; I
Mean, there's no second chance in Mikuyu Prison,

Is there? And that stupid traditional court
Judge, Moses, did he also ask you fellows to

Produce in court the person you'd sorted and
When you could not, did the devil also squeal:

*Go and wait for your victim at Mikuyu Prison?*
What village justice brought you to doom here?'

## Matthew 26:67a

Then they spat in his face and struck him.

# New Negro Sermon

## JACQUES ROUMAIN

Haiti, 1907–1944. In his short life, Roumain became a leading spokesman for Negritude, the movement of Blacks in Africa and the Caribbean to reject European cultural domination and recover their African heritage. "New Negro Sermon" voices, in the language of 1930s socialist humanism, Roumain's disgust at the existing institutions of church, Haitian government, and capitalism. After the poem was included in a widely read 1948 anthology compiled by SENGHOR, its final eight lines became a Negritude motto. "New Negro Sermon" is translated from the French by Ellen Conroy Kennedy.

In His face they spit their icy scorn,
As at a black flag flying windswept by snow
To make of Him, poor nigger, the god of those in power,
From His rags, relics to embellish altars;
From His gentle song of poverty,
From the trembling lamentation of His banjo,
The haughty thunder of the organ;
From His arms that hauled the heavy cotton
On the river Jordan,
The arms of those who wield the sword;
From His body, worn like ours from the plantations
Like a glowing coal,
Like a black coal burning in white roses,
The golden necklace of their fortune;
They whitened His black face beneath the spittle
      of their icy scorn,
They spit on Your black face,
Lord, our friend, our comrade;
You who parted on her face long hair that hid the harlot's tears,
Like a screen of reeds;
They the rich, the Pharisees, the owners of the land, the bakers,
From the bleeding man they made the bleeding god;
Oh, Judas snicker;
Oh, Judas laugh;
Christ, like a torch between two thieves,
At the summit of the world,
Lit the slaves' revolt.
But Christ today is in the house of thieves

And his spread arms in the cathedral spread a vulture shadow,
And in the monastery vaults priests
Count the interest of the thirty pieces
While church bells shower death on hungry multitudes.

We do not pardon them because they know what they do:
They lynched John who organized the union,
They chased him through the wood with dogs like a savage wolf,
Laughing there, they hanged him to the sycamore.
No, brothers, comrades,
We will pray no more.
Our revolt will rise like the stormbird's cry,
Above the putrid lapping of the swamps.
We'll no longer sing the sad, despairing spirituals!
Another song will spring forth from our throats
Our red flags we shall unfurl,
Stained by the blood of our upright brothers.
Beneath this sign we shall march,
Beneath this sign we are marching,
Standing tall, the wretched of the earth!
Standing tall, the legions of the hungry!

# John 18:28

Then they took Jesus from Caiaphas to Pilate's headquarters. It was early in the morning. They themselves did not enter the headquarters, so as to avoid ritual defilement and to be able to eat the Passover.

# Pilate's Headquarters

JEAN DE LA CEPPÈDE

France, 1548–1623. See page 414 for biographical information on this poet. "Pilate's Headquarters" is translated from the French by Keith Bosley.

Meanwhile the priests, who want to prove to Rome
How deeply they are religious one and all
For fear of taint before the Paschal lamb
Is eaten, stay outside the judgement hall.

O whited sepulchres, hearts full of filth
Who at sheer villainy do not bat an eyelid
These for whom murder brings no risk to health
Fear by a gentile roof to be defilèd!

Ha! How these grand robes, how these fancy titles
Cover Religion's maggot in the vitals:
But falsehood blows its cover in the end.

The hypocrite is like the ostrich, sham
Bird of the south that waving a vain plume
Pretends to fly, and never leaves the ground.

# Mark 15:2

Pilate asked him, "Are you the King of the Jews?" He answered him, "You say so."

# from *Cosmic Canticle*

ERNESTO CARDENAL

Nicaragua, 1925–. Father Cardenal, Nicaragua's major contemporary poet, has had a life almost as varied and expansive as the wildly-ranging verses of his *Cosmic Canticle*, in which he attempts to identify the Kingdom of Heaven with every imaginable vision—philosophical, scientific, historical, political, and religious—under the sun. THOMAS MERTON's student in the novitiate at Gethsemani Abbey, Cardenal returned home to become an early advocate of liberation theology and was declared an outlaw in 1977. He later served as Minister of Culture in the Sandinista government. *Cosmic Canticle* is translated from the Spanish by John Lyons.

Alfa and Omega.
The prophecy of the Gâthâs
that someone would come to "re-cloth the bodies."
On whose account in Western Africa the skulls
are painted red.
Killing a god dates from the most remote times according to Frazer.
Those Redskins
seeing the whole world full of blood,
as though painted with blood, they say,
and that's why there are red rocks,
and that's why the world is beautiful.
The hieroglyphics on the tombs of Tell-el Armana:
addressed to him.
in the XVI century Ricci encountered
most ancient Jewish communities in China
waiting for the *Moscia* (some time within 10,000 years).
And Confucius said:
You do not leave except by the door.
You do not walk except along the path.
He came to unite all our totems and all our clans.
To set us free from all the taboos.
The saviour of the tribe.
A Mediating Saviour in the Upper Nile,
who is not dead according to them in the Upper Nile.
*Mictlan Tecuhli* Nahuatl, the Lord of the Mansion of the Dead.
The sun.          The one that feeds us
and by night lights up our dead.

The primitives in their myths, according to Frobenius,
never mention the technical process of that discovery
(fire) but that it is always from a god, an outsider.
Fire was *stolen* also in Polynesia
(Island of Mangala). Thanks to a hero, people have light
            and can cook their food.
A humanity in deep darkness, the Zuni recall,
crowded together, climbing one on top of the other like reptiles,
until the great wise man brought them out of there
to the surface of the earth, to the Sun-Father.
The *agraphon* of Christ's:
            "Raise up the stone and there you will find me."
(He's been around since the Palaeolithic.)
The stone that God worked (Chilam Balam de Chumayel)
there where formerly there was no sky.
In the Strait of Torres
Mutuk was inside a shark.
Yetl (sun god) inside a whale.
Jonah, deeply rooted in the mind of primitive peoples
says Frobenius.
Once again Frobenius. Dear Pound.
The hero defeats the monster in the Pygmy myth
delivering from it the men that it had devoured.
"Difficult to know what he will be like" Confucius said,
"the saint awaited for a hundred generations."
A generation (*chi*) is 30 years;
that is, awaited for 3,000 years.
Also: That the two first dynasties have not
been able to satisfy the heavens.
"You have said it. I am king." He said in the praetorium.
Which you have to interpret in the orthodox manner:
I am the People. And the People are king.
            I am the proletariat.
                    And the proletariat is king of history.

# Mark 15:6—15

Now at the festival he used to release a prisoner for them, anyone for whom they asked. Now a man called Barabbas was in prison with the rebels who had committed murder during the insurrection. So the crowd came and began to ask Pilate to do for them according to his custom. Then he answered them, "Do you want me to release for you the King of the Jews?" For he realized that it was out of jealousy that the chief priests had handed him over. But the chief priests stirred up the crowd to have him release Barabbas for them instead. Pilate spoke to them again, "Then what do you wish me to do with the man you call the King of the Jews?" They shouted back, "Crucify him!" Pilate asked them, "Why, what evil has he done?" But they shouted all the more, "Crucify him!" So Pilate, wishing to satisfy the crowd, released Barabbas for them; and after flogging Jesus, he handed him over to be crucified.

# Pontius Pilate Discusses the Proceedings of the Last Judgment

VASSAR MILLER

U.S., 1924–. See page 146 for biographical information on this poet.

Unfortunate. Yet how was I to know,
appointed to preserve the Pax Romana,
that *he* was not another of these fools
whose crosses bristled on the hills like toothpicks.
And how were you to guess that the young girl
you burned one day in France for hearing Voices
was destined to be hailed as saint and genius,
not merely silly in the head from sex?
Most of her kind would be. And it's the duty
of men like us to save the world from madness.
Never mind who saves the world from sin.
For madness does the harm that we can see,
strangles the baby, sets the house on fire,
and rapes the women in the name of powers
we can't, nine times out of ten. And if
we're wrong the tenth time, why should we be blamed?
That judge, now, over there, he'll sit in honor
simply because he happened to follow the way
his nose led him to declare the fellow
who knelt barefooted at the Communion Rail
in a suburban parish a poor crazy
son-of-a-bitch. He bet on a sure thing
and won. Our gambles looked the same. We lost.
*He* really and truly was the Son of God?
I'm not surprised. The gods will play some joke—
and then get angry every time it works!

# The Crown of Thorns

## Mark 15:16–17

Then the soldiers led him into the courtyard of the palace (that is, the governor's headquarters); and they called together the whole cohort. And they clothed him in a purple cloak; and after twisting some thorns into a crown, they put it on him.

# The Coronet

ANDREW MARVELL

England, 1621–1678. A scholar, Latinist, and statesman, Marvell converted to Catholicism while at Cambridge University, though his father, an Anglican rector, soon reconverted him to his original faith. Marvell served as assistant to his friend JOHN MILTON, before being elected to Parliament. Now considered one of his century's major lyric poets, Marvell was known in his own time mainly as a man of public affairs and a political satirist. His fascination with gardens found its way into nearly all of his poems, even this one on the Crown of Thorns.

When for the Thorns with which I long, too long,
    With many a piercing wound,
    My Saviour's head have crown'd,
I seek with Garlands to redress that Wrong:
    Through every Garden, every Mead,
I gather flow'rs (my fruits are only flow'rs)
    Dismantling all the fragrant Towers
That once adorned my Shepherdesses head.
And now when I have summ'd up all my store,
    Thinking (so I my self deceive)
    So rich a Chaplet thence to weave
As never yet the king of Glory wore:
    Alas I find the Serpent old
    That, twining in his speckled breast,
    About the flow'rs disguis'd does fold,
    With wreaths of Fame and Interest.
Ah, foolish Man, that would'st debase with them
And mortal Glory, Heaven's Diadem!
But thou who only could'st the Serpent tame,
Either his slipp'ry knots at once untie,
And disentangle all his winding Snare:
Or shatter too with him my curious frame:
And let these wither, so that he may die,
Though set with Skill and chosen out with Care.
That they, while Thou on both their Spoils dost tread,
May crown thy Feet, that could not crown thy Head.

# In a Country Church

R. S. THOMAS

Wales, 1913–. See page 7 for biographical information on this poet.

To one kneeling down no word came,
Only the wind's song, saddening the lips
Of the grave saints, rigid in glass;
Or the dry whisper of unseen wings,
Bats not angels, in the high roof.

Was he balked by silence? He kneeled long,
And saw love in a dark crown
Of thorns blazing, and a winter tree
Golden with fruit of a man's body.

## Mark 15:18–19

And they began saluting him, "Hail, King of the Jews!" They struck his head with a reed, spat upon him, and knelt down in homage to him.

# Claudius: A Roman Sentinel

KAHLIL GIBRAN

Lebanon, 1883–1931. See page 204 for biographical information on this poet.

After he was taken, they entrusted Him to me. And I was ordered by Pontius Pilatus to keep Him in custody until the following morning.

My soldiers led Him prisoner, and He was obedient to them.

At midnight I left my wife and children and visited the arsenal. It was my habit to go about and see that all was well with my battalions in Jerusalem; and that night I visited the arsenal where He was held.

My soldiers and some of the young Jews were making sport of Him. They had stripped Him of His garment, and they put a crown of last year's brier-thorns upon His head.

They had seated Him against a pillar, and they were dancing and shouting before Him.

And they had given Him a reed to hold in His hand.

As I entered someone shouted: "Behold, O Captain, the King of the Jews."

I stood before Him and looked at Him, and I was ashamed. I knew not why.

I had fought in Gallia and in Spain, and with my men I had faced death. Yet never had I been in fear, nor been a coward. But when I stood before that man and He looked at me I lost heart. It seemed as though my lips were sealed, and I could utter no word.

And straightway I left the arsenal.

This chanced thirty years ago. My sons who were babes then are men now. And they are serving Cæsar and Rome.

But often in counselling them I have spoken of Him, a man facing death with the sap of life upon His lips, and with compassion for His slayers in His eyes.

And now I am old. I have lived the years fully. And I think truly that neither Pompey nor Cæsar was so great a commander as that Man of Galilee.

For since His unresisting death an army has risen out of the earth to fight for Him. . . . And He is better served by them, though dead, than ever Pompey or Cæsar was served, though living.

# The One People Once Called

ANNA AKHMATOVA

Russia, 1889–1966. See page 309 for biographical information on this poet. "The One People Once Called" is translated from the Russian by Judith Hemschemeyer.

The one people once called
King in jest, God in fact,
Who was killed, and whose implement of torture
Was heated by the warmth of my breast . . .
The disciples of Christ tasted death,
And the old gossips, and the soldiers,
And the procurator from Rome—all gone.
There, where once the arch rose,
Where the sea splashed, where the cliff turned black,
They were imbibed with the wine, inhaled with the stifling dust
And the fragrance of immortal roses.
Gold rusts and steel decays,
Marble crumbles away. Everything is on the verge of death.
The most reliable thing on earth is sorrow,
And the most enduring—the almighty Word.

# The Way of the Cross

*Mark 15:20b*

Then they led him out to crucify him.

# Salvator Mundi: Via Crucis

DENISE LEVERTOV

U.S., 1923 –. Daughter of a Russian Jew who had married a Welsh woman and become an Anglican clergyman, Levertov was born in England. She became a U.S. citizen after World War II and has been a leading American poet since the 1960s. She began writing from an agnostic standpoint, but a sense of mystery, of inspiration from an unknown source, always informed her poetry. Gradually, she has said, "the unknown began to be defined for me as God, and, further, as God revealed in the Incarnation." By the early 1980s she was avowedly writing from "a position of Christian belief."

Maybe He looked indeed
much as Rembrandt envisioned Him
in those small heads that seem in fact
portraits of more than a model.
A dark, still young, very intelligent face,
a soul-mirror gaze of deep understanding, unjudging.
*That* face, in extremis, would have clenched its teeth
in a grimace not shown in even the great crucifixions.
The burden of humanness (I begin to see) exacted from Him
that He taste also the humiliation of dread,
cold sweat of wanting to let the whole thing go,
like any mortal hero out of his depth,
like anyone who has taken a step too far
and wants herself back.
The painters, even the greatest, don't show how,
in the midnight Garden,
or staggering uphill under the weight of the Cross,
He went through with even the human longing
to simply cease, to not be.
Not torture of body,
not the hideous betrayals humans commit
nor the faithless weakness of friends, and surely
not the anticipation of death (not then, in agony's grip)
was Incarnation's heaviest weight,
but this sickened desire to renege,
to step back from what He, Who was God,
had promised Himself, and had entered
time and flesh to enact.
Sublime acceptance, to be absolute, had to have welled
up from those depths where purpose
drifted for mortal moments.

## Luke 23:32

Two others also, who were criminals, were led away to be put to death with him.

# Ride Upon the Death Chariot

OSWALD MBUYOSENI MTSHALI

South Africa, 1940–. See page 24 for biographical information on this poet.

They rode upon
the death chariot
to their Golgotha —
three vagrants
whose papers to be in Caesar's empire
were not in order.

The sun
shrivelled their bodies
in the mobile tomb
as airtight as canned fish.

We're hot!
We're thirsty!
We're hungry!

The centurion
touched their tongues
with the tip
of a lance
dipped in apathy:

"Don't cry to me
but to Caesar who
crucifies you."

A woman came
to wipe their faces.
She carried a dishcloth
full of bread and tea.

We're dying!

The centurion
washed his hands.

# Golgotha

## *Matthew 27:33–37*

And when they came to a place called Golgotha (which means Place of a Skull), they offered him wine to drink, mixed with gall; but when he tasted it, he would not drink it. And when they had crucified him, they divided his clothes among themselves by casting lots; then they sat down there and kept watch over him. Over his head they put the charge against him, which read, "This is Jesus, the King of the Jews."

# To Crucify the Son

MIGUEL DE GUEVARA

Mexico, 1585?–1646?. As a missionary Augustin monk, Fray Miguel de Gue-
vara went among the Aztecs, Tarascos, and Matlalzingos. Some of his sacred
sonnets, like "To Crucify the Son," are characteristic of the best seventeenth-
century Spanish poetry, with its tight paradoxical play of words and ideas. "To
Crucify the Son" is translated from the Spanish by Samuel Beckett.

> To Crucify the Son and pierce his breast,
> to sacrify him that I might not die,
> it is very sure proof, Lord, of love,
> to show thyself so full of love for me.
>
> So that—I God, thou mortal man—I should
> give thee the godly being then were mine,
> and in this my mortality lay me down
> that of so good a God I might have joy.
>
> And yet thy love received no recompense
> when thou didst raise me up to excellency
> of godhood, and to manhood God didst humble.
>
> I owe and rightfully shall ever owe
> the debt that by the Son upon the cross
> was paid for me that thou mightst be requited.

# That Yellowed Body

VLADIMIR LVOV

Russia, 1926–1961. Born in Moscow, Lvov seemed to cultivate obscurity. Solitary and depressed by an unhappy love affair, he drowned in a swimming pool in Moscow. "That Yellowed Body" is translated from the Russian by Sarah W. Bliumis.

> That yellowed body of the Lord
> Hanging on the cross,
> The face tormented with loss,
> And we do not adore him
> With his nails and small board.
> The radiance of his scarlet blood,
> That worn-out, mournful face.
> We can only pity Christ today,
> So, of course, he's no longer great.
> Our earth loves the victorious.
> O, dear old God, forgive me,
> But when the cup runneth over,
> It's not quite decent to suffer.

# Wonders Will Never Cease

AILEEN KELLY

England, 1939 –. Educated at Cambridge University, Kelly lives in Melbourne, Australia, where she works in adult education. A Roman Catholic, she draws in her poetry on two particular strands of that tradition: a passion for social justice, and the incarnational spirituality often called "nature mysticism." Her first book of poetry, *Coming up for Light* (1994), won the prestigious Mary Gilmore Award from the Association for the Study of Australian Literature.

So they lay themselves down for the small,
their own bodies bitten with frost and the death of children,
crawling in basements of black humour, black love.
And from that angle every dawn they see
how long the shadows are that darken the windows.

So they stand up to the great
       muscle-men and puzzle them;
       crowds and touch them;
       power-brokers and break the power
back.

       Hesitantly making progress towards
that unbelievable moment the first nail's
pain captures a wrist
                and small friends huddle
at a distance watching
silent

# Friday

## ELIZABETH JENNINGS

England, 1926–. Jennings began her career as part of Britain's "angry young men" literary movement during the 1950s. Since then her verse has become increasingly religious, with Gospel themes among the many subjects in her classically crafted verse. "Art is not self-expression," she says, "while, for me, 'confessional poetry' is almost a contradiction in terms." A prolific poet, with over twenty-five published volumes of verse, Jennings lives in Oxford.

We nailed the hands long ago,
Wove the thorns, took up the scourge and shouted
For excitement's sake, we stood at the dusty edge
Of the pebbled path and watched the extreme of pain.

But one or two prayed, one or two
Were silent, shocked, stood back
And remembered remnants of words, a new vision.
The cross is up with its crying victim, the clouds
Cover the sun, we learn a new way to lose
What we did not know we had
Until this bleak and sacrificial day,
Until we turned from our bad
Past and knelt and cried out our dismay,
The dice still clicking, the voices dying away.

# Christ

FAZIL HÜSNÜ DAĞLARCA

Turkey, 1914 –. The author of over sixty collections of poetry and a great quantity of political journalism, Dağlarca served as an army officer until his retirement in 1950. The recipient of numerous poetry awards, he ran for many years a famous Istanbul bookshop and literary gathering place. Though his influences derive almost exclusively from native Turkish and Islamic literatures, he is widely known for the originality and individuality of his voice and vision. "Christ" is translated from the Turkish by Talat Sait Halman.

1

Your body,
Like a hunted animal,
Is crucified,
But we sense your time
In four dimensions
As our life
Endures.

You hardly differ
From Buddha and the other idols,
But by rejection
And death
And ascension, myth by myth,
You are
Mightier.

Your light fills our room
Through our window.
Your endless presence
Eats, drinks, listens, thinks
Over vast stretches of land.
You unite the ages
Of men and nations.

2

Nails pierced your palms.
The pain is still warm.

Blood lives on,
Far from red.

They expand toward us,
Tired, desolate,
Little,
Yellow, dark and white.

Not gone from our world, not separated,
In a thousand laments
Your palms
Declare that we are friends.

# from *Divine Comedy*

DANTE ALIGHIERI

Italy, 1265–1321. Born in Florence into an affluent commercial family, Dante successfully combined a literary, scholarly, and active Florentine life until he was condemned to death for his political opposition to the papacy in 1302. Exiled from his beloved city, Dante spent the rest of his life wandering through Italy and writing his greatest work, and one of the greatest poems in any language, the *Divina Commedia*. The *Commedia* tells the story of Dante's visionary journey through Hell, Purgatory, and Paradise. In the excerpt below, Dante has reached the sphere of the planet Mars in Paradise and beholds there the vision of Christ on the Cross. This selection from *Divine Comedy* is translated from the Italian by John Ciardi.

I was made aware that I had risen higher
    by the enkindled ardor of the red star
    that glowed, I thought, with more than usual fire.

With all my heart, and in the tongue which is
    one in all men, I offered God my soul
    as a burnt offering for this new bliss.

Nor had the flame of sacrifice in my breast
    burned out, when a good omen let me know
    my prayer had been received by the Most Blest;

for with such splendor, in such a ruby glow,
    within two rays, there shone so great a glory
    I cried, "O Helios that arrays them so!"

As, pole to pole, the arch of the Milky Way
    so glows, pricked out by greater and lesser stars,
    that sages stare, not knowing what to say—

so constellated, deep within that Sphere,
    the two rays formed into the holy sign
    a circle's quadrant lines describe. And here

memory outruns my powers. How shall I write
    that from that cross there glowed a vision of Christ?
    What metaphor is worthy of that sight?

But whoso takes his cross and follows Christ
    will pardon me what I leave here unsaid
    when *he* sees that great dawn that rays forth Christ.

From arm to arm, from root to crown of that tree,
    bright lamps were moving, crossing and rejoining.
    And when they met they glowed more brilliantly.

So, here on earth, across a slant of light
    that parts the air within the sheltering shade
    man's arts and crafts contrive, our mortal sight

observes bright particles of matter ranging
    up, down, aslant; darting or eddying;
    longer and shorter; but forever changing.

And as a viol and a harp in a harmony
    of many strings, make only a sweet tinkle
    to one who has not studied melody;

so from that choir of glories I heard swell
    so sweet a melody that I stood tranced,
    though what hymn they were singing, I could not tell.

That it was raised in lofty praise was clear,
    for I heard "Arise" and "Conquer"—but as one
    may hear, not understanding, and still hear.

My soul was so enraptured by those strains
    of purest song, that nothing until then
    had bound my being to it in such sweet chains.

# Between Two Thieves

*Matthew 27:38*

Then two bandits were crucified with him, one on his right and one on his left.

# Knight

RUBÉN DARÍO

Nicaragua, 1867–1916. See page 49 for biographical information on this poet. "Knight" is translated from the Spanish by Lysander Kemp.

I am a semicentaur
with a rough, roguish look.
I imitate the Minotaur
and follow Epicurus.

The laurel on my forehead
predicts my future,
and under the sign of Taurus
I batter down strong walls.

I sing to Proserpina,
who burns hearts
in her smoking brazier.

I am Satan, and I am Christ
dying between two thieves—
Oh where do I exist?

# The Dreamer

WOLE SOYINKA

Nigeria, 1934–. See page 359 for biographical information on this poet.

Higher than trees a cryptic crown
Lord of the rebel three
Thorns lay on a sleep of down
And myrrh; a mesh
Of nails, of flesh
And words that flowered free

A cleft between the birches
Next year is reaping time
The fruit will fall to searchers
Cleansed of mould
Chronicles of gold
Mourn a fruit in prime.

The burden bowed the boughs to earth
A girdle for the see
And bitter pods gave voices birth
A ring of stones
And throes and thrones
And incense on the sea.

# Derision: Come Down from the Cross

## Mark 15:29–30

Those who passed by derided him, shaking their heads and saying, "Aha! You who would destroy the temple and build it in three days, save yourself, and come down from the cross!"

# The Day Zimmer Lost Religion

PAUL ZIMMER

U.S., 1934–. Zimmer worked as an editor and bookstore manager before assuming
the directorship of the University of Georgia Press. His "The Day Zimmer Lost
Religion" is typical of his self-parodic style in which the "Zimmer" persona bears
the brunt of the poet's pungent, thoughtful mockery.

> The first Sunday I missed Mass on purpose
> I waited all day for Christ to climb down
> Like a wiry flyweight from the cross and
> Club me on my irreverent teeth, to wade into
> My blasphemous gut and drop me like a
> Red hot thurible, the devil roaring in
> Reserved seats until he got the hiccups.
>
> It was a long cold way from the old days
> When cassocked and surpliced I mumbled Latin
> At the old priest and rang his obscure bell.
> A long way from the dirty wind that blew
> The soot like venial sins across the school yard
> Where God reigned as a threatening,
> One-eyed triangle high in the fleecy sky.
>
> The first Sunday I missed Mass on purpose
> I waited all day for Christ to climb down
> Like the playground bully, the cuts and mice
> Upon his face agleam, and pound me
> Till my irreligious tongue hung out.
> But of course He never came, knowing that
> I was grown up and ready for Him now.

# Father, Forgive Them

*Luke 23:34a*

Then Jesus said, "Father, forgive them; for they do not know what they are doing."

# *from* A Litany of Atlanta

W. E. B. DU BOIS

U.S., 1868–1963. Du Bois died in Ghana, having renounced his U.S. citizenship after persecution by the U.S. Government during the McCarthy era. In the years between, Du Bois had been one of America's few Renaissance men, contributing to the artistic, social, literary, and political environments. He is best known, however, for his sociological studies of the plight of the American Black and for his vigorous assault on racism from the columns of the NAACP's *The Crisis* magazine. The excerpt from the "Litany of Atlanta" shows the public use Du Bois made of poetry in expressing the anguish of his people.

Behold this maimed and broken thing; dear God, it was an humble black man who toiled and sweat to save a bit from the pittance paid him. They told him: *Work and Rise.* He worked. Did this man sin? Nay, but some one told how some one said another did—one whom he had never seen nor known. Yet for that man's crime this man lieth maimed and murdered, his wife naked to shame, his children, to poverty and evil.

*Hear us, O Heavenly Father!*

Doth not this justice of hell stink in Thy nostrils, O God? How long shall the mounting flood of innocent blood roar in Thine ears and pound in our hearts for vengeance? Pile the pale frenzy of blood-crazed brutes who do such deeds high on Thine altar, Jehovah Jireh, and burn it in hell forever and forever!

*Forgive us, good Lord; we know not what we say!*

Bewildered we are, and passion-tost, mad with the madness of a mobbed and mocked and murdered people; straining at the armposts of Thy Throne, we raise our shackled hands and charge Thee, God, by the bones of our stolen fathers, by the tears of our dead mothers, by the very blood of Thy crucified Christ: *What meaneth this?* Tell us the Plan; give us the Sign!

*Keep not Thou silence, O God!*

[ 466 ] THE PASSION

Sit no longer blind, Lord God, deaf to our prayer and dumb to our dumb suffering. Surely, Thou too art not white, O Lord, a pale, bloodless, heartless thing?

*Ah! Christ of all the Pities!*

Forgive the thought! Forgive these wild, blasphemous words. Thou art still the God of our black fathers, and in Thy soul's soul sit some soft darkenings of the evening, some shadowings of the velvet night.

But whisper—speak—call, great God, for Thy silence is white terror to our hearts! The way, O God, show us the way and point us the path.

Whither? North is greed and South is blood; within, the coward, and without the liar. Whither? To Death?

*Amen! Welcome dark sleep!*

# Riot

## A Poem in Three Parts

GWENDOLYN BROOKS

U.S., 1917–. See page 345 for biographical information on this poet. Biblical
images subtly suffuse Brooks' poetry, sometimes (as in "Riot") ironically, to
expose corruptions of Christianity.

> *A riot is the language of the unheard.*
> MARTIN LUTHER KING, JR.

John Cabot, out of Wilma, once a Wycliffe,
all whitebluerose below his golden hair,
wrapped richly in right linen and right wool,
almost forgot his Jaguar and Lake Bluff;
almost forgot Grandtully (which is The
Best Thing That Ever Happened To Scotch); almost
forgot the sculpture at the Richard Gray
and Distelheim; the kidney pie at Maxim's,
the Grenadine de Beouf at Maison Henri.

Because the "Negroes" were coming down the street.

Because the Poor were sweaty and unpretty
(not like Two Dainty Negroes in Winnetka)
and they were coming toward him in rough ranks.
In seas. In windsweep. They were black and loud.
And not detainable. And not discreet.

Gross. Gross. "Que tu es grossier!" John Cabot
itched instantly beneath the nourished white
that told his story of glory to the World.
"Don't let It touch me! the blackness! Lord!" he
whispered to any handy angel in the sky.

But, in a thrilling announcement, on It drove
and breathed on him: and touched him. In that breath
the fume of pig foot, chitterling and cheap chili,

malign, mocked John. And, in terrific touch, old
averted doubt jerked forward decently,
cried "Cabot! John! You are a desperate man,
and the desperate die expensively today."

John Cabot went down in the smoke and fire
and broken glass and blood, and he cried "Lord!
Forgive these nigguhs that know not what they do."

# Conversation with Two Thieves

## Luke 23:39−43

One of the criminals who were hanged there kept deriding him and saying, "Are you not the Messiah? Save yourself and us!" But the other rebuked him, saying, "Do you not fear God, since you are under the same sentence of condemnation? And we indeed have been condemned justly, for we are getting what we deserve for our deeds, but this man has done nothing wrong." Then he said, "Jesus, remember me when you come into your kingdom." He replied, "Truly I tell you, today you will be with me in Paradise."

# Luke XXIII

JORGE LUIS BORGES

Argentina, 1899–1986. See page 282 for biographical information on this poet.
"Luke XXIII" is translated from the Spanish by Mark Strand.


Gentile or Jew or simply a man
Whose face has been lost in time,
We shall not save the silent
Letters of his name from oblivion.

What could he know of forgiveness,
A thief whom Judea nailed to a cross?
For us those days are lost.
During his last undertaking,

Death by crucifixion,
He learned from the taunts of the crowd
That the man who was dying beside him
Was God. And blindly he said:

*Remember me when thou comest
Into thy kingdom*, and from the terrible cross
The unimaginable voice
Which one day will judge us all

Promised him Paradise. Nothing more was said
Between them before the end came,
But history will not let the memory
Of their last afternoon die.

O friends, the innocence of this friend
Of Jesus! That simplicity which made him,
From the disgrace of punishment, ask for
And be granted Paradise

Was what drove him time
And again to sin and to bloody crime.

# Gipsy Privilege

NIS PETERSEN

Denmark, 1897–1943. Born in southern Jutland, Petersen was orphaned as a young child and raised by a religiously strict grandmother, whose Christian influence he both respected and rebelled against throughout his hard-drinking bohemian life. The author of an internationally famous novel about ancient Rome, *The Street of the Sandalmakers* (1931), Petersen viewed love and charity as the great message of Christianity. His poetry often shows deep compassion for the poor and rootless. "Gipsy Privilege" is translated from the Danish by Robert Prescott Keigwin.

Those stains of crimson along the snowdrift
Were poor dead birds that had frozen stiff . . .
And green ones lay there and gray and white ones;
The wind blew icy from bay to cliff.
We saw them lying and feared to pass them;
But one of the tribe would pause, relenting,
And fold a bird to his naked bosom,
While Romany mourned with loud lamenting.

A robin it was, on its way to heaven;
And there's a legend you must have read,
That when our Lord on the cross was hanging
A bird came lighting upon his head;
Came down, that quivering tiny creature,
And robbed his brow of a thorn that tore him—
Then stabbed it deep in its own bird-bosom
And flew to the far-off lands before him.

And there's a tale that is old and trusty
How, when the Saviour was stricken down
With cold sweat shining on anguished forehead,
With bleeding back and his thorny crown,
They sought, those murderers' grisly henchmen,
The fourth great nail that escaped their clutches;
But Jesus smiled at the gipsy near him
Who stole for love . . . And the legend vouches

This was the promise the Saviour uttered:
That every gipsy through endless time,
For his mercy's sake, may go on thieving;

But if he traverse the snow and rime
And find a robin that's fallen, frozen,
His breast shall pity its desolation;
The tribe shall follow their little brother
With funeral grief and lamentation.

# Standing Near . . . His Mother

*John 19:25*

Meanwhile, standing near the cross of Jesus were his mother, and his mother's sister, Mary the wife of Clopas, and Mary Magdalene.

# Stabat Mater

## (attrib.) JACAPONE DA TODI

Italy, c.1230–1306. See page 291 for biographical information on this poet.
Though the perennially popular *Stabat Mater* ("The Mother Was Standing")
is traditionally attributed to Jacopone da Todi, modern scholars judge it not to
be his. "Stabat Mater" is translated from the Latin by George Dardess.

His mother stood there by the cross
Where her son was hanging,
His anguish sharing.
A sword pierced through her heart.

Though blessed and set apart
As mother of God's son,
Yet how great her painful sighing
To watch her child's slow dying.

Can there be one so cold
Who, seeing Christ's mother standing there,
Could watch her unconcernedly?
Not sorrowful himself, but hard and bold?

Not sharing her grief
To see him sliced by whips,
Split by nails,
In torment for our own sins and ills?
Her sweet son,
Abandoned, alone?

Mother, love's spring,
Pour out your pain on me
That with you I may mourn.
Make my heart burn
That I might love him too
And so bring joy to him and you.

O holy mother, drive the nails
Deep into my heart!

His wounds and dying—for whom else but me?
Let torment make us one,
Not drive us apart!

And may I also stand with you
Beside this cross,
Crying your tears,
Mourning your loss,
My life through.

Virgin above all virgins!
Do not shrug me away!
Wound me with his wounds.
Make me a drunkard of his cross
And of his blood—
My defense from fire and flame
On Judgment Day.

O Jesus, when it's my time to die,
Grant that through your mother's love
I might gain a place with you above.

Though my body fall away,
Lift my soul
To Paradise's eternal day!

# Lament of Our Lady under the Cross

ANONYMOUS

Poland, 15th century. "Lament of Our Lady under the Cross," said to be the best medieval poem in Polish, may be a fragment of an extinct mystery play for Good Friday. The Mary depicted here, in contrast to the saintly Mary in "Stabat Mater," begs for pity and gives free vent to her baffled resentment at not only the "infidel Jew" but also at Gabriel himself. "Lament of Our Lady under the Cross" is translated from the Polish by Jon Stallworthy.

Hear me, my dears, this bleeding head
I want to lament before you turn;
listen to this affliction that
befell me on Godd Friday.

Pity me, all of you, old and young,
The feast of blood will be my song.
I had a single son,
it is for him I weep.

A poor woman, I was rudely confused
when I saw my birthright in bitter blood.
Dreadful the moment and bloody the hour
when I saw the infidel Jew
beat and torment my beloved son.

Oh, son, sweet and singled-out,
share your pain with your mother.
I carried you near my heart, dear son.
I served you faithfully.
Speak to your mother. Console my great grief
now that you leave me and all my hopes.

Small boy, if you were only lower
I could give you a little help.
Your head hangs crooked: I would support it,
your dear blood flows; I would wipe it off.
And now you ask for a drink and a drink I would give you,
but I cannot reach your holy body.

Oh, angel Gabriel
where is that range of joy
you promised me would never change?
You said: "Virgin, you are filled with love,"
but now I am full of a great grief.
My body has rotted inside me and my bones moulder.

## John 19:26–27

When Jesus saw his mother and the disciple whom he loved standing beside her, he said to his mother, "Woman, here is your son." Then he said to the disciple, "Here is your mother." And from that hour the disciple took her into his own home.

# John Beseeches Her

KAROL WOJTYLA (POPE JOHN PAUL II)

Poland, 1920–. See page 190 for biographical information on this poet. "John Beseeches Her" is translated from the Polish by Jerzy Peterkiewicz.

Don't lower the wave of my heart,
it swells to your eyes, Mother;
don't alter love, but bring the wave to me
in your translucent hands.

He asked for this.

I am John the fisherman. There isn't much
in me to love.

I feel I am still on that lake shore,
gravel crunching under my feet—
and, suddenly—Him.

You will embrace His mystery in me no more,
yet quietly I spread round your thoughts like myrtle.
And calling you Mother—His wish—
I beseech you: may this word
never grow less for you.

True, it's not easy to measure the meaning
of the words He breathed into us both
so that all earlier love in those words
should be concealed.

# Darkness from Sixth to Ninth Hour

## Mark 15:33

When it was noon, darkness came over the whole land until three in the afternoon.

# Crucifixion

## FEDERICO GARCÍA LORCA

Spain, 1899–1936. Angered by what he saw as the Catholic Church's indifference to suffering, García Lorca wrote: "We must rescue Jesus' idea from your ruinous machinations." While visiting New York City, he composed the dark poems posthumously collected as *Poet in New York* (including "Crucifixion"), which bitterly condemn modern culture. Accused by Franco of being a Russian spy, García Lorca was executed by a firing squad during the Spanish Civil War. "Crucifixion" is translated from the Spanish by Greg Simon and Steven F. White.

The moon could rest in the end along the pure white curve of the
       horses.
A violent beam of light that escaped from a wound
projected the instant of a dead child's circumcision on the sky.

Blood flowed down the mountain and angels looked for it,
but the chalices became wind and finally filled the shoes.
Crippled dogs puffed on their pipes and the odor of hot leather
grayed the round lips of those who vomited on street corners.
And long southern howls arrived with the arid night.
It was the moon burning the horses' phallus with its candles.
A tailor, who specialized in purple,
had locked up three saintly women
and was showing them a skull through the window glass.
In the borough, three boys circled a white camel
that wept because at dawn
there was no other way except through the needle's eye.
Oh, cross! Oh, nails! Oh, thorn!
Oh, thorn driven to the bone until the planets rust to pieces!
Since no one turned to look, the sky could undress.
Then the great voice was heard, and the pharisees said:
That wicked cow has teats full of milk.
The multitude locked their doors
and rain flowed down the streets, determined to drench their hearts
while the evening clouded over with heartbeats and woodcutters
and the darkened city agonized under the carpenters' hammer.
That wicked cow
has teats full of bird shot,

said the blue pharisees.
But blood drenched their feet and unclean spirits
splattered drops of blistered ponds on the temple walls.
Someone knew the precise moment that our lives would be saved
because the moon washed the burns
of the horses with water
and not the living girl they silenced in the sand.
Then the chills went out singing their songs
and frogs ignited fires on the river's double shore.
That wicked cow, wicked, wicked, wicked,
won't let us sleep, said the pharisees,
and they withdrew to their houses through the riotous street,
pushing drunks aside and spitting sacrificial salt
while the blood followed them like a bleating lamb.

That's how it was
and the awakened earth cast off trembling rivers of moths.

# My God, My God . . .

*Mark 15:34*

At three o'clock Jesus cried out with a loud voice, "Eloi, Eloi, lema sabachthani?" which means, "My God, my God, why have you forsaken me?"

# Nocturne

GABRIELA MISTRAL

Chile, 1889–1957. See page 210 for biographical information on this poet. "Nocturne" is translated from the Spanish by Helene Masslo Anderson.

Our Father who art in heaven,
Why hast Thou forsaken me!
Thou did'st remember the February fruit,
When torn was its pulp of ruby.
My side is pierced also
Yet Thou will'st not look at me!

Thou did'st remember the dark grape cluster
And did'st give it to the crimsoned press,
And Thou did'st fan the poplar leaves
With thy breath of gentleness.
Yet in the deep wine press of death
Thou still would'st not my heart express!

As I walked I saw violets open;
And I drank the wine of the wind,
And I have lowered my yellowed eyelids
Never more to see Winter or Spring.
And I have tightened my mouth to stifle
The verses I am never to sing.
Thou hast wounded the cloud of Autumn
And Thou will'st not turn toward me!

I was sold by the one who kissed my cheek;
He betrayed me for the tunic vile.
I gave him in my verses, my blood-stained face,
As Thine imprinted on her veil,
And in my night of the Orchard I have found
John reluctant and the Angel hostile.

And now an infinite fatigue
Has come to pierce my eyes:
The fatigue of the day that is dying

And of the dawn that will arise;
The fatigue of the sky of metal
The fatigue of indigo skies!

And now I loosen my martyred sandal
And my locks, for I am longing to sleep.
And lost in the night, I lift my voice
In the cry I have learned from Thee:
Our Father who art in heaven,
Why hast Thou forsaken me!

# The Son of Man

RABINDRANATH TAGORE

India, 1861–1941. Tagore was awarded the 1913 Nobel Prize for Literature for his vision of life's beauty and sacredness, especially in the preciousness of childhood. His voluminous writings helped introduce the West to Bengali culture. Most of his poetry evokes a universal God; "The Son of Man" is rare in being inspired particularly by Christ.

From His eternal seat Christ comes down to this earth, where, ages ago, in the bitter cup of death He poured his deathless life for those who came to the call and those who remained away.

He looks about Him, and sees the weapons of evil that wounded His own age.

The arrogant spikes and spears, the slim, sly knives, the scimitar in diplomatic sheath, crooked and cruel, are hissing and raining sparks as they are sharpened on monster wheels.

But the most fearful of them all, at the hands of the slaughterers, are those on which has been engraved His own name, that are fashioned from the texts of His own words fused in the fire of hatred and hammered by hypocritical greed.

He presses His hand upon His heart; He feels that the age-long moment of His death has not yet ended, that new nails, turned out in countless numbers by those who are learned in cunning craftsmanship, pierce Him in every joint.

They had hurt Him once, standing at the shadow of their temple; they are born anew in crowds.

From before their sacred altar they shout to the soldiers, "Strike!"

And the Son of Man in agony cried, "My God, My God, why hast Thou forsaken me?"

# The Sponge Soaked in Vinegar

*John 19:28—29*

After this, when Jesus knew that all was now finished, he said (in order to fulfill the scripture), "I am thirsty." A jar full of sour wine was standing there. So they put a sponge full of the wine on a branch of hyssop and held it to his mouth.

# The Cruel Drink

JEAN DE LA CEPPÈDE

France, 1548–1623. See page 414 for biographical information on this poet. "The Cruel Drink" is translated from the French by Keith Bosley.

As soon as he has said 'I thirst,' a Jew
Impales a sponge which he has duly sunk
In vinegar until it is soaked through
Upon a stick, holds up the cruel drink.

This is the bitterness that pays the price
(Now that to you death stretches out its claws
O Christ) of sweetness, now a bait to entice
And hook the Old Man from the lord of lies.

Alas! Is this the fruit so long awaited
Is this the need to which your vine is fitted?
Who looked at it that it brought forth wild grapes?

Of all in those old oracles concealed
This only is left, unfolding at your lips:
In you now they are utterly fulfilled.

# The Sponge Full of Vinegar

THOMAS MERTON

U.S., 1915–1968. See page 125 for biographical information on this poet.

When Romans gambled in the clash of lancelight,
Dicing amid the lightnings for the unsewn mantle,
Thirst burned crimson, like a crosswise firebird
Even in the eyes of dying Christ.
But the world's gall, and all its rotten vinegar
Reeked in the sponge, flamed on His swollen mouth,
And all was paid in poison, in the taste of our feasts!

O Lord! When I lie breathless in Thy churches
Knowing it is Thy glory goes again
Torn from the wise world in the daily thundercracks of massbells,
I drink new fear from the four clean prayers I ever gave Thee!
For even the Word of Thy Name, caught from Thy grace,
And offered up out of my deepest terror,
Goes back gallsavored of flesh.
Even the one good sacrifice,
The thirst of heaven, comes to Thee: vinegar!
Reeks of the death-thirst manlife found in the forbidden apple.

# And He Died

## John 19:30b

Then he bowed his head and gave up his spirit.

# The Killing

EDWIN MUIR

Scotland, 1887–1959. Born in Deerness in the Orkney Islands, Muir wrote that he grew up in a "culture made up of legends, folk-song, and the poetry and prose of the Bible." But when he was 13 his family moved to industrial Glasgow, where within a year he was forced to leave school and where he lost both parents by the time he was eighteen. A highly repected literary critic as well as a poet and novelist, Muir was invited to give the prestigious Charles Eliot Norton lectures at Harvard in 1955–56.

That was the day they killed the Son of God
On a squat hill-top by Jerusalem.
Zion was bare, her children from their maze
Sucked by the demon curiosity
Clean through the gates. The very halt and blind
Had somehow got themselves up to the hill.

After the ceremonial preparation,
The scourging, nailing, nailing against the wood,
Erection of the main-trees with their burden,
While from the hill rose an orchestral wailing,
They were there at last, high up in the soft spring day.
We watched the writhings, heard the moanings, saw
The three heads turning on their separate axles
Like broken wheels left spinning. Round *his* head
Was loosely bound a crown of plaited thorn
That hurt at random, stinging temple and brow
As the pain swung into its envious circle.
In front the wreath was gathered in a knot
That as he gazed looked like the last stump left
Of a death-wounded deer's great antlers. Some
Who came to stare grew silent as they looked,
Indignant or sorry. But the hardened old
And the hard-hearted young, although at odds
From the first morning, cursed him with one curse,
Having prayed for a Rabbi or an armed Messiah
And found the Son of God. What use to them
Was a God or a Son of God? Of what avail

For purposes such as theirs? Beside the cross-foot,
Alone, four women stood and did not move
All day. The sun revolved, the shadow wheeled,
The evening fell. His head lay on his breast,
But in his breast they watched his heart move on
By itself alone, accomplishing its journey.
Their taunts grew louder, sharpened by the knowledge
That he was walking in the park of death,
Far from their rage. Yet all grew stale at last,
Spite, curiosity, envy, hate itself.
They waited only for death and death was slow
And came so quietly they scarce could mark it.
They were angry then with death and death's deceit.

I was a stranger, could not read these people
Or this outlandish deity. Did a God
Indeed in dying cross my life that day
By chance, he on his road and I on mine?

# The Earthquake

*Matthew 27:51*

At that moment the curtain of the temple was torn in two, from top to bottom. The earth shook, and the rocks were split.

# Antiphon for the Redeemer

HILDEGARD OF BINGEN

Germany, 1098–1179. See page 9 for biographical information on this poet.
"Antiphon for the Redeemer" is translated from the Latin by Barbara Newman.

> Blood that bled into a cry!
> The elements
> felt its touch and trembled,
> heaven heard their woe.
> O life-blood of the maker,
> scarlet music, salve our wounds.

# Song for Holy Saturday

JAMES KEIR BAXTER

New Zealand, 1926–1972. See page 99 for biographical information on this poet.

When His tears ran down like blood
I was sleeping in my clothes

When they struck Him with a reed
I cracked a very clever joke

When they gave Him a shirt of blood
I praised the colour of her dress

All the way up the hill
We were laughing fit to kill

When they were driving in the nails
I listened to the steel guitar

When they gave Him gall to drink
We were sipping the same glass

When He cried aloud in pain
We were playing Judases

When the ground began to shake
We pulled up the coverlet

Clean confessed and comforted
To the midnight mass I come

You who died in pain alone
Break my heart break my heart
*Deus sine termino.*

# A Stranger at the Fountain

## JABRĀ IBRĀHĪM JABRĀ

Palestine, 1919–. Born in Palestine, educated there and at Cambridge and Harvard, Jabrā left his native country for Iraq after the establishment of Israel. He is a leading novelist, poet, and critic of Arabic modernism. "A Stranger at the Fountain" shows T. S. Eliot's influence as well as the importance of Christ's resurrection as a significant if ambiguous metaphor for the revitalization of the Arabic soul. "A Stranger at the Fountain" is translated from the Arabic by Issa J. Boullata.

A blade of grass split a stone:
is it a cock's crow that resounded,
pierced the darkness, dragged the sun from his hair, and proclaimed
the sovereignty of day?
It is the miracle of thunder to the waste land,
to the parched lips which turned
wide open to the sky, and rain poured!
Take the soul, take the body,
take the mind, take, take
O fingers that have planted their nails
as rose bushes in my blood.
Your beloved carries the night and the sun together between his palms
and from the inside of the earth he comes
(like a blade of grass splitting a stone)
winged bedewed, he sprinkles
the deserts of your eyes, your hands,
O fingers that plant their nails
as fountains of love in my blood.

The breeze of the road surging at night with eyes,
sheltering strangers and prophets
in love with long sidewalks,
the breeze of the road that is heedless and roaring
descending from the house to the cave and the fountain,
ascending from the house to Golgotha,
from the bed of dreams to the Cross—
the breeze of the road, carrying the smell of dung and jasmine
of panting, death and the last laugh from beginning

and end, comes
in anger as smooth as a sleeping snake,
as a maiden of twenty kissing in the dark
a man for the first time, as a virgin with heated breasts
seeking pleasure and resisting it
swerving inveigling,
touching whispering burning
with the frenzy of flesh and blood,
uttering words that embody the spirit and drip with fragrance
on the tongue and the lips.

It is the spirit which causes ecstasy and pain. Like a mad man
it hits the corridors of the brains and the heart with its hoofs.
It is the inevitable lie, the lie whose
truth proceeds from the road beloved by prophets and fugitives.
The spirit is the road, the breeze is its whisper,
the touch of the loving breasts in the long heat of night.

The end of the trip is its beginning,
let the clocks of the city strike in vain!
Neither night now possesses its bats
nor morning threatens with coming death.
On the mountain, where the threatening Piece of Wood was set up,
the rock of water has exploded in cataracts
and the wild horses of night neighed
at the edge of the cool fountain.
A stranger in whose face are two dimples, in
whose hair is the taste of threshing-floors,
and in whose mouth is the summer of vineyards,
began dipping his feet in the flood
shouting: whose are these horses of night?
whose except the Stranger's who turned time into circles
and kissed the crown of thorns until
the horses, the night and all the clocks of the city went mad.

# Jesus's Side Pierced

## *John 19:31–37*

Since it was the day of Preparation, the Jews did not want the bodies left on the cross during the sabbath, especially because that sabbath was a day of great solemnity. So they asked Pilate to have the legs of the crucified men broken and the bodies removed. Then the soldiers came and broke the legs of the first and of the other who had been crucified with him. But when they came to Jesus and saw that he was already dead, they did not break his legs. Instead, one of the soldiers pierced his side with a spear, and at once blood and water came out. (He who saw this has testified so that you also may believe. His testimony is true, and he knows that he tells the truth.) These things occurred so that the scripture might be fulfilled, "None of his bones shall be broken." And again another passage of scripture says, "They will look on the one whom they have pierced."

# Vexilla Regis Prodeunt

## VENANTIUS FORTUNATUS

Italy, 530–609. Bishop of Poitiers, Fortunatus composed "Vexilla Regis Prodeunt," ("The Standards of the King Go Forth") on the occasion of the transference of a relic of the True Cross to Poitiers. The poem is regarded as one of the greatest hymns in the liturgy of Western Christianity. In the last Canto of the *Inferno*, DANTE has Virgil ironically quote the opening line of this hymn when the poets first catch sight of Satan. "Vexilla Regis Prodeunt" is translated from the Latin by Helen Waddell.

The standards of the King go forth,
    Shines out the blazoned mystery,
The Cross whereon the Lord of men
    As man was hung.

Where he was wounded by a thrust
    The edge of that sharp lance,
That he might wash us from our guilt;
    Water and blood flowed down.

Fulfilled are now the prophecies
    That David sang of, long ago,
Saying, The nations of the earth
    God ruleth from a tree.

O Tree of beauty and of light,
    With royal purple dyed,
Well wert thou chosen then to bear
    That sacred load.

Blessed, that on thy branches hung
    The ransom of the world,
The balance of his holy flesh.
    And hell despoiled.

# Nails and a Cross

R. A. K. MASON

New Zealand, 1905–1971. See page 109 for biographical information on this poet.

Nails and a cross and crown of thorn,
    here I die the mystery-born:
    here's an end to adventurings
    here all great and valiant things
    find as far as I'm concerned a grave.

God, I may say that I've been brave
    and it's led me—? Damned and deified
    here I spurt the blood from a riven side:
    blood, never revisit my heart again
    but suck the wisdom out of my brain
    I got in so many lonely days
    bruising my feet with flinty ways.

For I left my boyhood dog and fire
    my old bed and him I called my sire
    my mother my village my books and all
    to follow the wild and lonely call
    luring me into the solitary
    road that has brought me here to die.

And I see, if I squint, my blood of death
    drip on the little harsh grass beneath
    and friend and foe and men long dead
    faint and reel in my whirling head:
    and while the troops divide up my cloak
    the mob fling dung and see the joke.

# The Burial

*Matthew 27:57–60*

When it was evening, there came a rich man from Arimathea, named Joseph, who was also a disciple of Jesus. He went to Pilate and asked for the body of Jesus; then Pilate ordered it to be given to him. So Joseph took the body and wrapped it in a clean linen cloth and laid it in his own new tomb, which he had hewn in the rock. He then rolled a great stone to the door of the tomb and went away.

# God Speaks: Night, You Are Holy

CHARLES PÉGUY

France, 1873–1914. See page 300 for biographical information on this poet. "God Speaks" is translated from the French by Julian Green.

Night, you are holy, Night, you are great, Night, you are beautiful,
Night of the great mantle.
Night, I love you and greet you, and I glorify you, and you are my big
      daughter and my creature.
O beautiful night, night of the great mantle, daughter of the starry
      mantle,
You remind me, even me, you remind me of that great silence there
      was
Before I had opened up the floodgates of ingratitude,
And you announce to me, even me, you announce the great silence
      there will be
When I will have closed them.
O sweet, o great, o holy, o beautiful night, perhaps the holiest of my
      daughters, night of the long robe, of the starry robe,
You remind me of that great silence there was in the world
Before the beginning of the reign of man.
You announce to me that great silence there will be
After the end of the reign of man, when I will have resumed my
      scepter.
And at times I think of it beforehand, for that man really makes a lot
      of noise.
But specially, Night, you remind me of that night,
And I shall remember it eternally:
The ninth hour had struck. It was in the land of my people Israel.
All was over. That enormous adventure.
From the sixth hour, there had been darkness over all the land until
      the ninth hour.
All was over. Let us not mention it any more. It hurts me.
That unbelievable coming down of my son among men,
In the midst of men,
When you think what they made of it,
Those thirty years during which he was a carpenter among men,
Those three years during which he was a kind of preacher among men,

A priest,

Those three days during which he was a victim among men,

In the midst of men,

Those three nights during which he was a dead man among men,

In the midst of dead men,

Those centuries and centuries when he is a host among men.

All was over, that unbelievable adventure

By which I, God, have tied my arms for my eternity,

That adventure by which my Son tied my arms,

For eternally tying the arms of my justice, for eternally untying the
    arms of my mercy,

And against my justice inventing a new justice,

A justice of love, a justice of Hope. All was over.

That which was necessary. In the way that was necessary. In the way
    my prophets had announced it. The veil of the temple was
    rent in twain from top to bottom;

The earth did quake; the rocks rent;

The graves were opened; and many of the bodies of the saints which
    slept arose.

And about the ninth hour, my Son uttered

The cry that will never be still. All was over. The soldiers returned to
    their barracks,

Laughing and joking because that duty was over,

One more guard duty they would not have to stand.

Only one centurion remained, with a few men,

A very small post to guard that unimportant gallows,

The gallows on which my Son was hanged.

A few women only had remained.

The Mother was there.

And perhaps a few disciples too, and even so, one is not sure of that.

Now every man has the right to bury his son,

Every man on earth, if he has had the great misfortune

Not to have died before his son. And I alone, I, God,

Arms tied by that adventure,

I alone, at that moment, father after so many fathers,

I alone could not bury my son.

It was then, o night, that you came,

O my daughter, beloved among all, and I still see it, and I shall see
    that in my eternity.

It was then, o Night, that you came, and in a great shroud you buried
The centurion and his Romans,
The Virgin and the holy women,
And that mountain, and that valley on which evening was descending,
And my people Israel and the sinners, and together him who was
      dying, who had died for them,

And the men of Joseph of Arimathea who already were approaching,

Bearing the white shroud.

# The Messiah after the Crucifixion

BADR SHĀKIR AL-SAYYĀB

Iraq, 1926–1964. See page 177 for biographical information on this poet. Although a Muslim, al-Sayyāb often personally identifies in his poetry with the figure of Christ taking on suffering for the sake of his people. His famous poem "The Messiah after the Crucifixion" is set in Jaikur, the poet's native Iraqi village, under the tyrannical 1950s regime represented in the poem by Judas. The startling opening, in which the poet speaks as Christ from his tomb, is consistent with Muslim tradition, since the Qu'rān leaves unclear whether or not Jesus actually died on the Cross. "The Messiah after the Crucifixion" is translated from the Arabic by M. M. Badawi.

When they brought me down I heard the winds
In long lamentation weaving the leaves of palm-trees,
And footsteps receding far, far away. So the wounds
And the Cross to which I have been nailed all through the afternoon
Have not killed me. I listened: the wail
Traversed the plain between me and the city
Like a hawser tied to a ship
That is sinking into the depths. The cry of grief
Was like a line of light separating morning from night
In the sad winter sky.
Despite its feelings the city fell asleep.

When orange trees and the mulberry are in blossom
When Jaikur spreads out to the limits of fantasy
When it grows green with vegetation whose fragrance sings
Together with the suns that have suckled it with their brilliance
When even its darkness grows green,
Warmth touches my heart and my blood flows into its earth
My heart is the sun when the sun throbs with light
My heart is the earth throbbing with wheat, blossoms and sweet water
My heart is the water; it is the ear of corn
Whose death is resurrection: it lives in him who eats
In the dough that grows round, moulded like a little breast, the breast
     of life.
I died by fire: I burned the darkness of my mortal clay, there
     remained only the god.
I was the beginning and in the beginning was the poor man

I died so that bread might be eaten in my name,
That they might sow me at the right season.
Many are the lives that I shall live: in every pit
I will become a future, a seed, a generation of men,
In every heart my blood shall flow
A drop of it or more.

Thus I returned and as soon as he saw me Judas turned pale
For I had been his secret
He was a shadow of mine, grown dark, the frozen image of an idea
From which the spirit had been drawn out
He feared that it might betray death in the tears of his eyes
(His eyes were a rock
In which he tried to hide his tomb from the people)
He feared its warmth, its impossibility for him, so he informed
      against it.
'Is it you? Or is it my own shadow, grown white melting into light?
You struggling back from the land of the dead?
Men die only once, so our fathers said, so they taught us, was it a lie
      then?'
That is what he thought when he saw me, what his glance spoke.

I can hear footsteps of someone running, a step and a step and a step
The tomb shakes with their echo and almost falls apart.
Have they now come? Who else could it be?
A step and a step and a step.
I flung the rocks on my chest
Did they crucify me yesterday? Here I am in my tomb.
Who knows that I . . . ? Who knows?
And the friends of Judas? Who shall believe what they say?
A step and a step and a step.

Here I am now naked in my dark tomb
Yesterday I wrapped myself up like a thought, a bud
Under my shrouds of snow, the bloom of blood grows moist
Like a shadow I was betwixt night and day—
Then my soul burst open with treasure, unfolding like fruit.
When I tore off my pockets to make swaddling clothes and turned my
      sleeves into a cover

When one day I kept the bones of the little ones warm with my flesh
When I laid bare my wound and dressed the wound of another
The wall was demolished between me and God.

The soldiers surprised even my wound and my heart beats
Surprised all that was not death even if it was in a tomb,
Took me by surprise just as a flock of hungry birds storm a fruit-laden
      palm-tree in a deserted village.

The rifles' eyes devour my road
Pointed they are and the fire in them dreams of my crucifixion
Iron and fire they are made of, while the eyes of my people are
      fashioned
Of the light of skies, of memories and love.
They relieve me of my burden, and my cross then grows moist.
      O how small
Is that death, my death and yet how great!

When they had nailed me and I cast my eyes towards the city
I hardly recognized the plain, the wall and the tomb.
There was something, as far as the eye could see,
Like a forest in bloom.
In the place of every target there was a cross and a grieved mother.
Blessed be the Lord!
These are the pangs of the city in labour.

## Luke 23:55–56

The women who had come with him from Galilee followed, and they saw the tomb and how his body was laid. Then they returned, and prepared spices and ointments.

On the sabbath they rested according to the commandment.

# Easter Eve: A Fantasy

VASSAR MILLER

U.S., 1924–. See page 146 for biographical information on this poet.

The day does not speak above a whisper, is a high dividing
upon a moment into ebbing and flowing,
two pairs of lips neither pressing nor quite yet parting,
the twilight between sleep and waking,
the bowl of hush held lifted to the bird's first trilling.
Yet the day does not wait. It has become a waiting
as we have become our shadows stuffed full of wind and walking,
and if my hand reached toward you, it would pass through you.
For the world has become a dream of that sleeping Head
which on Friday we pierced and folded in dust
until He awakens tomorrow when the light of His Rising
hardens to hills and crystallizes to rocks and ripples to streams.

# PART NINE

# THE RESURRECTION

# The Stone Rolled Away

## Mark 16:1−2

When the sabbath was over, Mary Magdalene, and Mary the mother of James, and Salome bought spices, so that they might go and anoint him. And very early on the first day of the week, when the sun had risen, they went to the tomb.

# Mary Magdalene

## KASSIA

Greece, c.840. Kassia is the one woman poet whose work has survived from
Byzantine Greek. Her "Mary Magdalene" is still chanted during Holy Week in
the Eastern Orthodox Church. The poem's invention of metaphors in which
the Creation mirrors its Creator is in the Eastern tradition of EPHREM. "Mary
Magdalene" is translated from the Greek by Aliki Barnstone, Willis Barnstone,
and Elene Kolb.

Lord, this woman who fell into many sins
    perceives the God in you,
    joins the women bringing you myrrh,
    crying she brings myrrh before your tomb.
"O what a night   what a night I've had!
    Extravagant frenzy   in a moonless gloom,
    craving the body.
Accept this spring of tears,
    you who empty seawater   from the clouds.
Bend to the pain   in my heart, you
    who made the sky bend   to your secret incarnation
    which emptied the heavens.
I will kiss your feet, wash them,
    dry them with the hair of my head, those feet whose steps
Eve heard at dusk
    in Paradise   and hid in terror.
Savior of souls   who will trace the plethora
    of my sins or the knowable chasm of your judgments?
Do not overlook me, your slave,
    in your measureless mercy."

# Repentance

YŪSUF AL-KHĀL

Lebanon, 1917–1987. See page 253 for biographical information on this poet. "Repentance" is translated from the Arabic by Issa J. Boullata.

On the Mountain of Silence, at my appointment
With the penitent, I raised my brow
(My arms are tightly tied to a rock):
Father, when will my cup pass
Father, when will I descend on my way
To my brothers, stretch out my eyelids to them,
Laugh across my suspicions,
And weep,
Dream and lay my head—
Father, when will my cup pass?

Something reigned with Silence
Was it the fluttering of wings in the dark
Or the breaking of dawn?
                                        I see a ghost,
My God, and I hear footsteps
Like her footsteps:
O Beloved, I remember the ointment
On my feet and the hair,
I remember how my heart blossomed
And I revived a dead man,
How with your love I gave myself up
And became a symbol and a promise,
How for your sake I loved my neighbor
And raised the balcony of my house.
                                        And here I am alive . . .
And here I am alive
(My arms are tightly tied to a rock
My longing for my brothers is intense)
The dawn of day dresses my wounds.
My sail is free and my day as noble as my yesterday.
Father, when—
Father, when will my cup pass?

## Mark 16:3–4

They had been saying to one another, "Who will roll away the stone for us from the entrance to the tomb?" When they looked up, they saw that the stone, which was very large, had already been rolled back.

# African Easter: Easter Morning

ABIOSEH NICOL

Sierra Leone, 1924–. See page 380 for biographical information on this poet.

THE AFRICAN INTELLECTUAL:

*Ding dong bell*
*Pussy's in the well.*

Another day. . . .

Sleep leaves my opening eyes slowly
Unwillingly like a true lover.

But this day is different.
The lonely matin bells
Cut across the thin morning mist,
The glinting dew on the green grass,
The cool pink light before the heat of day,
The sudden punctual dawn of tropic skies,
Before the muezzin begins to cry,
Before the pagan drums begin to beat.

Easter morning.

But still for me
The great rock remains unrolled.

Within my wet dark tomb
Wounded peace remains embalmed,
The pricking thorns still yet my crown.

Easter morning.
Where are my ancestral spirits now?
I have forgotten for many harvests
To moisten the warm earth
With poured libations.
Where are you now, O Shango?

Two-headed, powerful
Man and woman, hermaphrodite
Holding your quivering thunderbolts
With quiet savage malice;
Brooding over your domain,
Africa, Cuba, Haiti, Brazil,
Slavery of mind is unabolished.
Always wanting to punish, never to love.

I have turned away from you
To One who stands
Watching His dying dispossessed Son
Shouting in Aramaic agony

Watching the white Picasso dove
Hovering above the Palestinian stream
Watching and waiting, sometimes
To punish, always to love.

Sleep confuses my tired mind
Still the bell rings
I must up and away.
I am a good Churchman, now.
Broadminded, which means past caring
Whether High or Low.
The priest may hold the chalice,
Or give it to me. It depends
On where he trained. I only mind
That he wipes the wet rim
Not to spread dental germs.
A tenth of my goods
I give to the poor
Through income tax

Easter morning.

Yet you Christ are always there.
You are the many-faceted crystal
Of our desires and hopes,

Behind the smoke-screen of incense,
Concealed in mumbled European tongues
Of worship and of praise.
In the thick dusty verbiage
Of centuries of committees
Of ecumenical councils.
You yet remain revealed
To those who seek you.
It is I, you say.
You remain in the sepulchre
Of my brown body.

Christ is risen, Christ is risen!

You were not dead.
It was just that we
Could not see clearly enough.
We can push out the rock from the inside.
You can come out now.
You see we want to share you
With our masters, because
You really are unique.

The great muddy river Niger,
Picks up the rising equatorial sun,
Changing itself by slow degrees
Into thick flowing molten gold.

# The Empty Tomb

*Luke 24:3*

But when they went in, they did not find the body.

# The Third Day

PHILLIS LEVIN

U.S., 1954–. Born in Paterson, New Jersey, Levin has published two collec-
tions of poetry: *Temples and Fields* (1988), which won the Norma Farber First
Book Award from the Poetry Society of America, and *The Afterimage* (1955). In
"The Third Day," she ponders the mystery of presence in the midst of loss, by
imagining the possibility that the disciples visiting Jesus' tomb found his dead
body there.

> When they came to the tomb
> What did they see?
> Only what they could not say.
>
> Too empty, too cold
> To say what they saw,
> Too full to say empty
>
> And cold, but full.
> They said what they said,
> Saw what they saw,
>
> And knew they could not
> Say what they saw.
> They did not know
>
> That whatever words they found
> To say would fill the world
> With those very words,
>
> The best they could find
> In that place, that time,
> When all words fail or fall.
>
> After the stone is rolled away,
> After the sky refuses to reply,
> Comes the heaviness of being there.

# The Abduction of Saints

ALICE WALKER

U.S., 1944–. Born in Eatonton, Georgia, Walker was educated at Spelman Col-
lege and at Sarah Lawrence, where she graduated in 1965. Awarded (among
other recognitions) the Merrill and Gugenheim Fellowships, Walker was the
first Black woman to win the Pulitzer Prize, for her 1982 novel *The Color
Purple*. Walker has always championed Black causes, but has been sardonically
aware at the same time—as is evident in "The Abduction of Saints"—of how
revolutionaries can fall victims to their most earnest followers.

As it was with Christ, so it is with Malcolm
and with King.
Who could withstand the seldom flashing smile,
the call to dance among the swords and barbs
that were their words? The men leaning from
out the robes of saints,
good and wholly kind? Though come
at last to both fists clenched and Voice
to flatten the ears
of all the world.

You mock them who divide and keep score of what
each man gave. They gave us rebellion as pure love:
a beginning of the new man.

Christ too was man rebelling. Walking dusty roads, sweating
under the armpits. Loving the cool of evening beside
the ocean,
the people's greetings and barbecued chicken; cursing under
his breath
the bruise from his sandal and his donkey's diarrhea.
Don't let them fool you. He was himself a beginning
of the new man. His love in front.
His love and his necessary fist, behind. (Life,
ended at a point, always falls backward into the
little that was known of it.)

But see how this saint too is hung defenselessly
on walls, his strong hands pinned:

his pious look causes us to blush, for him.
He belongs to Caesar.

It is because his people stopped to tally and to count:
Perhaps he loved young men too much? Did he wear his hair
a bit too long, or short? Weren't the strategies
he proposed all wrong,
since of course they did not work?

It is because his people argued over him. Denounced
each other
in his name. When next they looked they hardly noticed
he no longer looked himself.

Who could imagine that timid form with Voice like
thunder
to make threats, a fist enlarged from decking merchants?
That milkwhite cheek, the bluebell eye, the cracked
heart of plaster
designed
for speedy decay.

*Aha!* said a cricket in the grass (ancient observer of
distracted cross examiners);

*Now you've seen it, now you don't!*

And the body
was stolen away.

# The Angel's Message:
# He Has Risen

## Luke 24:4–5

While they were perplexed about this, suddenly two men in dazzling clothes stood beside them. The women were terrified and bowed their faces to the ground, but the men said to them, "Why do you look for the living among the dead? He is not here, but has risen."

# Easter Hymn

KU SANG

Korea, 1919–. See page 4 for biographical information on this poet. "Easter
Hymn" is translated from the Korean by Brother Anthony of Taizé.

> On an old plum tree stump,
> seemingly dead and rotten,
> like a garland of victory
> flowers gleam, dazzling.
>
> Rooted in you, even in death
> all things remain alive;
> we see them reborn, transfigured.
> How then could we doubt
> our own Resurrection since
> by your own you gave us proof?
>
> Since there is your Resurrection and ours,
>     Truth exists;
> since there is your Resurrection and ours,
>     Justice triumphs;
> since there is your Resurrection and ours,
>     suffering accepted has value;
> since there is your Resurrection and ours,
>     our faith, hope, love, are not in vain;
> since there is your Resurrection and ours,
>     our lives are not an empty abyss.
>
> In this lost corner of the earth,
> dappled by the spreading spring,
> as I imagine that Day's world,
> made perfect by our Resurrection,
> I am overwhelmed in rapture.

# Ecce Dies Celebris

## Sequence for Easter

ADAM OF ST. VICTOR

France, d.1192. See page 385 for biographical information on this poet. "Ecce Dies Celebris" ("Look! the Glorious Day!") is translated from the Latin by George Dardess.

It's come, the day we love to mark!
When light follows dark.
Resurrection, death.
Sad things yield to happy
Since there is a glorious resolution
Greater than the old confusion.
Type gives way to reality,[1]
The used-up to the new,
Sorrow to consolation.

Honor our new Passover!
The head leads;
Each member of the body heeds.
This new Passover is Christ,
Sinless lamb
Who bled for us.

Our enemy, the Devil, prowling at our door—
Christ snatched us from his grip:
A role that Samson played before
When he tore the lion apart,
And when that brave heart
David
From lion's jaw and bear's throat
Freed his flock:

1 A predominant medieval way of seeing Gospel events and characters was through biblical typology: as fulfillment of events and characters whose "types" are pre-figured in the Hebrew Scriptures. Here, in stanzas 3–4, Samson and David are seen as types of Christ; in stanza 5, some Hebrews, sent by Moses in Numbers 13 to spy out the land of Canaan, return carrying a pole with a cluster of grapes—the pole prefigures the Cross, and the grapes, referred to also in Micah 7, prefigure Christ, the true vine; in stanza 6, the sackcloth of Psalm 30 becomes the flesh of Christ; in stanza 7, the rejected stone which becomes the cornerstone, from Psalm 118, is one of the earliest typological references to Christ.

That same Samson
Who, dying himself, brought the temple down
On Philistines,
Prefiguring Christ,
Whose death our life has won.
If Samson's name meant "Their Sun,"
Then Christ is the light of each chosen one
Illumined by grace.

Already from the cross's tree
(Carried once by the Hebrew spies)
Prophet Micah's grapes fall free
Into the Church's sanctuary,
Where now their juice is tread,
And where is drunk, all sorrow sped,
The new wine
Of the first-fruits
Of every land.

Christ's flesh, once like sackcloth torn,
Is now a royal robe victoriously worn;
Tragedy's mask of pain, now Comedy's smile:
Flesh triumphant over Satan's wile.

Destroying the king,
They lost the kingdom.
But murderous Cain must not disappear.
He, like they, remains a sign to fear.

Condemned, rejected,
This stone, erected,
Is set as a sign of victory
And the cornerstone.
Destroying sin, not nature,
He creates a new creature,
Stretching himself to reconcile
Jew and Gentile.
Glory to our head!
And peace to every member. Amen.

# Easter Dawn

KOFI AWOONOR

[George Awoonor-Williams] Ghana, 1935–. Awoonor was born of mixed To-
golese and Sierra Leonian parentage. As a child he attended local funeral rites
of his region's Ewe sub-group, whose dirge forms shaped his early poetry. He
has since taught at the University of Ghana's Institute of African Studies, spe-
cializing in vernacular poetry. He edits the Ghanian literary journal, *Okyeame*.

That man died in Jerusalem
And his death demands dawn marchers
From year to year to the sound of bells.
The hymns flow through the mornings
Heard on Calvary this dawn.
  the gods are crying, my father's gods are crying
  for a burial—for a final ritual—
  but they that should build the fallen shrines
  have joined the dawn marchers
  singing their way towards Gethsemane
  where the tear drops of agony still freshen the cactus.
He has risen! Christ has risen!
  the gods cried again from the hut in me
  asking why that prostration has gone unheeded.
The marchers sang of the resurrection
That concerned the hillock of Calvary
Where the ground at the foot of the cross is level.
  the gods cried, shedding
  clayey tears on the calico
  the drink offering had dried up in the harmattan
  the cola-nut is shrivelled
  the yam feast has been eaten by mice
  and the fetish priest is dressed for the Easter service.
The resurrection hymns come to me from afar
touching my insides.
  Then the gods cried loudest
  Challenging the hymners.
  They seized their gongs and drums
  And marched behind the dawn marchers
  Seeking their Calvary
  Seeking their tombstones
  And those who refused to replace them
  In the appropriate season.

# Peter and John at the Tomb

## John 20:3–9

Then Peter and the other disciple set out and went toward the tomb. The two were running together, but the other disciple outran Peter and reached the tomb first. He bent down to look in and saw the linen wrappings lying there, but he did not go in. Then Simon Peter came, following him, and went into the tomb. He saw the linen wrappings lying there, and the cloth that had been on Jesus' head, not lying with the linen wrappings but rolled up in a place by itself. Then the other disciple, who reached the tomb first, also went in, and he saw and believed; for as yet they did not understand the scripture, that he must rise from the dead.

# The Answer

R. S. THOMAS

Wales, 1913–. See page 7 for biographical information on this poet.

Not darkness but twilight
in which even the best
of minds must make its way
now. And slowly the questions
occur, vague but formidable
for all that. We pass our hands
over their surface like blind
men, feeling for the mechanism
that will swing them aside. They
yield, but only to re-form
as new problems; and one
does not even do that
but towers immovable
before us.
       Is there no way
other than thought of answering
its challenge? There is an anticipation
of it to the point of
dying. There have been times
when, after long on my knees
in a cold chancel, a stone has rolled
from my mind, and I have looked
in and seen the old questions lie
folded and in a place
by themselves, like the piled
graveclothes of love's risen body.

# The Appearance to Mary Magdalene

## John 20:11–18

But Mary stood weeping outside the tomb. As she wept, she bent over to look into the tomb; and she saw two angels in white, sitting where the body of Jesus had been lying, one at the head and the other at the feet. They said to her, "Woman, why are you weeping?" She said to them, "They have taken away my Lord, and I do not know where they have laid him." When she had said this, she turned around and saw Jesus standing there, but she did not know that it was Jesus. Jesus said to her, "Woman, why are you weeping? Whom are you looking for?" Supposing him to be the gardener, she said to him, "Sir, if you have carried him away, tell me where you have laid him, and I will take him away." Jesus said to her, "Mary!" She turned and said to him in Hebrew, "Rabbouni!" (which means Teacher). Jesus said to her, "Do not hold on to me, because I have not yet ascended to the Father. But go to my brothers and say to them, 'I am ascending to my Father and your Father, to my God and your God.'" Mary Magdalene went and announced to the disciples, "I have seen the Lord"; and she told them that he had said these things to her.

# Hymn of the Magdalene

## MARBOD OF RENNES

France, c.1035–1123. Marbod became bishop of Rennes in 1096 after a distinguished career as a schoolmaster. His poetic gifts won him honor as one of the most eminent literary men of the eleventh century. Yet, loving simplicity and quiet and the countryside, he ended his days as a simple Benedictine monk. Marbod's warm heart and dislike of censoriousness are evident in his treatment of Mary Magdalene in "Hymn of the Magdalene." "Hymn of the Magdalene" is translated from the Latin by Helen Waddell.

Mary was Mother of the Lord,
And Lazarus' sister was a Mary too,
Both bright heavens to befriend men's souls.
The handmaid no way equal to her lady
But shares her radiant name.

The one is the very symbol of repentance,
The other the mother of all pardon.
The one was the virgin of virgins, saint of all saints,
The other had known all sin and company kept with sinners.
One Mary bore the feet that the other held, weeping,
And because she greatly loved she was purified of her stain . . .
To her the risen Lord had first shown himself
And made his first apostle
A woman of ill fame.

# The Arisen

RAINER MARIA RILKE

Germany, 1875–1926. See page 107 for biographical information on this poet.
"The Arisen" is translated from the German by Edward Snow.

He was never able, right up to the end,
to refuse her or break by saying "no"
her way of feeling famous in her love;
and she sank at the cross in the costume
of a grief that was completely studded
with her love's most ostentatious stones.

But when she then, meaning to anoint him,
arrived at the tomb, with tears in her face,
he had risen just for her sake, that he
might say to her with deeper bliss: Don't—

She only understood it in her cave—
how he, grown stronger through his death,
at last forbade her the oil's assuaging
and the presentiment of touch,

in order to make from her the lover
who is drawn no longer toward the loved,
since she, transported by enormous
storms, ascends beyond his voice's reach.

# When I Went into My Garden

SISTER BERTKEN

Netherlands, 1427?–1514. Sister Bertken lived in a Utrecht convent for fifty-seven years. Very little is known of her life. In such poems as "When I Went into My Garden," she allegorically combines both Old and New Testament imagery. "When I Went into My Garden" is translated from the Dutch by Willis Barnstone.

When I went into my garden, I found
only nettles and thorns.

The nettles and thorns I threw out.
I seeded some flowering plants.

I found someone who knew his work,
willing to help me in my task.

The tree was in such a hurry to climb,
I couldn't dig it out in time.

In my dilemma he had a remedy.
Alone he pulled up the tree.

Now I must ask advice from him
or he won't help me again.

However much I weed and clear,
the poison grass appears.

I'd like to seed lilies on this site
before the day is bright.

If my lover feeds it with dew,
it will richly bloom.

He loves among all flowers,
the lily in its white splendor.

Red roses unfurl.
In their calices burns the pearl.

Then the pearl is dressed in sun.
The strong heart looks on.

Jesus is the gardener's name.
I am his. One being, we are the same.

His love is sweetest breath,
beyond all things on earth.

# Magdalene's Song

HAE-IN LEE (CLAUDIA LEE)

Korea, 1945–. See page 191 for biographical information on this poet. "Magdalene's Song" is translated from the Korean by Brother Anthony of Taizé.

I beg you, open
the door.

I do not wish to recall again
the times when I was battered by an anguish
that came so bitterly piercing.

Hour duller and darker than death
when you were not
and pain lamented the blood-like hour
as I stood weeping choking
on and outside the sepulchre

until you slipped off the raiment of death
and came forth living robed in light
all resplendent
through the sepulchre's tightly closed door.

Ah! Rabboni!
The song of sorrow buried now
waving victory's banner of white

my joy
restored to life
with ever trembling heart
dawn of glory bright sun rising
by your resurrection.

Dear master, you cleansed with dazzling love
my pathway of shame
and henceforth I will never
turn aside.

My way
in life
restored to life at the sight of you
this one single life of mine
loving
dying

Lord
Come
and open, I beg you.

# Mary of Magdala in the Garden

THOMAS IMMOOS

Switzerland, 1919–. See page 170 for biographical information on this poet.
"Mary of Magdala in the Garden" is translated from the German by Dalma
Hunyadi Brunauer.


One should go into the garden again and again,
even though His absence resounds throughout the world,
into the garden where the empty grave yawns.
But no garden blooms
in the black ghettos' burnt ruins
in the city
from which the good angels have flown long ago.
No garden blooms in the slums of Peru
where the cholera stinks.
The last gardens have withered
in the hail of grenades in Sarajevo.
The stones of the intefada
are covering the gardens
where the Holy Sepulcher once was.
And when He appears in the thrashed body of Rodney King,
we recognize Him not.
And yet, there arises, forever new,
Hope, the absurd,
that Love overcomes Hate
that He rises up in the hearts,
He, Who is Way, and Truth, and Life.

# Magdalene

## KÓSTAS VÁRNALIS

Greece, 1884–1974. Born in Bulgaria of Greek parents, Várnalis completed his
university education in Athens, studied at the Sorbonne, and returned to
Greece to teach literature until he was fired for his left-wing views in 1925. A
Marxist, whose poetry often combined polemic and satire, Várnalis received
the Lenin Peace Prize in 1958. "Magdalene" is from *The Burning Light* (1922),
a volume that celebrates the modern proletarian spirit as it issues from such
heroic forerunners as Prometheus and Jesus. "Magdalene" is translated from
the Greek by Kimon Friar.


In palaces where music echoed as in caves,
where clustered lights and burnished metals gleamed and glittered,
aromas glid like sweet narcosis on my cheeks,
that no sun ever saw, and bit them deep like vipers;
in my pellucid voice a husky, dim note slid.

In the four kingdoms of Judea, I was the Fountain:
the unwithering and musk-fragrant citrons of my breasts.
Earth never before had known such flames as in my body,
never had such ripe calm been found as in my arms,
my love games conquered even Rome the conqueror.

But darkness lay within me, stretches of vast, dry sand,
and on my dulcet lips my laughter would turn bitter.
Fears of the great unknown would suddenly shake my heart
and stop my breathing in my rich embroidered gowns.
There high on Triumph's peak I saw the world's destruction.

It was no sudden lightning bolt, for it came slowly . . .
You were not handsome or noteworthy in any way.
Your eyes cast down on pebbles, you talked slowly, calmly,
but on the third or the fourth time, my weak mind shuddered,
and when you raised your eyes, I could not bear their gaze.

I longed impetuously to cast myself at your feet,
and felt a still immaculate soul trembling within me.
I knew clean happiness in giving without fee,

freedom in slavery to a certain true ideal,
and noble knowledge, ultimate pleasure found in pain.

When I had given all my possessions to the poor,
my diamonds, silver, gardens, palaces, and silks,
I followed in your footsteps, and though the night wind always
erased them on the sand, they still remained forever
like sweet lights still on sand, on soul, in ears, in eyes.

You never said anything new, nor clad old things afresh.
All had been said by many men in times long past.
But yours the power to hear the silence of the heavens;
and men and all inanimate things, and even the heart
of God became for you—for me—transparent glass.

No one (not wise men, students, parents or multitudes)
could sense the agony behind your miracles;
and if you ever hoped to be saved from a death unjust,
then only I, who once was whore and mud, have felt
how mortal you were, Christ! And I shall resurrect you!

# The Appearance to the Women

## Matthew 28:8–10

The women left the tomb quickly with fear and great joy, and ran to tell his disciples. Suddenly Jesus met them and said, "Greetings!" And they came to him, took hold of his feet, and worshiped him. Then Jesus said to them, "Do not be afraid; go and tell my brothers to go to Galilee; there they will see me."

# Epigram VII

FILIPPO PANANTI

Italy, 1766–1837. Born in Tuscany, Pananti began studying for the priesthood but left the seminary to pursue a degree in law from the University of Pisa. He traveled extensively and lived for a time in London, where he fell under the literary spell of Lawrence Sterne's novels. Pananti's humor and wit are revealed in his celebrated Epigrams. "Epigram VII" is translated from the Italian by Joseph Tusiani.

> Christ, risen from his sepulcher at last,
> appeared to women first
> so that the news would travel very fast.

# The Bribing of the Guards

*Matthew 28:11–15a*

While they were going, some of the guard went into the city and told the chief priests everything that had happened. After the priests had assembled with the elders, they devised a plan to give a large sum of money to the soldiers, telling them, "You must say, 'His disciples came by night and stole him away while we were asleep.' If this comes to the governor's ears, we will satisfy him and keep you out of trouble." So they took the money and did as they were directed.

# A Guard of the Sepulcher

EDWIN MARKHAM

U.S., 1852–1940. Markham truly spanned epochs. Born in the Oregon territory before the Civil War, Markham became, thanks to William Randolph Hearst's publication of "The Man with the Hoe," an early media celebrity, touring America for decades to promote his mystically Christian version of socialism, and being hailed at the 1915 Panama-Pacific Exhibition as "the greatest living poet." "A Guard at the Sepulchre" shows well his rhetorical idiom and his emphasis on the corruption of the "little man" by money.

I was a Roman soldier in my prime;
Now age is on me and the yoke of time.
I saw your Risen Christ, for I am he
Who reached the hyssop to Him on the tree;
And I am one of two who watched beside
The Sepulcher of Him we crucified.

All that last night I watched with sleepless eyes;
Great stars arose and crept across the skies,
The world was all too still for mortal rest,
For pitiless thoughts were busy in the breast.
The night was long, so long, it seemed at last
I had grown old and a long life had passed.
Far off, the hills of Moab, touched with light,
Were swimming in the hollow of the night.
I saw Jerusalem all wrapped in cloud,
Stretched like a dead thing folded in a shroud.

Once in the pauses of our whispered talk
I heard a something on the garden walk.
Perhaps it was a crisp leaf lightly stirred —
Perhaps the dream-note of a waking bird.
Then suddenly an angel burning white
Came down with earthquake in the breaking light,
And rolled the great stone from the Sepulcher,
Mixing the morning with a scent of myrrh.
And lo, the Dead had risen with the day:
The man of Mystery had gone his way!

Years have I wandered, carrying my shame;
Now let the tooth of time eat out my name.
For we, who all the wonder might have told,
Kept silence, for our mouths were stopt with gold.

# In the Key of Resurrection

## TÁKIS PAPATSÓNIS

Greece, 1895–1976. Descended on his father's side from a famous military family and on his mother's from a prominent Catholic family, Papatsónis is one of the few Greek poets whose traditions are Roman Catholic rather than Orthodox. Educated in law and economics, he was also a distinguished statesman whose many high government positions included Secretary General of the Ministry of Economics. Proficient in several ancient and modern languages, he published translations of Hölderlin, Claudel, Saint-John Perse, Edgar Allan Poe, and T. S. Eliot's "The Waste Land." "In the Key of Resurrection" is translated from the Greek by Kimon Friar.

The voice in Byzantine psalms has come true,
now that the transitory shadows have dissolved
in the inaccessible light of a certain Dawn.

Indeed, do You think the dead will praise You?
We the living will praise You now.
Or indeed the cold ones, whose blood has been depleted?
To us has it befallen to taste
the benevolence of the Omnipotent, the wish of the earth-born.
To us has it befallen to stress
in a loud, descanting voice,
"death has been seen to be futile,"
and who would have imagined it
a few hours earlier when the Veil
was rent in twain and the Cherubim frowned.
No, we shall not go away, one by one,
this world will not be wholly darkened,
we shall not retreat to the Cemeteries.

Holding his reed with its funnel
and sponge—exotic image
of an Unknown Spearman at Golgotha—
the Sacristan, after the end of the Service,
puts out the Altar candles, one by one.
There were you ministered and shone, my God,
darkness now reigns. In a hidden corner
only a wick illuminates the well

of Charity, the last trace of adoration,
and whatever still remains of aromatic incense.
The portals also close, the belfry left in solitude.

Not so for us: the dead will open
the new-dug graves for their own dead;
let the dead bury their dead, not we;
"all the Fellowship of the Apostles, as it theologizes,
buries deeply the dead voice of the Hellenes."
Let them do the burying, but not we.
And in a moment of arrogance
they even said, with narrow heart: "Peter orates,
Plato is silenced; Paul teaches,
Pythagoras sets like the sun." But not we,
we shall not say it. We proclaim both Peter
and Pythagoras with his triangles. And Paul of Tarsus
and soaring Plato, and all groups
timeless and spiritual, all in the name of Christ.
Hebrews and Hellenes, stumbling block and foolishness,
Jesus Christ and He Crucified,
Jesus Christ with a banner who was verily
resurrected, the true and living accusation
for drowsy and false witnesses
who scowl, and sentries
bribed and terrified.

# The Road to Emmaus

## Luke 24:13–32

Now on that same day two of them were going to a village called
Emmaus, about seven miles from Jerusalem, and talking with each other
about all these things that had happened. While they were talking and
discussing, Jesus himself came near and went with them, but their eyes
were kept from recognizing him. And he said to them, "What are you
discussing with each other while you walk along?" They stood still,
looking sad. Then one of them, whose name was Cleopas, answered
him, "Are you the only stranger in Jerusalem who does not know the
things that have taken place there in these days?" He asked them, "What
things?" They replied, "The things about Jesus of Nazareth, who was a
prophet mighty in deed and word before God and all the people, and
how our chief priests and leaders handed him over to be condemned to
death and crucified him. But we had hoped that he was the one to
redeem Israel. Yes, and besides all this, it is now the third day since these
things took place. Moreover, some women of our group astounded us.
They were at the tomb early this morning, and when they did not find
his body there, they came back and told us that they had indeed seen a
vision of angels who said that he was alive. Some of those who were with
us went to the tomb and found it just as the women had said; but they
did not see him." Then he said to them, "Oh, how foolish you are, and
how slow of heart to believe all that the prophets have declared! Was it
not necessary that the Messiah should suffer these things and then enter
into his glory?" Then beginning with Moses and all the prophets, he in-
terpreted to them the things about himself in all the scriptures.

As they came near the village to which they were going, he walked
ahead as if he were going on. But they urged him strongly, saying, "Stay
with us, because it is almost evening and the day is now nearly over."
So he went in to stay with them. When he was at the table with them,
he took bread, blessed and broke it, and gave it to them. Then their
eyes were opened, and they recognized him; and he vanished from
their sight. They said to each other, "Were not our hearts burning
within us while he was talking to us on the road, while he was opening
the scriptures to us?"

# That Day

HAROLD McCURDY

U.S. 1909–. As Professor of Psychology at Chapel Hill, McCurdy tried—not
always successfully, by his own estimation—to use his field of study as a bridge
between the poetry he loved and the "brutal assault" of technology. In "That
Day," Cleopas seems to play McCurdy's own baffled role, while the risen
Christ alone succeeds in bridging the worlds.

Cleopas and another, unaware
Of who it was walked with them as they walked
Wearily from Jerusalem to their town,
Listened with growing wonder as he talked
Of how the ancient Scriptures had led down
To this their day, this day of their despair.

Tongue-tied they were, or simply too polite
To interrupt a stranger's eloquence:
It did at least divert their troubled minds
From the unbearable burden of events
Summed up at Golgotha.
       (And the sun blinds
Them at its setting, westering into night.)

Still, with a care for him, they bid him dine
At their villatic board. Slender the fare,
But he, their guest, soon was their generous host,
Blessing, breaking the bread. Caught in a stare
At more than meets the eye, they staring lost
The seen man in the unseeable Divine.

Off in a stunned trice then, they hurried back
To drear Jerusalem in time to hear
Simon's adventure and relate their own
Before their Subject chose to reappear
And satisfy his famished flesh and bone
With a broiled fish plucked smoking from the rack.

Mangled his wrists and ankles, gashed his side,
Yet death had not undone him—no, no more

Than black holes can the Lord God's radiance.
No bar to him, that day, tomb, doubt, or door.
Now pity holds him aloof. Were he to advance
Two inches nearer, we'd be terrified.

# The Half-way House

GERARD MANLEY HOPKINS

England. 1844–1889. Hopkins studied with Walter Pater at Oxford and took a degree in classics. Profoundly influenced by John Henry Newman, Hopkins converted to Roman Catholicism. He destroyed his early poetry when he took Jesuit orders, but resumed writing in 1875. At the time of his death, he was professor of Greek at the Royal University of Ireland in Dublin. His astonishingly innovative poetry, with its enormous influence on twentieth-century metrics, was collected and published by his friend Robert Bridges in 1918.

Love I was shewn upon the mountain-side
And bid to catch Him ere the drop of day.
See, Love, I creep and thou on wings dost ride:
Love, it is evening now and thou away;
Love, it grows darker here and thou art above;
Love, come down to me if thy name be Love.

My national old Egyptian reed gave way;
I took of vine a cross-barred rod or rood.
Then next I hungered: Love when here, they say,
Or once or never took Love's proper food;
But I must yield the chase, or rest and eat.—
Peace and food cheered me where four rough ways meet.

Hear yet my paradox: Love, when all is given,
To see thee I must see thee, to love, love;
I must o'ertake thee at once and under heaven
If I shall overtake thee at last above.
You have your wish; enter these walls, one said:
He is with you in the breaking of the bread.

# The Appearance
# in the Locked Room

*John 20:19–20*

When it was evening on that day, the first day of the week, and the doors of the house where the disciples had met were locked for fear of the Jews, Jesus came and stood among them and said, "Peace be with you." After he said this, he showed them his hands and his side. Then the disciples rejoiced when they saw the Lord.

# Wherefore the Scars of Christ's Passion Remained in the Body of His Resurrection

THEODULF OF ORLEANS

Spain, c.750–821. See page 357 for biographical information on this poet. "Wherefore the Scars. . ." is translated from the Latin by Helen Waddell.

When Christ came from the shadows by the stream
   Of Phlegethon,
Scars were upon his feet, his hands, his side.
  Not, as dulled souls might deem,
  That He, who had the power
Of healing all the wounds whereof men died,
  Could not have healed his own,
But that those scars had some divinity,
   Carriage of mystery,
Life's source to bear the stigmata of Death.

By these same scars his men
Behind the very body that they knew,
   No transient breath,
   No drift of bodiless air,
And held him in their hearts in fortress there.
They knew their Master risen, and unfurled
The hope of resurrection through the world.

By these same scars, in prayer for all mankind,
   Before his Father's face,
He pleads our wounds within his mortal flesh,
And all the travail of his mortal days:
   For ever interceding for His grace,
   Remembering where forgetfulness were blind,
   For ever pitiful, for ever kind,
Instant that Godhead should take thought for man,
   Remembering the manhood of His Son,
   His only Son, and the deep wounds he bore.

By these same scars his folk will not give o'er
   Office of worship, whilst they see,

Passion, thy mystery:
In those dark wounds their weal,
In that descent to hell their climb to the stars,
His death, their life,
Their wreath, his crown of thorns.

# Weep for Balder

OLE WIVEL

Denmark, 1921–. One of Denmark's major modernist poets, Wivel has owned
a publishing house and edited a literary magazine. His earlier poetry was in-
fluenced by RILKE and Eliot. In the 1960s Wivel's poetry broke out of its ear-
lier confessional mode and engaged such contemporary issues as nuclear arms
and the Vietnam war. "Weep for Balder" is translated from the Danish by
Martin S. Allwood.

> Weep for Balder—for the mistletoe
> Struck the gentle God who had already
> Feared for his death in sudden dreams.
> Victory is Loke's. Nana, pale, is
> Laid to slumber by her fair Lord's side—
> Burning, bound for Hell their funeral ship.
>
> Weep for Orpheus—see Eurydice
> With slender arm across her eyes
> And hidden face, descending now to Hades.
> Hermes knew it, when the god of song
> Took from his lip the flute's sweet sound away,
> Stopping at the last turn of the road,
> There where lights from human worlds were seen—
> Hermes knew Euridice was damned.
>
> Weep for Jesus—he who only said:
> "Take your bed and go", and who commanded
> Waves to bear him safely to the boat.
> He was powerless like mortal men
> When he stood again in Galilee
> In their midst, and his disciples would
> Not believe that it was he who spoke—
> Would but see his bleeding hands and wounds.

# Walking Through Walls

X. J. KENNEDY

U.S., 1929–. See page 196 for biographical information on this poet.

Passing through doors unopened, He appeared
   in His disciples' midst as might a wind
hurtling through branches. One not to be feared,
   opening walls with living, nail-pierced hand.

In Sundayschool that story made a dent
   far deeper in my brain-pan than His pains
upon the cross. Superior to Clark Kent
   whose gaze pierced brick, somehow not Lois Lane's

clothing, He had to be. I'd read a tale
   perhaps apocryphal or utterly false
about a man who'd walked out a jail
   by lining up his atoms with the wall's.

I'd try. So I pretended to be Him
   and Superman, approached my bedroom door,
eyes tight shut, took a giant step and—*wham.*
   Mortal I was. For days my dome felt sore.

# Doubting Thomas

## John 20:24–29

But Thomas (who was called the Twin), one of the twelve, was not with them when Jesus came. So the other disciples told him, "We have seen the Lord." But he said to them, "Unless I see the mark of the nails in his hands, and put my finger in the mark of the nails and my hand in his side, I will not believe."

A week later his disciples were again in the house, and Thomas was with them. Although the doors were shut, Jesus came and stood among them and said, "Peace be with you." Then he said to Thomas, "Put your finger here and see my hands. Reach out your hand and put it in my side. Do not doubt but believe." Thomas answered him, "My Lord and my God!" Jesus said to him, "Have you believed because you have seen me? Blessed are those who have not seen and yet have come to believe."

# Adoro Te

## (attrib.) THOMAS AQUINAS

Italy, 1227–1274. Best known for the *Summa Theologica*, his massive harmoniza-
tion of Christian faith and Aristotelian rationalism, Aquinas was also a poet. The
hymns he composed for the Feast of Corpus Christi are among the greatest me-
dieval Latin lyrics. "Adoro Te" ("I Worship You"), another beloved lyric of the
period, is commonly ascribed to him. "Adoro Te" is translated from the Latin by
Helen Waddell.

> With my heart I worship,
>     O hidden Deity.
> Thou that dost hide Thyself
>     Beneath these images
>         In full reality.
>
> My heart submits to Thee,
>     Yea, all my thought:
> For contemplating Thee,
>     All else is naught.
>
> I cannot touch, I cannot taste, I cannot see.
>     All sense is cheated of Thee, but the ear.
> The Son of God hath spoken: I believe:
>     For naught hath truth beyond the world I hear.
>
> Upon the cross Thy Deity was hid,
>     And here is hidden Thy humanity:
> Yet here I do acknowledge both and cry,
>     As the thief cried to Thee on Calvary.
>
> I do not gaze, like Thomas, on Thy wounds,
>     But I confess Thee God.
> Give me a stronger faith, a surer hope,
>     More love to Thee, my Lord.
>
> O thou memorial of the dying Lord,
>     O living Bread that givest life to men,
> Make strong my soul that it may live by Thee,
>     And for all sweetness turn to Thee again.

O Christ that gave Thy heart to feed Thy young,
  Cleanse Thou my foulness in Thy blood was spilt.
One single drop of it would save a world,
  A whole world from its guilt.

The veil is on Thy face: I cannot see.
  I cry to Thee for grace,
That that may come to pass for which I thirst,
  That I may see Thee with Thy face unveiled,
    And in that vision rest.

# Via Negativa

R. S. THOMAS

Wales, 1913–. See page 7 for biographical information on this poet.

Why no! I never thought other than
That God is that great absence
In our lives, the empty silence
Within, the place where we go
Seeking, not in hope to
Arrive or find. He keeps the interstices
In our knowledge, the darkness
Between stars. His are the echoes
We follow, the footprints he has just
Left. We put our hands in
His side hoping to find
It warm. We look at people
And places as though he had looked
At them, too; but miss the reflection.

# The Appearance on the Shore of Tiberias

*John 21:1a, 15—19*

After these things Jesus showed himself again to the disciples by the Sea of Tiberias. . . . When they had finished breakfast, Jesus said to Simon Peter, "Simon son of John, do you love me more than these?" He said to him, "Yes, Lord; you know that I love you." Jesus said to him, "Feed my lambs." A second time he said to him, "Simon son of John, do you love me?" He said to him, "Yes, Lord; you know that I love you." Jesus said to him, "Tend my sheep." He said to him the third time, "Simon son of John, do you love me?" Peter felt hurt because he said to him the third time, "Do you love me?" And he said to him, "Lord, you know everything; you know that I love you." Jesus said to him, "Feed my sheep. Very truly, I tell you, when you were younger, you used to fasten your own belt and to go wherever you wished. But when you grow old, you will stretch out your hands, and someone else will fasten a belt around you and take you where you do not wish to go." (He said this to indicate the kind of death by which he would glorify God.) After this he said to him, "Follow me."

# Back from the City

JANE KENYON

U.S., 1947–1995. Born in Michigan, Kenyon lived her adult life in New England, an area whose literary and natural environment—evident in "Back from the City"—suited her disciplined, meditative approach to life and poetry.

After three days and nights of rich food
and late talk in overheated rooms,
of walks between mounds of garbage
and human forms bedded down for the night
under rags, I come back to my dooryard,
to my own wooden step.

The last red leaves fall to the ground
and frost has blackened the herbs and asters
that grew beside the porch. The air
is still and cool, and the withered grass
lies flat in the field. A nuthatch spirals
down the rough trunk of the tree.

At the Cloisters I indulged in piety
while gazing at a painted lindenwood Pietà—
Mary holding her pierced and desiccated son
across her knees; but when a man stepped close
under the tasseled awning of the hotel,
asking for "a quarter for someone
down on his luck," I quickly turned my back.

Now I hear tiny bits of bark and moss
break off under the bird's beak and claw,
and fall onto already-fallen leaves.
"Do you love me?" said Christ to his disciple.
"Lord, you know
that I love you."
                    "Then feed my sheep."

# Peter

BÉLA CSENDES

Hungary, 1921–1996. Though born of peasant parents, Csendes managed to obtain the highest education, receiving a doctorate to teach Latin. Accused by the Communist government of conspiracy, he spent most of his life in prisons and brutal labor camps; the descriptions of torture in "Peter" are autobiographical. A fellow prisoner later remarked that he hadn't known that Csendes was a poet, but that in prison "he was always singing." In his poems, written in classical Latin style, Csendes identifies with Gospel figures; his retrospective volume is titled *Lamb—Peter—Thomas*. "Peter" is translated from the Hungarian by Dalma Hunyadi Brunauer.


My fellow-apostle, see; Our Lord indeed
from mixed materials our selves did knead:
soul and body each other prepare
for good and evil and for betrayal.

The rooster didn't even call out twice
you had already betrayed your Master trice;
although your well-honed sabre previously
sliced off the Chief Priest's servants's ear right smartly.

Perhaps you sensed instinctively, this instant
is the last opportunity to run away—or else
the crazed mob will tear you to pieces, and
your only escape will be to cold death.

This way: you will not be pulped soft to make confessions—
as one hurled into a fall-pit—nightly beatings
will not rain down on your soles—and when
willpower is destroyed and the decision-making mind

disintegrates, wishing nothing more
than to save its bare existence—or not even that—
so you may choose the hard wall, made of stone,
to beat your head to pieces if you bang it;

if nothing remains to separate you
from dishonor, except death, then die;

then they cannot make you confess as equally true
that which was, and that which never was:

equate your friend and yourself, and the stranger,
whom you did not know and never even met;
you are not forced to declare him an accomplice;
they cannot force dead lips to implicate him.

That's why your sabre sliced, that's why you ran away,
that's why you made denial trice and loud,
that's why you slunk away from Golgotha
on that Friday, disappearing even before the others.

And you were not moved to turn back again
by the Lord's eyes which followed you, nor his past
words, "You are the rock, and on this rock
I must establish my Holy Church."

Those are the facts, my Friend. And then the Rising—
there, by itself, even though at the empty tomb
you were allowed to stand, did not make you Confessor
yet, nor did the questioning

glances of the other disciples make you speak
in a way to inspire minds and hearts;
with prophesying faith creating faith
dispelling mute indifference;

even though already there had been the promise
of the Spirit to come, the Holy One, the one
to be sent by the Lord in the future
to console us and to strengthen,

yet, only on the fiftieth day,
in the wind's roar, did fire alight in your heads,
and drove you with flaming tongues, so you may speak
for the understanding of the many-tongued multitude.

Peter, it's in you the Holy Spirit slumbers,
in you and in us, and it is brought forth

by the wind, which bloweth where it wilt,
kindling and holding flame on flame.

Transfigured, it waits in the free matter's
depths, but it needs multiple promptings to rise,
once at the coming of Whitsuntide
and at the daily promptings springing up in us.

The rock is a rock. Unshakeable, solid.
The Absolute No and the Yes it is also.
A whole in its wholeness. You, Peter,
derive your strength from this—your failing too.

Know this: you have been called, and while the tear, shed for your sins,
for your betrayal, daily etches wounds,
falling on your face, it lays down scab on scab,
from wound to wound, providing strength for you,

and also to teach you that Salvation
has been ordained for every sinner, for you and for all
peoples: Beware! in your heat
don't go overboard trying to prove it.

Not even the Holy Ghost can light up
the offshoot paths of justice and goodwill:
it's possible for you to make a choice,
blind-alone, but op'ning on the Wrong.

In your hard skull, keep the teaching whole,
but let the New quicken and ferment it,
so shall development rise ever and ever,
while you yourself shall be the Lord's good tool.

Your burden shall not be out of time, crippling you.
When you'll be gray, you shall spread out your arms;
unbidden, someone else will gird you up and save you
on that spot where stands a cross in Rome.

# The Ascension

*Luke 24:50—51*

Then he led them out as far as Bethany, and, lifting up his hands, he blessed them. While he was blessing them, he withdrew from them and was carried up into heaven.

# The Ascension

FRAY LUIS DE LEÓN

Spain, 1527?–1591. His family were *conversos*: Jews who in 1492 converted to
Catholicism rather than leave Spain. This fact, and Fray Luis' criticism of the
Latin Vulgate Bible, landed him in prison during the Inquisition. An Augis-
tinian monk, professor, translator from Hebrew, Latin, and Greek, Fray Luis
was most famous for his prose treatise *On the Names of Christ*. His poetry is
mystical, focusing on the contrast between earthly and spiritual realities. "The
Ascension" is translated from the Spanish by George Dardess.

How can you leave your flock,
O holy shepherd,
in this valley deep and dark,
while you break the pure
air, departing to regions immortal and secure?

Those once blessed,
now sad, afflicted,
those nourished at your breast
and now by you dispossessed,
where will they turn their faces?

Can their eyes,
having seen the beauty of your face,
see anything now that does not fret them?
And to ears that heard your sweetness,
is not all else clamor and dullness?

And that swollen sea,
who now shall calm it?
Who tame the burning wind?
With you in eclipse,
what star shall guide the ship to port?

O envious cloud,
do you grudge even our brief delight?
Where do you fly in such haste?
Your departure, so splendid and bright!
But how poor and blind you leave us!

# Ascension

DENISE LEVERTOV

U.S., 1923–. See page 448 for biographical information on this poet.

Stretching Himself as if again,
    through downpress of dust
        upward, soil giving way
to thread of white, that reaches
    for daylight, to open as green
        leaf that it is . . .
Can Ascension
    not have been
        arduous, almost,
as the return
    from Sheol, and
        back through the tomb
into breath?
    Matter reanimate
        now must relinquish
itself, its
    human cells,
        molecules, five
senses, linear
    vision endured
        as Man—
the sole
    all-encompassing gaze
        resumed now,
Eye of Eternity.
    Relinquished, earth's
        broken Eden.
Expulsion,
    liberation,
        last
self-enjoined task
    of Incarnation.
        He again

Fathering Himself.
    Seed-case
        splitting,
He again
    Mothering His birth:
        torture and bliss.

# Beware, Soul Brother

CHINUA ACHEBE

Nigeria, 1930–. Achebe's first novel, *Things Fall Apart*, is a modern classic, translated into nearly forty languages. Written as British colonial rule of Nigeria ended, it is, in the author's words, "an act of atonement with my past, the ritual return and homage of a prodigal son." Primarily a novelist, Achebe turned to poetry during the disruptive years of the Nigerian civil war. "Beware, Soul Brother" brings the Christianity of the author's youth (his parents were Anglican missionaries) into play within his Igbo religion. Currently, Achebe holds an endowed professorship in English Literature at Bard College.

> We are the men of soul
> men of song we measure out
> our joys and agonies
> too, our long, long passion week
> in paces of the dance. We have
> come to know from surfeit of suffering
> that even the Cross need not be
> a dead end nor total loss
> if we should go to it striding
> the dirge of the soulful *abia* drums . . .
>     But beware soul brother
> of the lures of ascension day
> the day of soporific levitation
> on high winds of skysong; beware
> for others there will be that day
> lying in wait leaden-footed, tone-deaf
> passionate only for the deep entrails
> of our soil; beware of the day
> we head truly skyward leaving
> that spoil to the long ravenous tooth
> and talon of their hunger.
> Our ancestors, soul brother, were wiser
> than is often made out. Remember
> they gave Ala, great goddess
> of their earth, sovereignty too over
> their arts for they understood
> too well those hard-headed
> men of departed dance where a man's

foot must return whatever beauties
it may weave in air, where
it must return for safety
and renewal of strength. Take care
then, mother's son, lest you become
a dancer disinherited in mid-dance
hanging a lame foot in air like the hen
in a strange unfamiliar compound. Pray
protect this patrimony to which
you must return when the song
is finished and the dancers disperse;
remember also your children
for they in their time will want
a place for their feet when
they come of age and the dance
of the future is born
for them.

# Credits

Achebe, Chinua. "Beware, Soul Brother" from a collection of a book of poems *Beware, Soul Brother and Other Poems* by Chinua Achebe. First published by Nwamife Publishers Limited, Enugu, in Nigeria, in 1971.

Adcock, Fleur. "Mary Magdalene and the Birds." Copyright © Fleur Adcock 1983. Reprinted from Fleur Adcock's *Selected Poems* (1983) by permission of Oxford University Press.

Ahluwalia, Jasbir Singh. "Autobiography of Mr. X." Translated from the Punjabi by the poet. From *The Voices of Indian Poets: An Anthology of Indian Poetry*, edited by Pranab Bandyopadhyay. Calcutta: United Writers, 1975.

Akhmatova, Anna. "Knock with your little . . . ," "And once more . . . ," and "The one people once called . . . ," translated by Judith Hemschemeyer. Reprinted from Volume II of *The Complete Poems of Anna Akhmatova* with the permission of Zephyr Press of Somerville, Massachusetts. Copyright " 1990 by Judith Hemschemeyer.

Alcuin. "Brief Is Our Life,"and "In the Refectory," translated from the Latin by Helen Waddell, from *More Latin Lyrics: From Virgil to Milton*. Copyright © 1976 by Victor Gollancz. Reprinted by permission of Stanbrook Abbey, Worcester, England.

Anonymous. "Lament of Our Lady Under the Cross." Translated from the Polish by Jon Stallworthy. Copyright © Oxford University Press 1970. Reprinted from *Five Centuries of Polish Poetry 1450-1970* by Jerzy Peterkiewicz and Burns Singer (2nd ed. 1970) by permission of Oxford University Press.

Aquinas, Thomas. "Adoro te," translated from the Latin by Helen Waddell, from *More Latin Lyrics: From Virgil to Milton*. Copyright © 1976 by Victor Gollancz. Reprinted by permission of Stanbrook Abbey, Worcester, England.

Atwan, Robert. "Good Friday, 1993: Heading." From *Image: A Journal of the Arts and Religion* No.10, Summer 1995. Reprinted by permission of the author.

Atwood, Margaret. "Resurrection" from *The Journals of Susanna Moodie* by Margaret Atwood. Copyright © Oxford University Press Canada 1970. Reprinted by permission of Oxford University Press Canada.

Auden, W. H. "The Temptation of Joseph" from *W. H. Auden: Collected Poems* by W. H. Auden. Copyright © 1944 and renewed 1972 by W. H. Auden. Reprinted by permission of Random House, Inc.

Avejina, Funso. "And so it came to pass . . ." From *A Selection of African Poetry*, edited by K. E. Senanu and T. Vincent, Essex: Longman, 1988.

Awoonor-Williams. "Easter Dawn." From *Rediscovery*. Ibadan: Mbari Publications, 1964.

Baudelaire, Charles. "Saint Peter's Denial." from *Les Fleurs du Mal* by Charles Baudelaire. Translated by Richard Howard. Reprinted by permission of David R. Godine, Publisher, Inc. Copyright © 1982 by Richard Howard.

Baxter, James Keir. "The Maori Jesus," "Lazarus," "Theif and Samaritan," "Ballad of Dives and Lazarus," and "Song for Holy Saturday." From *Collected Poems*. New Zealand: Oxford Unversity Press, 1979.

Belli, Giuseppe. "Martha and Magdalene" from *Sonnets of Giuseppe Belli*, translated, with an introduction by Miller Williams. Translations copyrights © 1981 by Miller. Reproduced by permission of Louisiana State University.

Bertken, Sister. "When I went into my garden . . ." Translated from the Dutch by Willis Barnstone. From *A Book of Women Poets from Antiquity to Now* by Willis and Aliki Barnstone. Copyright © 1980 by Schocken Books, Inc. Reprinted by permission of Schocken Books, published by Pantheon Books, a division of Random House, Inc.

Bolander, Nils. "Christianity Was Once an Eagle." From *20th Century Scandinavian Poetry*, edited by Martin S. Allwood. Sweden: Marston Hill Mullsjo, 1950.

Borges, Jorge Luis. "Matthew XXV, 30" and "Luke XXIII." Reprinted from *Jorge Luis Borges Selected Poems 1923–1967* by Jorge Luis Borges. Copyright © 1968, 1969, 1970, 1971, 1972 by Jorge Luis Borges, Emece Editores, S. A. and Norman Thomas Di Giovanni. Used by permission of Delacourte Press/Seymour Lawrence, a division of Bantam Doubleday Dell Publishing Group, Inc.

Brooks, Gwendolyn. "In Emanuel's Nightmare: Another Coming of Christ" from *Blacks* by Gwendolyn Brooks,© 1991, published by Third World Press, Chicago. Reprinted by permission from the author. "Riot." Reprinted by permission of Broadside Press, 1969.

Cardenal, Ernesto. From *Cosmic Canticle*. Excerpted from *Cosmic Canticle* by Ernesto Cardenal (1993, Curbstone Press). Reprinted by permission of Curbstone Press.

Chakrabarti, Nrendra Nath. "Christ of Calcutta." Translated from the Bengali by Provat Guha. From *The Voices of Indian Poets: An Anthology of Indian Poetry*, edited by Pranab Bandyopadhyay. Calcutta: United Writers, 1975.

Cisneros, Antonio. "Sunday in St. Christina's in Budapest and Fruitstand Next Door," translated from the Spanish by Wayne H. Finke. Reprinted from the *Anthology of Contemporary Latin American Literature, 1960–1984* edited by Barry J. Luby & Wayne H. Finke. Copyright © 1986 by Fairleigh Dickinson University Press. Used by permission from Associated University Presses.

Clinton, De Witt. "In My Father's House." From *Cross Currents*, Winter 1993–94. Reprinted by permission of the author.

Cohen, Leonard. "I Am Too Loud When You Are Gone." © 1968 Leonard Cohen. Originally printed in "Selected Poems, 1956–1965." New York, Viking Press, 1968. Used by Permission/All Rights Reserved.

Hahn, Oscar. "The Last Supper," translated from the Spanish by Wayne H. Finke. Reprinted from the *Anthology of Contemporary Latin American Literature, 1960–1984* edited by Barry J. Luby & Wayne H. Finke. Copyright © 1986 by Fairleigh Dickinson University Press. Used by permission from Associated University Press.

Hāwī, Khalīl. "Magi in Europe." Translated from Arabic by Diana Der Hovanessian and Lena Jayyusi. From *Modern Arabic Poetry: An Anthology*, edited by Salma Khaddra Jayyusi. New York: Columbia University Press, 1987.

Hildegard of Bingen. "Antiphon for the Virgin," "Song to the Virgin" and "Antiphon for the Redeemer." Reprinted from St. Hildegard of Bingen, *Symphonia: A Critical Edition of the Symphonia armonia celestium revelationum.* Edited and translated by Barbara Newman. Copyright © 1989 by Cornell University. Used by permission of the publisher, Cornell University Press.

Holloway, Marcella. "The Risk" in *The Bible Today* (March 1985). Reprinted by permission of the poet.

Hope, A. D. "A Bidding Grace." *Collected Poems 1930-1965.* Viking, Penguin, 1966.

Hopkins, Gerard Manley. "The Half-Way House." Copyright © The Society of Jesus 1967. Reprinted from *Poems of Gerard Manley Hopkins* edited by W. H. Gardner and N. H. MacKenzie (4th ed. 1967) by permission of Oxford University Press.

Huygens, Constantijn, "Christmas." From *Coming After: An Anthology of Poetry from the Low Countries*, edited by Adrian J. Barnouw, Rutgers University Press, 1948.

Immoos, Thomas. "Kyrie Eleison I" from *Missa Mundi* (Verlag Styria, 1988). Used by permission of Verlag Styria. Translation by Dalma Hunyadi Brunauer used by permission of the translator. "Mary of Magdala in the Garden" translated by Dalma Hunyadi Brunauer. Used by permission of the poet and translator.

Jabra, Jabra Ibrahim. "A Stranger at the Fountain." From *Modern Arab Poets*, translated and edited by Isaa J. Boullata. London: Heinemann, 1976.

Jacob, Max. "Love of One's Neighbor." Translated from the French by Wallace Fowlie. From *Mid-Century Poet*, edited by Wallace Fowlie. New York: Twayne, 1955.

Jennings, Elizabeth. "Friday" from *Collected Poems* by Elizabeth Jennings. Copyright © 1986 by Carcanet Press. Reprinted by permission of David Higham Associates.

Jiminez. Juan Ramon. "The Lamb Baad Gently." Reprinted from *Three Hundred Poems, 1903-1953*, by Juan Ramon Jiminez, translated by Eloise Roach. Copyright © 1962. Used by permission of the University of Texas Press.

John of the Cross. "The Incarnation," from *The Collected Works of St. John of the Cross* translated by Kieran Kavanaugh and Otilio Rodriguez. © 1979, 1991 by Washington Province of Discalced Carmelites. Reprinted by permission from ICS Publications, 2131 Lincoln Road, N.E., Washington, D.C. 20002.

Karlfeldt, Erik Axel. "Black Yule." Translated from the Swedish by C. D. Locock. From *A Selection of Modern Swedish Poetry*, New York: Macmillan, 1929.

Kassia. "Mary Magdalene." Translated from the Dutch by Willis Barnstone. From *A Book of Women Poets from Antiquity to Now* by Willis and Aliki Barnstone. Copyright © 1980 by Schocken Books, Inc. Reprinted by permission of Schocken Books, published by Pantheon Books, a division of Random House, Inc.

Kelly, Aileen. "Wonders Will Never Cease," from *Coming Up for Light* by Aileen Kelly. Copyright © 1994 by Pariah Press. Reprinted by permission of author.

Kennedy, X. J. "A Scandal in the Suburbs" and "Walking Through Walls." Used by permission from the author.

Kenyon, Jane. "Back from the City." Copyright © 1986 by Jane Kenyon. Reprinted from *The Boat of Quiet Hours* with the permission of Graywolf Press, Saint Paul, Minnesota.

Kerouac, Jack. "A Pun for Al Gelpi." From *Scattered Poems* by Jack Kerouac, City Lights Books, Pocket Poet Series 28, 1971.

al-Khāl, Yūsuf. "The Eternal Dialogue," and "Repentance." From *Modern Arab Poets*, translated and edited by Isaa J. Boullata. London: Heinemann, 1976.

Lacaba, Emmanuel. "When a Cloud Shades the Sun." Reprinted from *Salvaged Poems*. Edited by Jose F. Lacaba. Manila: Salinhali Publishing House, 1986. Copyright Miriam V. Lacaba and Emanwelga Lacaba.

Lawrence, D. H. "The Lord's Prayer." From *The Complete Poems of D. H. Lawrence* by D. H. Lawrence, edited by V. de Sola Pinto & F. W. Roberts. Copyright © 1971 by Angelo Ravagli and C. M. Weekley, Executors of the Estate of Frieda Lawrence Ravagli. Used by permission of Viking Penguin, a division of Penguin Books USA Inc. and Laurence Pollinger Ltd. and the Estate of Frieda Lawrence Ravagli. "As Thyself!" From *The Complete Poems of D. H.Lawrence* by D. H. Lawrence, edited by V. de Sola Pinto & F. W. Roberts. Copyright © 1964 by Angelo Ravagli and C. M. Weekley, Executors of the Estate of Frieda Lawrence Ravagli. Used by permission of Viking Penguin, a division of Penguin Books USA Inc. and Laurence Pollinger Ltd. and the Estate of Frieda Lawrence Ravagli.

Lee, Hae-in [Sr. Claudia Lee]. "Like the Samaritan Woman by the Well" and "Magdalen's Song." Used by permission of the poet.

Levertov, Denise. "Ascension," and "Salvator Mundi: Via Crucis," from *Evening Train* by Denise Levertov. Copyright © 1992 by Denise Levertov. Reprinted by permission of New Directions Publishing Corp. and Laurence Pollinger Limited.

Levi, Primo. "Annunciation" from *Collected Poems*. Italian text © Garzanti Editore s.p.a., 1984, 1991. English translation © Ruth Feldman and Brian Swann, 1988. New material English translation © Ruth Feldman, 1992. Reprinted by permission of Faber and Faber, Inc.

Levin, Phillip. "The Third Day," from *Afterimage*, published by Copper Beech Press, 1995. Copyright © by Phillip Levin, as first published in *The Atlantic Monthly*.

Li, Wu. "Late in Han . . ." and "Song of the Fisherman," translated from the Chinese by Jonathan Chaves. Reprinted from "Music of Harmonious Heaven in Reverent Thanks to the Lord of Heaven" in Jonathan Chaves, *Singing of the Source*, copyright © 1993. Used by permission of the University of Hawaii Press.

Lorca, Frederico Garcia. "Crucifixion" from *Poet in New York*, edited by Christopher Maurer. Translation copyright © 1988 by the Estate of Frederico Garcia Lorca, and Greg Simon and Steven F. White. Reprinted by permission of Farrar, Strauss & Giroux, Inc.

Lowell, Robert. "The Holy Innocents" from *Lord Weary's Castle*, copyright © 1946 and renewed 1974 by Robert Lowell, reprinted by permission of Harcourt Brace & Company.

Lvov, Vladimir. "That Yellowed Body" by Vladimir Lvov. Translated by Sarah W. Bliumis. From *20th Century Russian Poetry* by Yevgeny Yevtushenko. Copyright © 1993 by Doubleday, a divsion of Bantam Doubleday Dell Publishing Group, Inc. Used by permission of Doubleday, a division of Bantam Doubleday Dell Publishing Group, Inc.

Lynch, John. Reprinted from *A Woman Wrapped in Silence* by John Lynch. Copyright 1941 and 1968 by John Lynch. Used by permission of Paulist Press.

Lyon, George. "The Foot-Washing" by Geroge Ella Lyon, appearing in *Appalachian Journal*, vol. 9:4 (Summer 1982), p. 288. Copyright 1982 by Appalachian State University/Appalachian Journal. All rights reserved.

Machado y Ruizo, Antonio. "Christ Teaches," poem XLII of "Proverbs & Songs," p. 187 of Antonio Machado, *Selected Poems* translated by Alan S. Trueblood. Cambridge, Mass.: Harvard University Press, Copyright © 1982 by the President and Feloows of Harvard College. "Lord, You Have Ripped." Reprinted from *Times Alone: Selected Poems of Antonio Machado* translated by Robert Bly, Wesleyan University Press, Middletown, CT, 1983. Copyright 1983 by Robert Bly. Reprinted with his permission.

Malmberg, Bertil. "Christ Meets Lucifer." From *20th Century Scandinavian Poetry*, edited by Martin S. Allwood. Sweden: Marston Hill Mullsjo, 1950.

Mapanje, Jack. "The Tale of a Dzeleka Prison Hard-Core Hero." From *The Chattering Wagtails of Mikuyu Prison* by Jack Mapanje. Oxford, England: Heinemann, 1993. African Writers Series. Reprinted by permission of Heinemann Educational Books.

Marbod of Rennes, "Hymn of the Magdalen," translated from the Latin by Helen Waddell, from *More Latin Lyrics: From Virgil to Milton*. Copyright © 1976 by Victor Gollancz. Reprinted by permission of Stanbrook Abbey, Worcester, England.

Mason, R. A. K. "Oils and Ointments," "On the Swag," "Judas Iscariot," "Nails and a Cross," and "Footnote to John ii.4." From *Collected Poems*, Pegasus Press, 1962.

McAuley, James. "Jesus" from *Collected Poems* © 1971. Reprinted by permission from HarperCollins Publishers.

McCurdy, Harold. "That Day" is reprinted with the permission of Harold McCurdy and America Press, Inc., 106 West 56th Street, New York, NY 10019. Originally published in *America*'s April 15, 1995 issue.

Merton, Thomas. "The Widow of Naim," and "The Sponge Full of Vinegar," from the *The Collected Poems of Thomas Merton* by Thomas Merton. Copyright © 1948 by New Directions Publishing Corporation, 1977 by The Trustees of the Merton Legacy Trust. Reprinted by permission of New Directions Publishing Corp. and Laurence Pollinger Limited.

Miller, Vassar. "Oblation," "Self-Ordained," "Paradox," "Pontius Pilate Discusses . . . " and "Easter Eve: A Fantasy" from *If I Had Wheels or Love* (Dallas, Southern Methodist University Press). Copyright © 1991 by Vassar Miller. Used by permission of Southern Methodist University Press.

Milosz, Czeslaw. "Readings," from *Bells in Winter* by Czeslaw Milosz. Copyright © 1974, 1977, 1978 by Czeslaw Milosz. First published by The Ecco Press in 1974. Reprinted by permission.

Mistral, Gabriela. "Martha and Mary," from *Selected Poems of Gabriela Mistral*, trans and edited by Doris Dana, copyright © 1971. Reprinted by permission of the John Hopkins University Press. "Nocturne," translated from the Spanish by Helene Masslo Anderson. Reprinted from *Gabriela Mistral: The Poet and Her Work*, by Margot Arce de Vazquez, copyright " 1964. by permission from New York University Press.

Moraes, Dom. "At Seven O'Clock." From *Modern Indian Poetry in English*, edited by P. Lal. Calcutta: Writers Workshop, 1969.

Morsztyn, Andrej. "To St. John the Baptist." Translated by Jerzy Peterkiewicz and Burns Singer with Jon Stallworthy. Copyright © Oxford University Press 1970. Reprinted from *Five Centuries of Polish Poetry 1450-1970* by Jerzy Peterkiewicz and Burns Singer (2nd ed. 1970) by permission of Oxford University Press.

Mtshali, Oswald Mbuyoseni. "An Abandoned Bundle," "An Old Man in Church," and "Ride Upon the Death Chariot." From *Sounds of a Cowhide Drum*. The Third Press, Joseph Okpaku Publishing Co.: New York, 1972.

Muir, Edwin. "The Killing" from *Collected Poems* by Edwin Muir. Copyright © 1960, 1979 by Willa Muir. Reprinted by permission of Faber and Faber, Ltd. and Oxford University Press, Inc.

Nicol, Abioseh. "African Easter: Easter Eve," "African Easter: Good Friday," and "Easter Morning." From *Poems from Balck Africa*. Edited by Langston Hughes. Bloomington: Indiana University Press, 1963.

Norris, Kathleen. "Luke 14: A Commentary." From *Cross Currents*, Winter 1994–95. Reprinted by permission of the author.

Oberg, Robert. "Rooster." *Commonweal*, March 11, 1994. Copyright © Commonweal Foundation, 1994. Reprinted with permission of the Commonweal Foundation.

Ofeimun, Odia. "Judgement Day." From *The Poet Lied* by Odia Ofeimun. Lagos: Updated Communications, 1988.

Österling, Anders Johan. "Unemployed" From *20th Century Scandinavian Poetry*, edited by Martin S. Allwood. Sweden: Marston Hill Mullsjo, 1950.

Pananti, Filippo. "Epigram VII." Translated from the Italian by Joseph Tusiani. From *From Marino to Marinetti*, edited by Joseph Tusiani. New York: Baroque Press, 1974.

Papatsonis, Takis. "In the Key of Resurrection," from *Modern Greek Poetry*, edited by Kimon Friar © 1973, published by Simon and Schuster. Reprinted by permission from Dino Friar.

Pascoli, Giovanni. "Jesus." Translated from the Italian by Joseph Tusiani. From *From Marino to Marinetti*, edited by Joseph Tusiani. New York: Baroque Press, 1974.

Pasolini, Pier Paolo, "The Day of My Death," from *The New Italian Poetry*, ed. Lawrence R. Smith. Copyright © 1981. Reprinted by permission of University of California Press.

Pasternak, Boris. "Miracle" translated by Nina Kossman. From *The Gospels in Our Image*, edited by David Curzon (New York: Harcourt Brace & Company, 1995). Reprinted by permission of the editor and translator.

Péguy, Charles. "I Am Their Father, Says God," and "God Speaks: Night, You are Holy." From *God Speaks* by Charles Peguy, translated from the French by Julian Green, Pantheon, a division of Random House Inc., 1945.

Pellicer, Carlos, "Sunday," translated from the Spanish by Dudley Fitts, from *Anthology of Contemporary Latin-American Poetry* by Dudley Fitts. Copyright © 1948 by New Directions Corp. Reprinted by permission of the New Directions Publishing Corp.

Petersen, Nis. "Gipsy Privelege" From *20th Century Scandinavian Poetry*, edited by Martin S. Allwood. Sweden: Marston Hill Mullsjo, 1950.

Pozdnyayev, Mikhail. "Remembrances of Five Loaves" by Mikhail Pozdnyayev. Translated by Lunnis and Todd. From *20th Century Russian Poetry* by Yevgeny Yevtushenko. Copyright © 1993 by Doubleday, a divison of Bantam Doubleday Dell Publishing Group, Inc. Used by permission of Doubleday, a division of Bantam Doubleday Dell Publishing Group, Inc.

Prévert, Jacques. "The Last Supper." Translated from the French by Lawrence Ferlinghetti. From *The Random House Book of Twentieth Century French Poetry*, edited by Paul Auster, New York: Random House, 1984.

Prudentius. "A Hymn After Fasting," translated from the Latin by Sr. M. Clement Eagan C.C.V.I. Reprinted from *The Poems of Prudentius*, © 1962 by Catholic University of America Press, Father of the Church Series Volume 43. Used by permission of the Catholic University of America Press, 620 Michigan Avenue, N.E., Washington, D.C. 20064.

Randall, Julia. "Miracles." Reprinted from *Contemporary Religious Poetry* by Paul Ramsey. © 1987 by Paul Ramsey. Used by permission of Paulist Press.

Revius, Jacobus. "Foot-Washing." From *Jacob Revius*, edited and translated by Henrietta Ten Harmsel, Wayne State University Press, 1968.

Rilke, Rainer Maria, "The Arisen" from *New Poems (1908): The Other Part* by Rainer Maria Rilke, translated by Edward Snow. Reprinted by permission of North Point Press, a division of Farrar, Straus & Giroux, Inc. "Of the Marriage at Cana," and "The Last Supper" translated by David Curzon and Will Alexander Washburn. From *The Gospels in Our Image*, edited by David Curzon (New York: Harcourt Brace & Company). Reprinted by permission of David Curzon.

Romanos. "On the Woman with an Issue of Blood," and from *Homily on Dives and Lazarus*. From *Kontakia of Romanos*, vol. I and II, translated by Marjorie Carpenter. University of Missouri Press, 1970.

Rónay, György. "Stones and Bread," translated from the Hungarian by Dalma Hunyadi Brunauer, from *Isten erkezese* by Mora Ferenc Konyvkiado. © 1991 György Rónay. Reprinted by permission from the Hungarian Clearinghouse.

Roumain, Jacques. "The Negro Sermon." Translated from the French by Ellen Conroy Kennedy. From *The Negritude Poets*, edited by E. C. Kennedy. New York: Viking, 1975.

Rozewicz, Tadeusz. "Unknown Letter" and "The Dream of John," translated from the Polish by Victor Contoski, from *Unease*, copyright © 1980. Reprinted by permission from New Rivers Press.

Rubisova, Yelina. "Humility is the Eye of the Needle" by Yelina Rubisova. Translated by Thomas E. Bird. From *20th Century Russian Poetry* by Yevgeny Yevtushenko. Copyright © 1993 by Doubleday, a divison of Bantam Doubleday Dell Publishing Group, Inc. Used by permission of Doubleday, a divison of Bantam Doubleday Dell Publishing Group, Inc.

Ryan, Patrick H. "Mary Sat." Source: Meredith Parsons Lillich, ed., *Studies in Cistercian Art and Architecture*, volume 4, Cistercian Studies Series, Number 143. Copyright, Cistercian Publications, Kalamazoo, Michigan-Spencer, Massachusetts, 1993.

Sanchez–Baudy, Jose. "To Saint Lazarus," translated from the Spanish by Claudio Freixas. Reprinted from *Afro-Cuban Poetry/De Oshua Yemaya*. 1978 by Ediciones Universal, Miami, Florida. Reprinted by permission from the author.

Sang, Ku. "The True Appearance of the Word," "Christmas Lament," "Mysterious Wealth," and "Easter Hymn" from *Wasteland of Fire: Selected Poems of Ku Sang*. (London: Forest Books, 1989.) Translated from the Korean by Anthony of Taizé. Reprinted by permission of the poet and translator.

Sarton, May. "Lazarus," copyright © 1966 by the estate of the late May Sarton, from *Collected Poems 1930–1993* by May Sarton. Reprinted by permission of W. W. Norton & Company, Inc and A M Heath & Company Limited.

Sayigh, Tafiq."The Sermon on the Mount." From *An Anthology of Modern Arabic Poetry*, edited and translated by Mounah A. Khouri and Hamid Algar. Berkeley: University of California Press, 1974. Used by permission of the Regents of the University of California and the University of California Press.

al-Sayyāb, Badr Shākir. From *City of Sinbad*. From *An Anthology of Modern Arabic Poetry*, edited and translated by Mounah A. Khouri and Hamid Algar. Berkeley: University of California Press, 1974. Used by permission of the Regents of the University of California and the University of California Press. "The Messiah after the Crucifixion." Translated from the Arabic by M. M. Badawi, from the *Journal of Arabic Literature*, Vol. VI, 1975.

Senghor, Leopold. "Snow in Paris" and "Return of the Prodigal Son" translated from the French by Melvin Dixon. From *Leopold Senghor, The Collected Poetry*. Charlottesville, University Press of Virginia, 1991. Reprinted with permission of the University Press of Virginia.

Sikelianos, Angelos. "Unrecorded," from *Modern Greek Poetry*, edited by Kimon Friar © 1973, published by Simon and Schuster. Reprinted by permission from Dino Friar.

Sinka, Istvan. "Jesus Leaves Nazareth Forever," translated from the Hungarian by Dalma Hunyadi Brunauer, from *Isten erkezese* by Mora Ferenc Konyvkiado. © 1991 Istvan Sinka. Reprinted by permission from the Hungarian Clearinghouse.

Soyinka, Wole. "Easter" and "The Dreamer" from *Idanre and Other Poems* by Wole Soyinka. Copyright © 1967 by Wole Soyinka. Reprinted by permission of Hill & Wang, a division of Farrar, Straus & Giroux, Inc and by Reed Consumer Books Ltd.

Tagore, Rabindranath. "The Son of Man" by Rabindranath Tagore. Reprinted with the permission of Simon & Schuster from *The Collected Poems and Plays of Rabindranath Tagore* (New York: Macmillan, 1949).

Teresa of Avila. "On the Circumcision" and "For the Veiling of Sister Isabel de los Angeles," from *The Collected Works of St. Teresa of Avila Volume Three*, translated by Kieran Kavanaugh and Otilio Rodriguez. © 1985 by Washington Province of Discalced Carmelites. Reprinted by permission from ICS Publications, 2131 Lincoln Road, N.E., Washington, D.C. 20002.

Theodulf of Orleans, "Wherefore the scars of Christ's passion remained in the body of his resurrection," translated from the Latin by Helen Waddell, from *More Latin Lyrics: From Virgil to Milton*. Copyright © 1976 by Victor Gollancz. Reprinted by permission of Stanbrook Abbey, Worcester, England.

Thomas, R. S. "The Answer" from *Frequencies* by R. S. Thomas. (London: Macmillan, 1978). "The Bright Field" from *Laboratories of the Spirit* by R. S. Thomas. (London: Macmillan, 1978). "The Coming" and "Via Negativa" from *H'M* by R. S. Thomas. (London: Macmillan, 1972). "In a Country Church" from *Songs at the Year's Turning* by R. S. Thomas. (London: Thames & Hudson, 1958).

Tūqūān, Fadwā. "To Christ." From *Modern Poetry of the Arab World*, translated and edited by Abdullah al-Udari, New York: Penguin, 1986.

Unamuno, Miguel de. "Cloud-Music." From *Poetry*, February 1963. Translated by Anthony Kerrigan.

U Tam'si, Gerard Felix Tchicaya."The Scorner (2)," "The Scorner (6)," and "Communion."From *Selected Poems*, translated by Gerald Moore, London: Heinemann: African Writers Series, 1970. Reprinted by permission of the Peters Fraser & Dunlap Group Ltd.

Valdivielso, José de. "Seguidilla." Translated from the Spanish by Thomas Walsh. From *The World's Great Catholic Poetry: The Catholic Anthology*, edited by T. Walsh. Macmillan, 1927 and 1940.

Vallejo, César. "Stumble Between Two Stars." From *Nine Latin American Poets*, translated and edited by Rachel Benson. Cypress Books, Las Americas Publishing Co., 1968.

Varnalis, Kostas. "Magdalene," from *Modern Greek Poetry*, edited by Kimon Friar © 1973, published by Simon and Schuster. Reprinted by permission from Dino Friar.

Vega y Carpio, Felix Lope de. "Shepherd Who With Your Tender Calls." Translated from the Spanish by Kate Flores. From *An Anthology of Spanish Poetry from Garcilaso to Garcia Lorca*, edited by Angel Flores, Anchor Doubleday, 1961.

Verlaine, Paul, "Lord, I'm Afraid . . .," translated from the French by C. F. MacIntyre. Reprinted from *Selected Poems* by Paul Verlaine, copyright © 1948, with permission of the University of California Press.

Villa, José Garcia. "Does a Mirror Forget?" From *Collected Poems and New*. New York: McDowell, Obolensky, 1942.

Vondel, Joost van den. "Christmas Night." From *Coming After: An Anthology of Poetry from the Low Countries*, edited by Adrian J. Barnouw, Rutgers University Press, 1948.

Wakefield, Kathleen. "Mary's Poem." from *There and Back* (Brockport, NY: State Street Press, 1993). Used by permission of the poet.

Walker, Alice. "The Abduction of Saints," from *Good Night Willie Lee, I'll See You in the Morning* by Alice Walker. Copyright © 1975, 1977, 1979 by Alice Walker. Used by permission of Doubleday, a division of Bantam Doubleday Dell Publishing Group, Inc.

Wilbur, Richard. "A Wedding Toast," from *The Mind Reader*, copyright © 1972 by Richard Wilbur, reprinted by permission of Harcourt Brace & Company.

Wivel, Ole. "Weep for Balder." From *20th Century Scandinavian Poetry*, edited by Martin S. Allwood. Sweden: Marston Hill Mullsjo, 1950.

Wojtyla, Karol. "The Samaritan Woman" and "John Beseeches Her" from *Collected Poems* by Karol Wojtyla, translated by Jerzy Peterkiewicz. Copyright © 1979, 1982 by Libreria Editrice Vaticana, Vatican City. Reprinted by permission of Random House, Inc.

Xingyao, Zhang. "How Wonderful Was Peter," translated from the Chinese by D. E. Mungello. Reprinted from *The Forgotten Christians of Hangzhou* by D. E. Mungello, copyright © 1994. Used by permission of the University of Hawaii Press.

Yeats, W. B. "The Travail of Passion" by W. B. Yeats. Reprinted by permission of Simon & Schuster from *The Poems of W. B. Yeats: A New Edition*, edited by Richard J. Finneran (New York: Macmillan, 1983).

Zagajewski, Adam. "Palm Sunday" from *Tremor: Selected Poems*. Tranlsation by Renata Gorczynski copyright © 1985 by Farrar, Straus & Giroux, Inc. Reprinted by permission of Farrar, Strauss & Giroux, Inc.

Zerov, Mikola. "Salome," from *The Ukranian Poets: 1189–1962* edited by C. H. Andrusyshen and Watson Kirkconnell, copyright © 1963. Reprinted by permission from University of Toronto Press.

Zhao, Simon. "Explanation Without Words." Translated from the Chinese by Kim-Kwong Chan and Alan Hunter. From *Prayers and Thoughts of Chinese Christians*, by Chan and Hunter, Cowley Publications, 1991. Reprinted by permission of Cowley Publications, 28 Temple Place, Boston, MA 02111.

Zimmer, Paul. "The Day Zimmer Lost Religion." From *The Zimmer Poems*. Dryad Press, 1976.

# Index of Titles

# Index of Poets